The Long Way Home

Angels, Liars, and Thieves
Boston 1946-2016

Book Four: 1994 to 2016

Memoir by David Scondras
Second edition, January, 2018

Dedicated to Raffi Freedman-Gurspan

Raffi Freedman-Gurspan was the first openly transgendered legislative staffer in the Massachusetts House of Representatives. I knew we were getting somewhere when Raffi told me she was to be appointed as the first transgendered woman to work at the White House.

At first, there was only one, and it was a guy:
One god; one guy; one owner; one boss; one president; always cis-gender.
Later, they figured out there were two:
Men and women; boys and girls; blue and pink.

It took a while,
but they figured out the bi's were actually another group.
Then the drag queens.
Then the transgendered.

First there was homophobia.
Then queer-phobia.
Now trans-phobia.

At first there was LG.
Then there was LGB.
Then there was LGBT.
Then there was LGBTQ.
Someday soon, we're gonna figure out that the real word
uses every letter in the alphabet.

Introduction to Book Four

Leaving the City Council gave me the opportunity to pivot my focus to a smaller number of very significant issues, especially AIDS in the United States, India, and Africa. We revived the non-profit Boston Human Rights Institute, renaming it *Search For A Cure*, which focused on dealing with the AIDS epidemic. In the United States, we concentrated on accelerating research as well as the way that companies priced drugs. In India, we helped put together a non-profit AIDS foundation which resulted in countrywide educational movies on HIV protection, and raising awareness in general. In Africa, we focused on treatment. This was particularly so in Malawi, where we secured the largest grant to fight AIDS of any country in the world, structuring and funding their test-and-treat program. This book explores my post-electoral career on these and other issues.

Table of Contents

Chapters 1 through 131 appear in Books One through Three.
Chapters 132 through 142 appear in Book Four (here).

Chapter in Book Four ....Page
132 /   1994: A New Chapter..5
        Search For A Cure 6
        The Politics of AIDS 20
        Like a Bird...26
133 /   March, 1995: Haiti 33
134 /   1996 Vancouver: "One World One Hope"...........41
135 /   1996: Another Gay Bashing 44
136a /   An HIV textbook?...58
136b /   India and HIV..67
        Voodoo, Mumbai's gay bar................................78
        JJ Hospital..82
        World AIDS Day...85
        GATT? Whazzat? A Glossary of Financial Terms....88

137 /	Comeback	90
138 /	Geneva	96
139 /	Africa	100
	Lake Malawi	107
	Mbeki and AIDS	116
	Durban, South Africa: July, 2000	135
	Return to Malawi: October, 2000	139
	Interview in AIDS Treatment News	148
140 /	Another old friend dies	158
141 /	Thought Crime	167
	Part One: War Crime and Sex Crime	167
	Part Two: The Columbus Day Massacre	173
	Part Three: Child Molester	186
	Part Four: Computer War	191
	Part Five: Guilty Until Proven Innocent	196
	Part Six: Thought Crimes and Plea Bargains	199
	Part Seven: The fires of San Diego	205
	Part Eight: Whining	209
142 /	God Bless America, by Big Brother	216
Epilogue /	Notes to the Survivors on What We Learned	218
	I / The Heart of the Problem	218
	II / What is limiting our progress	220
	III / The Architecture of Power	221
	IV / Costs of keeping things the way they are	223
	V / What keeps us from our own interests	226
	VI / What we can do about it	230

132 /   1994: A New Chapter

The rocks were flat and white on the graves of my two uncles, one with my own name on it, creating a mystery and a prophecy for me. I remember the trips to the silent stones, me not understanding the tear that fell from my father's eye until now.

As the demon AIDS swept the world, I would come to see the others of my generation as living memories, as silent as those stones about the ones we lost, as if our dead friends hovered around us but we could not speak of them. Perhaps it was fear of the flood of emotion that would follow, as we tried to have their presence guide us without distracting us with the thoughts of the possible futures we could never share with them. We needed to focus on finding what would work to stop the killing. In a way, we put our grief on hold.

The great AIDS doctor and gay friend Ken Mayer looked at me after our friend Fred Mandel died and said, "We should have been able to save him." I remembered Fred's laughter and his face that mixed love and merriment with stern cautions that befitted the lawyer he was. He was the first of those who directed the Boston Human Rights Commission that my office and others created. It was the first institution in Massachusetts history to protect gay people from bigotry, and an institutional testament to the battles of the days that created the first law to protect gay people. It was for me an institution solid as hope, that made me remember the strength and silence of the little man that ran it and the dead men and women who wrote the law and lobbied it through the council, and cheered when it passed while our enemy Dapper O'Neil yelled "Welcome to Cuba!" So many of the bravest and brightest of us fell victims to the plague.

In the gay community, AIDS led to the ascendancy of the assimilationists and the end of the gay revolution. What is now thought of as the gay revolution has become the assimilationist Andrew Sullivan 1990 version of freedom: the right to be the same.

It made sense for me to turn attention after losing the election to the beast that forced me to choose between fight and flight, between bottles of booze and laboratory beakers of brews that might save millions of people.

It did not take me long to decide to focus on the institute we had begun with Coors money known as the *Boston Human Rights Foundation*, then *The Boston Human Rights Institute* and finally *The Search For A Cure*, which you can read about today at www.searchforacure.org, for I am still hunting the animal that tore apart half the heartmates of my younger years.

Search For A Cure

My friends, Robert, and I decided to develop a non-profit to find ways to manage, treat, research and ultimately cure HIV. By March 19th, 1995 that effort had created and developed the Massachusetts AIDS Fund (a project launched while I was still in office but which took much time after I left to implement), funded by a line on the state income tax which by then raised $1.3 million for research and education by the state. It created the SMART team, a group of scientists who met regularly to advise us on what public policy and political actions made sense given their understanding of AIDS; the "Bomb Squad," a group of people with HIV in which we would use a group of antiviral medicines as a cocktail (we were right but too afraid to try it!); and public events to talk about the results of research with the public. *For A Cure,* would last for some 25 years and helped move the fight against AIDS forward.

A Sunday Section Of The Paper

Mary Hurley wrote a long piece in the *Boston Sunday Globe* (November 24th, 1994) about me saying my loss begets a book and perhaps a comeback. She said I had not yet decided on a title. *The Kiss* was one possibility and *Out* was another. She made it clear I was not in a mood to retire from life.

This was not the typical response of the media to my efforts to redefine the trajectory of my life. They kept asking if I would 'return' when I had never left. And this would continue until 1999.

Will Scondras seek old seat?

PAGE 4 • MARCH 18, 1999 • BAY WINDOWS

Continued from page 1

might replace him on the 13-member council, serving the Back Bay/Beacon Hill/Fenway/Mission Hill neighborhoods. Scondras was attending a seminar on complications from protease inhibitors in Santa Monica, Calif., when he was paged with an urgent call. The caller was a Boston Globe reporter, asking Scondras if he was going to attempt a political comeback. Scondras said he didn't even know that Keane wasn't running, much less what his own plans were. He didn't mind the question, but bristled at the implication.

"I was polite; but do people think I've been sitting around for five years waiting for this? Since I left the Council, I started a non-profit agency (Search for a Cure); I write a regular AIDS news and research column ("Reasons for Hope," published by Bay Windows and other periodicals); I'm still an activist who will file bills whether or not I'm on the Council," Scondras said. A longtime resident of the Fenway, Scondras made his reputation as a grassroots neighborhood activist by fighting an arson ring in his neighborhood in the 1970s and by co-founding the Fenway Community Health Center.

A graduate of Harvard University, with a Master's Degree in Economics from Northeastern, Scondras is now finishing a book about his 10 years on the Boston City Council which he hopes will be published next year.

He is quick to differentiate himself from "politicians who [serve] only to feed their pathetic egos."

"David Scondras has a life. I am committed to eradicating AIDS from this planet," said Scondras. "If serving on the Council is useful to me, and if people feel I can make a difference, then it is an attractive prospect."

Scondras is well aware that a run for his old seat will dredge up embarrassing episodes in his past that many say contributed to the downfall of a politician once regarded as one of Boston's brightest and fastest rising stars. Scondras is blunt about the circumstances that led to his narrow defeat by Keane in 1983.

"I screwed it up," he said. "When my partner of 20 years, Robert [Krebs], was diagnosed with AIDS, I fell apart." Scondras, who is HIV-negative, was ridiculed publicly — particularly by Boston Herald columnist Howie Carr — for a series of 911 calls to the Boston Police Department which Scondras has admitted he made while drunk and on pain medication. Coming just a few months before the Nov., 1983, election, the negative publicity was widely seen as the major reason for Scondras' narrow defeat.

"Five years ago, I believed Robert would be dead by now. Instead, he's OK. The new therapies are working and his name is now on the cornerstone of our new house (which Krebs, an architect, designed) and not on a grave," said Scondras.

Despite the turnaround in his personal life, in 1996 Scondras again found himself mired in negative publicity when he was badly beaten by a 16-year-old whom

Scondras had taken to an afternoon movie at a popular Back Bay theater. Scondras denies he made a sexual advance at the youth, as the young man had claimed. Scondras was hospitalized with a broken jaw, nose and other injuries he suffered in the theater beating. But what angers him to this day is that he was cast as the villain, he said, and that it was "a few loudmouths" in the gay community doing the finger-pointing.

Scondras was initially charged by police in October, 1996, with sexual assault on the

An example of the question I was asked for five years

I decided in part not to participate in the old boy network of politics because it had become assimilationist and I felt then, as I do now, that this is a mistake. This way of trying to get acceptance, respectability and power is a misread as we are in a war and what is needed is organizing our side, not getting the blessings of our enemies. I know these words sound harsh, but the way we run our politics, research, business and education is not reaching for growth that empowers us all, but rather chasing delusions that protect the status quo of a handful of powerful people and their brokers — a situation I feel will lead virtually all of us to unhappiness and extinction.

David Munshine, a political science major at Northeastern, worked with me, helping me in the Washington, D.C. lobbying effort for money to test AIDS vaccines, among many other initiatives. I also was involved in drafting state bills, many of them – but I made it clear I did not want to run for office at that point in time. Of the city council I said, "It's hard to rate something that hasn't done anything." About Tom Keane I had no comment and still don't.

I told *Bay Windows* I would pen my experiences as the city's only openly gay elected official during the Reagan administration.

Sporters, the Beacon Hill bar where I gave Robert his first ever kiss, closed its doors for the last time by May of 1995 after 38 years. It had been the home of those who had no home, the church of those who had no church, who were condemned by religion, the place young people met the mentors that parents never were to them. It was one of the great institutions of the Boston gay world passing. The gay community had moved to the South End, faded into obscurity and had changed from underground to assimilationist.

Goodbye to Peter

I remember once that we went bowling in Boston — somewhere in West Roxbury I think — with a bunch of our friends.

Anyway Peter Medoff, who had joined us, was in pain and nausea from his HIV, and smoked a joint to help. Peter was always in pain. The marijuana helped a lot. A police officer started yelling at the top of his lungs at Peter telling him this was a 'family' place, arrested him, pushing his frail body against the wall and putting him in manacles, dragging him off to a police station a few blocks from the bowling alley.

I had to follow the group and I demanded to talk to the chief, and read him the riot act. I told him to call the police commissioner, and after a lot of fuss I managed to get the whole thing dropped. If I had not been a powerful city councilor at the time, Peter might have had his death in jail with far more pain and with far fewer friends around than what actually happened.

This made the perhaps hundredth time I had to do something about the arrogant bullying of police — a group I had learned over the years to hate. It amazed me how stupid, insensitive and bigoted many of them were. If you think I am exaggerating, read the final report of the St. Clair Commission on the Boston Police Department, which gives you a polite version of what an independent investigation concluded.

I walked into the Arlington Street Church on Saturday, May 14th, 1994, which was full for the memorial service of Peter Medoff. My efforts to get him a therapeutic vaccine called MGS120 produced by a company called MicroGenesis run by a short, fast talking guy named Frank Volvovitz, had Robert and Peter going week after week to Greenwich, Connecticut, but the vaccine did not seem to help. I remember once Peter and Robert got stuck in a snowstorm on the way back and had to get a neighbor to help. It was a difficult thing to keep going on with this therapeutic effort but at the time, there was little else to go on, except for "the Bomb" (we now call this "cocktails"), which we were too afraid to use. Dr. Alfred DeMaria, who was one of the top three people at our Department of Public Health, knew about our plans and much later noted how far ahead of anyone else our thinking on how to treat AIDS had been.

Walking into the church did not make me feel particularly good.

Peter had hung on to finish his book, *Streets of Hope* which he wrote with Holly Sklaar, and Robert and I went to the book signing where it was clear this was what he wanted to do as the final chapter of his life here on earth. Hundreds of people came to the signing in a ballroom of a hotel in downtown, with Peter at a table with piles of books. He signed them and said goodbye to all the people who were part of his life. My copy had a note from Peter saying, "David — thanks for your political inspiration and insights. They're in this book! Enjoy it! Love, Peter."

Later, in his apartment, he put on a cult classic movie we loved – "Harold and Maude" – and took enough pills to go to sleep forever. With the help of several friends he put an end to the daily pain and despair that marked HIV in those days. As so many of his friends did, Robert and I waited quietly at home during that afternoon vigil, waiting in near silence for the news of his passing.

I was the closing speaker for the memorial ceremony, listed as from the "Human Rights Institute," and I spoke from my heart, poetically, honestly, at times making people a bit uncomfortable, for Peter was part of the sexual revolution that AIDS was rapidly extinguishing.

Peter was big on reality. Not so long ago I remember a sunny day in Washington: Gays in the Millinery were marching, Peter in the middle of this mad group, a dozen or two strong among the million who came to freedom day, yelling, "Make hats not war," making fun for fans of gay political theater and among the many marchers, the cheers and TV cameras went for the queers in hats with feathers in their hair.

He could have managed Hartford, Connecticut — there was an offer — but would not begin what he could not finish. He was one of those who chose to make history without trying to stand in its center. He understood forces larger than himself — knew himself to be a passenger on the ship, but determined to be the uppity passenger. He's probably having a fight with the captain right now.

I loved him. He was part of our family He gave me hope and laughter and lots of advice, not all of which was easy to hear. I'm angry he left us.

Peter knew how to have fun. To dance, to sing off key. He did not think life was just to sip and taste. He wasn't afraid to swallow.

*And as we move forward without forgetting him, and witness
the genocide of a twelve-year epidemic, remember that we
have witnessed regicide as well... for Peter was a Prince.*

The Recessional Music was "If You Wanna Be" from "Harold and Maude."

Neil Sullivan, with whom I had worked for ten years, told me I had done well, passing over his uncomfortableness at my mentioning sex, and a woman whom I had known for years was touched by the poetry of my spontaneous closing speech.

I loved Peter and wanted to say goodbye the way I wanted to say goodbye. I think the passion moved people.

If you want to know who Peter really was, go to the part of Boston called the "Dudley Street Neighborhood Initiative" which, under Peter's leadership, transformed itself from a bombed out, bummed out place to a place filled with hope. It is flowering in the depression with parks, gardens, businesses, youth camps and new homes. Peter helped get the neighborhood so strong it got eminent domain powers. It made housing that could not be sold as speculation by ensuring the neighborhood owned the land. Peter understood that the revival of America requires a change of values from what makes the most money to what best serves the folks who live in a real community: a completely different way of organizing a society. To this day money spent on making the most money is destroying our society.

What we went through with Peter we went through with many of our friends.

I Continue To Work

I wrote a lengthy letter July 1st 1995 in which I called the 'temporary' homeless shelters which were now 12 years old as being intellectually bankrupt; that profit had reduced the 20,000 rooming house living spaces which housed mostly poor old people to fewer than 200; that as rents rose every business lost money because the poor spent while the rich hoarded; that rich landlords got money through untaxable loans against their holdings which they used to gamble with on nonproductive financial 'instruments' passing on the cost of the loans to the rents paid by tenants. I argued that as landlords upped rents the city should force them at least to fix the broken buildings, bring them up to the housing codes, and that universities should be forced to build housing and provide apartments for its students rather than letting the 'market' destroy one community after another.

I fought against my self-centered colleagues raising their pay by $10,000 during a holiday when no one was paying attention, raising their salaries way above what the average Bostonian earned. I pointed out that councilors spent a lot of their time at other jobs like law offices and that their tax returns should be made public. I wrote this in a *Globe* article.

Menino was such a horrible mayor that the *Herald*'s Joe Sciacca wrote that I was considering running against him. He was a pathetic leader not much more creative than what was required of him when his job was driving Senator Joe Timilty's car, his background for his job running the city. In fact, as temporary mayor, he promised the department heads and other administration officials that if they helped elect him, he would do his best to keep everything the same. (Except, apparently, for contributing developers!)

In November, I went to Seattle to meet with gay officials, now 60 of them, and the *New York Times* pointed to me as a founder of the group — I asked, "Who else can you talk to about your problems besides your domestic partner?"

I hosted a weekly show on *Radio Free Allston*, which made the papers, which I called "Truth Talk Radio." I said, "The radical thing is the truth. It's not on the left or on the right. We can disagree but there needs to be an area where we can agree at least about the facts. For example, if we are going to talk about welfare and welfare recipients, well, most of them are white; most are on for about two years. Welfare occupies about

2 percent of the budget. Any talk about welfare needs to begin with the facts, the real context."

I argued that most problems can be solved right here on the city level.

Charles E. Reade
1960-1995

This is very difficult for me to write, as I am sure around the world there are too many difficult stories of those who died. It is one reason I still try to help see an end to the killer epidemic whose beginning I had watched.

Robert and I lived in the Fenway and once there was a market called "The Bostonian" — a small superette whose owner was always in the store, which we used a lot because it was very close to our house.

One day, while I was looking for something in the market, I noticed a young man with blond hair who seemed to me the most beautiful man I had ever met. I spoke with him, and he was laid back, gentle, smiled a lot, and agreed to come to our house and meet Robert and check out where we lived.

Eventually Charles helped Robert rebuild our first home in the Fenway and we grew quite close. Charles became for a short while, a lover, sweet and kind and full of a gentleness that made me feel protective. Robert grew very close to Charles, and it was common to come home and find Charles there, talking about something or another.

I found out, from Robert, that Charles had a somewhat abusive lover whom we thought beautiful but there was no way to pry Charles away from being pushed around — perhaps he needed that.

· A SERVICE ·
in CELEBRATION of the LIFE of
Charles E. Reade
1960 - 1995

June 12, 1995
at 1 o'clock in the afternoon

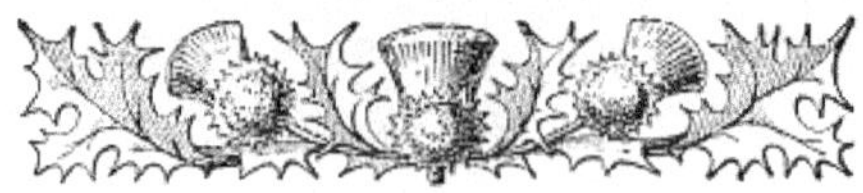

Later it became clear to Robert (who always has an intuition about these things) that Charles' lover clearly was ill, and I suppose it was inevitable that Charles as well would grow ill of the gay plague, and Robert spent hours with him, at his various homes, watching Charles create art and being one of the most wonderful people we have ever met.

Robert gave permission for Charles to die, for he struggled so mightily to keep alive even though he desperately wanted to leave it all behind. Robert could tell this, his grandmother having had died a little earlier. He told Charles, as Charles lay in bed struggling, that there would be people waiting for him and that he would not be alone. That we would miss him, but that it was ok for him to leave. Robert was with Charles when he died, standing next to the bed. He breathing was getting slower and slower and then he took a gasp and then he didn't breathe again. For Robert it seemed like the light in the room changed.

Launching a New Effort

Either AIDS would end me by turning me into a driveling bag of sadness or I would have to fight back. Robert Folan-Johnson started the Boston chapter of ACT UP and we had meetings at our house every week. As *Search For A Cure*, we wrote articles for *Bay Windows* weekly and over the years ended up being published in some 400 gay and lesbian publications.

Robert went weekly for vaccine shots to Connecticut. I was hopeful that a therapeutic vaccine therapy would lengthen his life. The creator of this vaccine was a guy named Frank Volvovitz. To be an advocate, I decided I had to learn about viruses, vaccines and AIDS.

It turns out that the U.S. Army had put together an actual plan for mobilizing resources to find a way to end the epidemic. I got a copy of and decided I would have to contact people in the Army.

In the meantime the gay community was inventing safer sex; trying out curcumin powder; using Ayurvedic cures from India; trying to heat up blood high enough to kill HIV and then reinfuse it; pray; used the armamentarium of medicines for opportunistic infections for both treatment and prophylaxis; invented the use of aerosolized pentamadine to treat PCP pneumonia; even using trampolines to see if jumping up and down would help. *Search For A Cure* was given "magnetized water" from the OhNo institute to use as a therapy and dozens of other far out ideas. We tried everything.

I was increasingly convinced that "The Bomb" cocktail would be what worked.

Anyway, I didn't know enough immunology. I didn't know any really except the little I learned years earlier from my penicillin allergy.

Apparently Congress had raised a few million to test the Army-developed vaccine but Congressional hearings began dragging and there was an argument about whether Congress could direct how money should be spent on research. It was a stupid hearing, and a stupid argument.

Keep in mind the Congress did not suddenly decide to test an AIDS vaccine: scientists who had been working on vaccines with the US Army for half a century were telling it that we needed to test this vaccine now.

I eventually convinced Al DeMaria to push for enough money to have Massachusetts conducted the only trial of a vaccine done by a state in the USA. We eventually got maybe $5 million to pull this off. But it all worked out somehow.

JOHN JOSEPH MOAKLEY

COMMITTEE ON RULES
CHAIRMAN

Congress of the United States
House of Representatives
Washington, DC 20515-2109
November 7, 1994

Mr. Steven Morin
Legislative Assistant
The Honorable Nancy Pelosi
240 Cannon House Office Building
Washington, D.C. 20515

Dear Mr. Morin:

The Commonwealth of Massachusetts has formally requested five million dollars from the federal government for the Massachusetts Department of Public Health in order to continue and expand its trials of potential therapies to combat HIV/AIDS. The attached letters from Massachusetts Lieutenant Governor Paul Cellucci and Assistant Commissioner of Public Health Dr. Alfred DeMaria highlight some of their concerns surrounding the redirection of a 1992 Congressional Appropriation of twenty million dollars for large scale domestic efficacy trials of therapeutic AIDS vaccines.

The Boston Human Rights Institute is sponsoring a briefing, which I am hosting in the House Rules Committee hearing room, located in H-312 of the Capitol Building. The briefing will take place on November 15, 1994 from 11:00 am to 3:00 pm. Lunch will also be provided by the Boston Human Rights Institute. The briefing will include a presentation by Dr. DeMaria, who will be joined by a small group of independent researchers who have been Principal Investigators for clinical trials of promising HIV/AIDS therapies.

The intent of the briefing is to provide Congress with the scientific edification needed to pursue the funding request. During the course of these presentations, there will be a brief exploration of how the study undertaken by the Massachusetts Department of Public Health was intended to complement federally sponsored trials which have never taken place.

I hope to see you on the 15th of November and please RSVP to Kathleen Taixeira of my staff at 225-8273 if you are able to attend.

Sincerely,

JOHN JOSEPH MOAKLEY
Member of Congress

JJM:xx

The effort to get money for testing the vaccine and other aggressive research efforts was not easy. Our non-profit got letters of support from Governor William Weld's office, from the State Department of Public Health over the Assistant Commissioner Alfred DeMaria's signature, and got Congressman Moakley to host a briefing in the Capitol Building at which *Search For A Cure* presented the scientific rationale for requesting $5 million to help the state research the disease.

At the briefing many people from groups like the National Association of People with AIDS to leaders in the scientific research testified to congressional staff about the need for help.

Tramont

I needed to be able to understand the difference between an idea with merit and a stupid idea if I was going to be an effective AIDS activist. We were sneaking into the yearly national scientific meetings with thousands of scientists, talking to everyone we could, and attending the talks, but much was beyond us. I got some time with a man named Ed Tramont, who was in the Army, and had created a new institute for the study of medicine at University of Maryland, which would become the "Institute for Human Virology."

My first meeting with Ed Tramont: a tall man with grey hair walked into the room. He took one look at me, told me to sit down, got a big pad of paper on a tripod with magic markers and said, "First, let's explain what correlates of immunity are."

Ed was amazing. He spent his life trying to make our society better. Over the next 20 years he gave me all the time I needed to understand everything from the science of immunology to the intramural political fights within the world's largest medical university, the National Institutes of Health (NIH).

As the story unfolds it becomes important to know a little bit about vaccines, so I apologize for a short digression about what Ed taught me.

The US Army invented many vaccines, perhaps the majority of those approved by the FDA. This made sense as soldiers would travel to many places which harbored diseases that, for the most part, did not exist in the United States. Tramont told me the Army had invented a vaccine for venereal diseases, which for some reason did not end up getting used. Some day I want to study this more as such a vaccine would be of great use to humanity.

Anyway, the way vaccines were developed, after the thousand years of fumbling, was to find someone who did not get sick from the disease and figure out what part of our immune system protected them, then invent a type of vaccine that created the same kind of protection.

The ways that those who got well after getting a virus were called the "correlates of immunity," a kind of road map that guided scientists in finding a successful vaccine.

There was a big problem with the virus HIV. Nobody got better. There was no road map. I was lost in the talk about helper T cells, B cells, and humoral vs. cellular responses, so I asked for help and Ed arranged for it.

After books and training, conferences and reading articles, I finally began to understand a little about the immune system and in the process met many of the leading figures in immunology and got to understand how extraordinary both the science and the people working on it were.

The Politics of AIDS

I co-authored two articles in 1994 with well known scientists spelling out how pissed off we were getting that the search for a vaccine was going nowhere.

Until the gay community essentially reformed the way the world of medicine developed cures — from the notion of "compassionate use" and "fast tracking," to participation by those fighting the disease on state decision-making panels, and participation in yearly scientific meeting — there was little direction. Ronald Reagan had difficulty saying 'AIDS,' but I have to hand it to him that he appointed an amazing man, Dr. Anthony 'Tony' Fauci, to run the effort to find a cure. Fauci still remembers me from the day that all of the gay elected officials came to see him – I stood on his desk – and ranted over the denial of AZT, the first AIDS medicine which Rock Hudson went to Paris to get, to be given to people with HIV here in the United States.

The search for a vaccine would not take a clear form until President Clinton created a vaccine center for this purpose and until the

Leadership needed in development of an AIDS vaccine

BOSTON GLOBE 8-5-94

DAVID SCONDRAS and DR. PAUL EPSTEIN

Most of us think of vaccines as a way of helping our immune systems prevent disease, but in recent years, some have been used to alleviate illness after it occurs. This approach would be of extraordinary help to the hundreds of thousands of people infected with the HIV virus in this country, if only the government and private industry would work together to expedite research.

The prospects for a vaccine to prevent HIV are less promising. A few weeks ago the National Institutes of Health AIDS Research Advisory Committee correctly voted not to begin national testing of one vaccine that might have some protective value because there is as yet no compelling evidence that it might work better than other vaccine products. But it did not take the next crucial step – to formulate a coherent strategy for vaccine development. These tests and that strategy are long overdue.

In the interim, the manufacturer of the rejected vaccine has boldly stated that it will attempt to get Congress and the president to overturn the NIH decision. The lack of a plan to test vaccines creates the vacuum in which such an effort might well succeed.

The NIH, Congress and the president have a fundamental decision to make: Now that there is evidence that vaccines may help people with HIV infection, and may possibly prevent disease, they must provide the leadership and federal resources necessary to see that promising therapies are quickly tested. The 1.5 million Americans infected with the virus deserve no less.

Because there is a lack of central leadership and a strategic plan, millions of dollars are being spent on projects of questionable worth in the midst of a worldwide pandemic. While 40 million people infected with HIV worldwide wait for a cure, the NIH is spending money on determining whether alcohol-

affects HIV in some way, whether HIV affects the heart muscle and a thousand other projects not targeted on finding a way to manage the disease. And the new director of the NIH is committed to moving even more money away from patient-oriented research.

Meanwhile, we lack funds for urgent and relevant research. For example, we need behavioral research to learn how effective the use of nonoxynol-9, a common spermicide, is against HIV alone or in helping condoms slow down the spread of the virus. What kinds of sexual practices are really safe? To what extent can vaccines that have been available since 1987 help infected people? Crucial studies of vaccines that seem to have some good effects on the immune system are going unfunded.

All of this reflects the lack of focus and the lack of a clear and compelling plan that has characterized the NIH's AIDS efforts for over a decade. Without immediate intervention, the problem will grow worse.

In 1987 Jonas Salk, famous for the development of the polio vaccine, expressed his belief that a therapeutic AIDS vaccine could be developed. Within the last few years, vaccines to treat herpes, leprosy, leishmaniasis, tuberculosis and hepatitis B have been developed and are being tested. The first to be completed shows that the herpes vaccine reduces recurrences in people with herpes by 30 percent. The results from the leprosy vaccine are very encouraging – 60 percent of people with severe forms of the disease in combination with medications that didn't work alone got the immune system to clear the lesions and control the leprosy bacillus.

The first therapeutic AIDS vaccine, called VaxSyn, was tested at Walter Reed Hospital in Washington, the Army and in Montreal, Sweden and Connecticut. The results have been very encouraging. The second, developed by Salk, has shown in a controlled trial that it slows down the rate at which the virus grows. Still other vaccines, like one called Genrpg 120, has produced antibodies that have protected chimps from the virus.

KEVIN KRENECK ILLUSTRATION

safety, decided it was necessary to do large scale tests and as was customary, went to Congress and got $20 million to do them. The NIH board of advisers voted unanimously to move forward with testing of several vaccines.

These tests were never done.

Politics interfered. No new data undermined these tests, and they still must happen if we are to move forward, but a series of events, unrelated to science and involving political infighting among companies, agencies and some politicians, killed these tests.

In the meantime, given the lack of consistent support and the tendency of the NIH to lurch from one incompleted project to the next, companies are starting to find it impossible to continue to develop the vaccines. Repligen just announced it was abandoning its vaccine efforts. Wyeth pulled out of the ef-

having trouble finding funding.

In the face of multiple emerging and resurging diseases, a new theory for managing infections is needed. The NIH, the drug companies and the scientific community need to develop a clear collaborative plan and implement it this fall, so that we can quickly test the efficacy of the therapeutic vaccine approach and other immune therapies to help control the AIDS epidemic. We must learn to augment, retune and modulate the immune system to help it identify and take action against a new set of clever enemies that are eluding our existing medicines.

David Scondras, a former Boston city councilor, is a member of the Massachusetts AIDS Fund Advisory Board. Paul Epstein, M.D., is chairman of the Cambridge AIDS

Funds sought for AIDS vaccine testing

By Scott S. Greenberger
STATES NEWS SERVICE

WASHINGTON – Massachusetts health officials and AIDS researchers and activists yesterday lobbied Capitol Hill lawmakers for $5 million to expand a promising trial of a therapeutic vaccine to treat the disease.

The group charged that the federal government has ignored a hopeful track in the AIDS fight by withholding research money slated for vaccines that strengthen the immune system. They say that $20 million appropriated by Congress in 1992 for the research has been "redirected."

Assistant Public Health Commissioner Dr. Alfred DeMaria, the principal investigator in the trial, said the gp160 vaccine has been administered to 139 HIV-infected Bay State residents with encouraging results.

He told congressional staffers that the vaccine, made from synthetic pieces of the AIDS virus' outer coat called gp160, has elicited antibody responses to HIV in 30 percent to 40 percent of the patients in the trial. The federal funding would enable researchers to include up to 2,400 people in the study, he said.

Several potential HIV vaccines are being tested on patients infected with the virus in hopes of slowing the progress of the disease as well as preventing it.

The National Institutes of Health has overlooked immune-based solutions to AIDS and has focused federal dollars on attempts to eradicate the virus with a "magic bullet," charged David Scondras of the Massachusetts AIDS Fund Advisory Board, a former Boston city councilor.

"The feds have a good deal of money that is being spent in ways that do not reflect congressional appropriations and which defy common sense," Scondras said.

'There is no team effort in the AIDS fight. There is no collaboration and no strategy.'

DR. CALVIN COHEN
Of the New England
Community Research Initiative

He said NIH is only now conducting a trial of the therapeutic HIV vaccine developed in 1987 by Dr. Jonas Salk, who developed the polio vaccine.

Scondras said "magic bullet" studies should continue, but federal dollars should support other avenues as well.

Several researchers joined Scondras in criticizing NIH's co-ordination of the AIDS battle.

"There is no team effort in the AIDS fight," argued Dr. Calvin Cohen of the New England Community Research Initiative. "There is no collaboration and no strategy."

Cohen charged that NIH refused to fund research on an antibiotic later used effectively against the pneumonia that kills many AIDS patients; neglected to investigate German research on an ulcer drug that can boost depleted immune system T-cells in AIDS patients; and has ignored "provocative, promising data" on a drug made from an Indian herb.

Most importantly, said Cohen, NIH has failed to promote "community-based" research, like the gp160 study in Massachusetts.

A spokesman for NIH said the government is beefing up its investigation into the HIV virus and centralizing its efforts, but did not answer any of the specific charges.

At yesterday'sthe meeting in the Capitol, the researchers said Massachusetts can launch in six weeks a research trial that can take up to a year for the federal government to get under way.

"The state efforts should be part of the team effort to check this stuff out," said Cohen.

Scondras said a letter he recently received from NIH epitomizes the problem.

"I asked them for an AIDS research agenda and they sent me a list of projects," he remarked. "A list is not a plan."

Robert and Dr. Tony Japour

In Boston an experiment was beginning. Scientists would use two medicines, Ritonavir and Saquinavir together and see if a one-two punch of powerful antivirals could contain the virus. A non-profit called "Community Research Initiative" headed up this project. Robert got into the trial testing this idea, which was the only kind of 'bomb' that we could try because he had already used up the other medicines, and his virus was already resistant to them.

The early results were looking good.

In the meantime, Dr. Tony Japour was working on a new drug and Robert met him — we were interested in using it when it was ready. Tony left to work at Abbott and would eventually come in second when George Bush appointed a new director for the NIH. That new drug would eventually become 'Kaletra' which Robert successfully used for 13 years.

Search For A Cure Continues

The January 19th (1994) edition of the Northeastern News had an article detailing a frat's (Theta Delta Chi) efforts to help *Search For A Cure* build its office in a run down building owned by Northeastern University.

In between dealing with issues around AIDS I was constantly being reviewed by the media about my decision on whether or not to run for office again. This would continue for five years. Even when I was in California dealing with an AIDS vaccine in 1998, the newspapers called me to check and see if I would run. articles which essentially asked if I would 'return' to public life would lead you to believe I had left it. I never left it because it had always been the same effort: to make a difference in the world that helps everyone live a life more full, happy and meaningful. That did not necessitate running for office.

I was also growing tired of the assimilationist tendencies of the newer generation of political people, for they had lost their way by thinking that obedience to the status quo would gain acceptance, respect and power. In a war this only makes you vulnerable.

Search For A Cure continued for twenty-five years, which was not what I had in mind when Elaine Noble and so many others helped me put it together. I figured it would take two, maybe four, years to deal with this disease. I was so wrong.

It turned out that my articles on vaccines and the growing popularity of *Search* led to an unexpected adventure that continues through today. I was approached, I forget exactly how, by two men in suits who seemed rather like security guards. They wanted us to go to a hotel in Cambridge, which we did. Up some stairs in a lobby of potted plants and wide expanses — I always liked lobbies, kind of indoor gardens — and at the top of the stairs in a chair against a wall, facing the widest part of the corridor and surrounded by the suits, was an older man with white hair who looked through eyes that were intense.

His name was Jonas Salk.

"Do you want to live?" he said. "Do you want the vaccine?" I was not sure what he was talking about. "You have to go get it," he said. It was clear he meant forming a political effort to get the government to give it out, but I was not aware of any vaccine.

It turns out that in 1987 Jonas Salk announced in Europe that he had completed work on a whole-killed vaccine. The process of killing the virus to the satisfaction of the FDA removed its outer garments, the glycosylated envelope that so many viruses wear, but the parts of the virus that made it work were still intact and that was what was needed for the body to 'see' in order to make a response to kill the virus.

Salk's vaccine, called "Remune," had been tested on hundreds of people in California who had HIV to see if it could help, because California had its own FDA and could grant permission to test drugs without the sanction of the Federal FDA, but now to get permission to move into much larger studies across the country, Salk's company, the Immune Response Corporation, would have to get permission from the federal FDA, which was not too happy with California for sidestepping it. Only Massachusetts and California can do this.

I was getting increasingly upset over the vaccine effort. When you asked scientists if a whole-killed vaccine, the kind that is used on every single virus ever successfully stopped by a vaccine, would work they would knowingly say "no." When you asked them why, they could not answer, coming up with theoretical gibberish like "the envelope changes too fast to get a vaccine that could elicit responses to the rapidly changing clothing of the virus." When you asked whether they had tried this old approach, which so far had always worked, they said "no." When you asked if they knew the correlates of immunity they said "no." So they knew that something, which they never tested, which had always worked before, would not work now about a virus that they knew next to nothing about based on their speculations about how HIV worked.

"Why not try the old ways and if they don't work, then go looking for some new never before done way?" I would ask, and no one had any answer.

I think it was because people hated Salk, who had a habit of calling big shots at the FDA "idiots" in public. Anyway, I didn't see how I could help, but got an invitation to come to California. to a place near San Diego, and see the data for myself along with many other AIDS activists.

In California, I met Dennis Carlo, who ran the company Jonas set up to make Remune, and Ron Moss, who worked there.

The data that was presented about the vaccine showed that people who took Remune had their T-cells decline more slowly than those who did not. At the time we did not have a lot of ways to figure out if something worked — T-cell decline and getting sick with opportunistic infections toward the end of the disease were the only markers you could use to decide if something was helping or not.

We went to the Salk Institute, where we first met Jonas' son Peter Salk, who has become a lifelong friend. He explained his father's thinking and I remember talking slowly about Peter's vision of a world connected to every piece of itself in ways, if woken up, that might bring a new kind of consciousness to bear on the pain of the planet. I liked Peter. I tried to convince him to participate in getting his father's vaccine tested, but I came to realize that Peter was a very private person not comfortable with the kinds of social interaction that would be needed for him to be of help.

Like a Bird

I could not believe my ears. Robert had been on gp160, the vaccine made by MicroGenesis, for a long time, when Frank Volvovitz gave me a call. Apparently there was the next day going to be a meeting in Greenwich, Connecticut of the board of directors of the company that made the vaccine to shut it all down, to end making any more of it. For me, it was a disaster. Hope is what keeps us alive, and to take away the hope would leave Robert and me with less to fight with. I had to do something about it.

But I had promised Ralph Martin, the district attorney of Suffolk County, that I would be at a press conference to endorse him along with Rosaria at one o'clock — there was no way to get from Greenwich, Connecticut, talk to the board of directors, and get back to Boston by 1 PM in a car.

I had an idea. I called my old friend Gwen Bloomingdale who had moved to Provincetown with her lover where they ran the Boston to P-Town airline. Gwen's lover, Barbara Gard, loved planes and had a single engine. I begged. It turned out that they had formed an organization of people who flew small planes to get people with HIV to medical help quickly when needed. So it was not so weird a request.

There was an airstrip near Waltham or somewhere nearby, and first thing in the morning Dave Munshine and I sped to an airstrip, my heart beating fast, as a one-engine plane lands and a woman waves her hand at us. We run up to the plane and I get in the co-pilot's seat and Munshine in the back.

This was my first time in a small plane and it was wonderful. I was allowed to fly the plane for most of the trip, going over hills, feeling like someone in a Hollywood scene.

We landed near MicroGenesis where a car was waiting that rushed us to the board meeting. I was barely in time. We interrupted the proceedings and I gave a passionate speech on why the company needed to finish what it began, for its own integrity, for those taking the vaccine, for the future in which people would wonder if the company had staying power, and because the vaccine might work. I won the vote and the vaccine stayed in production.

Back we flew to Boston. On the steps near the Suffolk Superior Courthouse, Rosaria and I had our press conference. Rosaria was annoyed that I looked a little disheveled but then, she really didn't know what I had been through that morning.

Years later, Gwen and Barbara, trying to fly around the world, disappeared from this earth off the coast of Iceland. They were some of the greats, worthy of emulation, as over and over again when faced with a decision fraught with danger they always said, "Why not?"

Washington, D.C., 1995

I attended the first White House Conference on AIDS – I felt odd being on the inside of a meeting that my friends were picketing on the outside – a reversal of roles for me. In my heart, I felt the people on the outside were basically right, but I felt their choice of tactic gave potential help to Bob Dole's efforts to unseat Clinton. I didn't trust Bob Dole.

I was assigned to the working group on AIDS treatment, and got lost in the Executive Office Building, as did many of the senior members of the Clinton administration. It's a giant gray stone wedding cake of a building with an internal labyrinth of small rooms and narrow hallways. There were maybe 20 people in the small conference room, including some of the most famous of scientists and the leadership of the National

Institutes of Health. Among them was the photogenic, soft spoken and persuasive Tony Fauci, the most consistent point person for several administrations on the effort to find a cure and vaccine for the disease. There were members of the President's Commission on AIDS, virologists, bench scientists, clinicians. It was a meeting of some of the country's most brilliant and powerful scientific administrators and researchers.

We drew up over 40 things the President could do to help speed up the search for a cure, and the tone of the meeting was optimistic. But when I raised the issue of Clade E, the new, more infectious strain of the virus, once again the most powerful people in the country panicked and basically said that we should not tell the country about the new version of the virus. The virus had mutated and one new form of it had spread across Asia, reached Japan, and now had been found in American soldiers – a new form that is primarily heterosexually transmitted and more infectious than the kind that has primarily affected gay men in America.

The people around the table, who disagreed about most things, were unanimous in not frightening the public about the new virus. I thought this was irresponsible, because kids across America were not being told that the virus that infected their gay brothers and drug users had a cousin that preyed on them as well.

I guess my friends at the Massachusetts Department of Public Health were right – nobody wanted to be Chicken Little, and everyone was willing to wait to see if the epidemic spread to straight young people, and only then call for action. Of course, since the disease is so slow to show symptoms, this means waiting until it is too late for hundreds of thousands of children. I just hoped in my heart that I was wrong about all this, but so far everything pointed to my being right and I was frightened.

I almost was cut out of seeing the President in the afternoon, at the meeting of two hundred AIDS activists with Clinton in which he listened to reports from nine workshops, including the one I was part of, which would say nothing about Clade E.

On some level, there would be a tragic kind of justice involved if the country found out too late for so many of its children. My whole life had been spent coping with coming out as a gay person in a place that hated people like me. Most Americans don't realize that in some countries, like Holland, gays can get political asylum from the United States because the oppression is so barbaric here. So when in America mostly gays got sick, there was no sense of urgency – no Manhattan Project toward a cure, no money to build new vaccines. Just that year more money had been spent to build a nuclear sub we didn't need than the entire effort to find a cure to AIDS. We didn't even have the money to test the vaccines that already existed.

If Americans cared about their poor and gay and drug-addicted and black members as much as they did about their suburban straight white children, we would already have had a vaccine and a cure — even with the underfunded, disorganized effort of the previous fifteen years, a great deal had been accomplished. But prejudice produces blindness, and it had not yet occurred to America that the virus, which mutates so fast, might eventually take a form that attacks everybody.

Lots of people think that the notion that oppression of anyone anywhere is oppression of everyone everywhere is just an unrealistic moral goal, but in fact it is a practical operating principle. Human history is littered with the bones of those who underestimated the danger of teaching people to hate each other, from the sands of the Middle East to the funeral parlors of America. So maybe on some higher level, the head-in-the-sand attitude of our leaders about the new strain of the virus is part of a painful lesson.

But I couldn't get it out of my head that a lot of beautiful, innocent kids might pay for the cowardice of the nation's guardians.

I wanted to tell the president to speed up the research, to grab the bull by the horns and test the new drugs that seem to work but which we don't know how to use, to test the vaccines we already have but are too frightened to try out and too underfunded to improve, to warn people about the new strain of the virus.

Again and again over the past 25 years I have seen how often people most affected by decisions had to take actions to make sure their voices, feelings and solutions to problems are heard by decision makers. The AIDS issue is no exception.

Bill Clinton came into the room with the traditional standing ovation, and proceeded to deliver a 20 minute set of promises and analysis to a room filled with the finest minds on AIDS – an impressive performance in which he showed a grasp of subtleties and specifics that reflected great staff work and a quick mind. He listened patiently for over an hour to the reports from each of the groups, and then engaged in an unorchestrated give and take with the audience.

It was clear that Clinton actually understood many of the complex issues the audience was raising, and I felt uplifted that we finally had a president willing to talk about finding a cure and a vaccine for AIDS, willing to use the word homophobia as a cause of part of the trouble, willing to commit an administration to an upgraded effort to cut red tape toward a cure. He repeatedly asked us to remember as we criticize the way the country has responded to AIDS that "Americans are essentially good people. When the chips are down, they do the right thing."

Sometimes they do, and sometimes they don't. I translated the president's caution as "don't trash the people you're trying to get help from."

Americans are good people if they know what's going on (which they rarely get a chance to do) and when they overcome their sense of powerlessness that is programmed into them all their life.

Given that the last two years of my life had been spent trying to cut red tape toward finding a cure for AIDS, this attitude of the president's of focusing on "a cure and a vaccine" was great to hear. Now hopefully the rhetoric would be matched by actions that reflected the spirit of the spoken commitments.

I knew how many of us at the conference felt tired, bitter, frustrated, hurt and depressed from watching their friends and lovers die slowly while the so-called national effort to find a therapy for the disease progressed slowly, without any sense of urgency. I knew how cynical most of us were, but I also knew that we collectively were the last best hope for some 20 million people around the world and over a million Americans, and that we had to do the best we could to push the administration to cut red tape toward finding a cure.

Washington, like all of America, is a set of contradictions. Mostly, what it promises is contradicted by what it delivers. Speeches are made here daily on the grandeur of our society, its wealth and majesty, its fairness, compassion and sensitivity. These speeches have a hollow ring to the gays and lesbians who feel betrayed by that grand Supreme Court building that ruled it's okay to go into gay people's bedrooms and arrest them for being gay. They have a hollow ring to the poor who watch Newt Gingrich and his friends in Congress take away the pittance grudgingly thrown to them, and turn it over to the members of America's privileged, rich ruling class that is offended when someone points out that they even exist. A hollow ring to those without health insurance, those unable to buy a home, those who cannot find work, those whose work is underpaid and unsatisfying.

A city that proclaims its delight at the end of apartheid in South Africa with marches and fanfare, while practicing social apartheid against gays and economic apartheid against blacks. A city in which there is a color line anyone can see who has eyes not trained by D.C. double talk. The Capitol's lawns are cut by blacks, garbage is collected by blacks, taxis are driven by blacks; a city of white rulers serviced by black and Hispanic low income workers.

A city that sat impassively as the AIDS epidemic which killed more people than all the wars America fought in the 20th century continued to ravage families across the continent because society believed AIDS only killed people nobody likes.

Yet it is the place of power, and the place of decisions that create and destroy hope and happiness, so all of those like myself who spent their lives trying to make the planet a little more peaceful, a little kinder, a little more open-minded and a little more empowering to all of the people that live together on this little whirling globe found ourselves dragged by a force almost magnetic in its insistence to this city of living monuments.

During the years Bill Clinton wasn't inhaling, I was marching in Washington, getting arrested by Richard Nixon's paranoid police as I tried to help stop the war in Vietnam. Now, in 1995, more than 25 years of trips to the land of Oz later, I found myself invited by a President into the White House, to the first-in-history White House Conference on AIDS.

During the afternoon, I went to a reception at the Renwick Gallery. Hillary Clinton spoke to us of her husband's veto of Medicaid cuts, the federal program that pays for much of the medicine for people with AIDS, and I felt hopeful for all of us because it is clear that for whatever reason, this administration has some level of genuine concern for the elderly, the sick and the needy.

Hillary was a fighter. I could hear it in her voice. When she finished the speech that was interrupted often by applause, I told her that when her husband finishes, I'd work on her campaign for President. She laughed and shook her head, saying "No way. Eight years is enough of this for anyone."

Soon after the Washington reception, we traveled to Canada to the international AIDS conference, which could not be held in the U.S.A. because the country refused to allow people with HIV to enter. But we would go first to Haiti.

133 /   March, 1995: Haiti

The years after losing the city council election I felt little confused on what I wanted to do. Whatever I would eventually decide, it seemed important to do what I could to help, wherever I could.

I decided to go to Haiti in part because I had met Jean Bertrand Aristide, the elected president of Haiti who was ousted by a coup primarily supported by the "Tonton Macoutes," a violent group some of whom wore cowboy hats. When he came to Boston, I lent him my bullet proof vest. I told friends that I was going to Haiti because I wanted it back. Aristide eventually would be re-installed in Haiti with American support in return for giving up on the socialism and independence of the movement that brought him to power and his support for the "American Plan."

Tonton Macoutes with cowboy hats: see takshzilabeta.com

I went to Haiti with a group to see if I could help in any way with the efforts to fight AIDS. On March 1st, 1995 I left from JFK for Port-au-Prince. We were a motley crew. On the other hand, everyone not a fascist belongs to a motley crew.

Ellen Israel – one member of our group – said she was concerned that my going to a gay bar in Haiti might be dangerous to me and also might 'discredit' the delegation. I have grown rather tired over the decades of wearing a scarlet letter — of constantly being concerned with how the uneducated, the small-minded, the mean and the bullies feel.

My own feeling was that a delegation, which gets 'discredited' by association with gays, is dealing with a society I feel had no credit to begin with. I was determined to interact with gay people in Haiti, and with the Health Ministry on the issue of an AIDS vaccine and how gays are treated. The whole thing was a moot point, as Haiti had no gay bars according to my most recent information. There is a "gathering place" at a family restaurant near the Holiday Inn, which is also near the cruising area.

One of my gay Haitian students (I have had several as students) spent time sharing aspects of being "in the life" in Haiti. Clearly the society is schizoid about it — violently homophobic yet with lots of gay sex.

The equation between gay and HIV was made clear when the government of Haiti, learning that scientists had determined that some of the HIV that reached the United States had come from Haiti, said that this was impossible because Haiti did not have any gay people. It is said that the dictator of Haiti had been gay and that many in the government were gay.

This combination of action and denial seems a characteristic of totalitarian mindsets. I do not know why. Perhaps being gay is genetic and the more oppressive a culture the more gays pass on their genes? Now there is an argument for total freedom that a 'phobe could support!

In any event, I went to the cruising areas. And I decided to try hard to get Haiti to use an attenuated live vaccine as soon as possible to save people's lives.

First Impressions of Port-au-Prince

Landing at Port-au-Prince, the mountains in the background were beautiful but clearly showed signs of deforestation. At the airport there are children with guns — lots of very young soldiers — along with UN personnel. I noticed that Haitian men touched each other a lot and acted friendly. Porters at the airport pressured the arrivals to use them — I found it hard to say no — people needed money pretty badly. Kids aged 8-12 stayed next to the cars hoping to get a handout.

Many people in Haiti spoke Creole, but a surprising number who had gone to school had learned French. Because I spoke some French, I found myself from time to time switching languages to help explain what I was thinking to people that were amazingly caring.

Although I was staying with a family whose son spoke with me often, wanting to come to the United States — I wanted to help him achieve his dream but I was never able to – I found that the best place to learn about Haiti was at The Oloffson, an elaborate old wood and yellow brick hotel filled with upper class people of all sorts.

We were being oriented to serve as election observers. The military had deposed Aristide and seized power in 1991. They appointed Marc Bazin, who had been a World Bank official. Bazin represented the interests of the wealthy and was a favorite of George H.W. Bush. The coup collapsed in 1994 under pressure from the US and Aristide returned to Haiti, leading to the 1995 elections. There were essentially three forces: 'democratic,' 'reactionary,' and 'popular'. The reactionaries were the privileged who wanted to keep things the same way they had always been under Papa Doc Duvalier, the dictator. There were two factions among the reactionaries in Haiti: the *Tonton Macoutes* (the folks who got their way through terror), and the monopolists (much of Haiti's economic activity was owned and controlled by a handful of people). The popular forces were part of a loose democratic movement, with several reformist groups and Aristide. They embraced social liberalism without economic reform.

When Aristide had been elected in 1990 he supported political efforts by community groups and civilian power. He was overthrown immediately.

It became clear to me that like Boston politics, learning about Haiti would take a lifetime — there was no shortcut to understanding the complexities of the society and the issues with which its people were grappling.

Election Commission and Clinics

Up at 6:55 a.m. — I couldn't figure out where this "get up at daybreak" politically correct crap came from — for an early ride to the election commission offices.

Mostly Macoutes had been hired to work in the new elections. We decided to go to the election commission in order to ascertain if the concerns we heard about them were real. I noticed a lot of 'femme' behavior among the workers at the election commission. Also it seems that people in the place are quite clothes conscious. The femme behavior is either gay or possibly a class affectation.

On statues are signs saying, "He has come back."

There is a "truth commission" made up of seven members, three Haitians, three international members, and the president. It seems to have no mandate to do anything but research.

The new Haitian government was trying to transform institutions from engaging in arbitrary repression. It would be difficult to accomplish this given the way the country was structured: for example there were very tight relationships between the army, the police, and the judicial system. Many people were waiting to speak before the truth commission and seemed to trust it to do the right thing. The people I spoke with did not see their country, the 'real' people of their country, as killing, maiming, or terrorizing.

The day ended with us having some hope that Haiti was trying to recreate itself and I noted that some of the efforts Haiti was making such as those with the judiciary would benefit the USA.

In 1991, when Aristide was banished from Haiti in a coup, people in the streets and famous musicians sang a song called "Fèy." A verse from this traditional Voodoo lamentation was "My only son, they made him leave the country.". The military leaders of Haiti in 1991 that had ousted the elected President Aristide banned the song from the radio, increasing its popularity. The military leaders had to give up and allow Aristide to return in small part from the movement the song helped galvanize.

We would see a clinic today and speak with representatives from the main political movement in the country, the MPP.

I noticed a clinic, *Partners in Health,* which involved Paul Farmer and the Harvard School of Public Health. The clinic had family planning assistance. There was a consultation room with no equipment.

I noticed that the way the slums were constructed, there was no place to drain sewage at all. So people waited for rain. Even where there were latrines, rain and overflows contaminated sources of water.

We learned a great deal about the public health crises that impacted Haiti. There were limited condom distribution perhaps 10 condoms per month per person. We asked many questions and got a plethora of information about the efforts being made to bring public health to Haiti and its obstacles.

People argued that the CIA and other American forces were using the Macoutes to destabilize the society as a reaction to the progressive agenda of the MPP. For example, there are huge mass meetings for training on how to avoid AIDS. The previous Saturday, some 10,000 people came to be trained on AIDS. At the end of the meeting, the Macoutes came and destabilized the effort by shooting into the crowd. According to the MPP, the CIA uses the Macoutes to destabilize the society in order to get people in power that would obey the US directives.

The people we met characterized the US involvement as an "occupation," making it harder for the movement to fight. Aristide was characterized as having become an American puppet with Haiti entering into the "New World Order." It was difficult to disentangle the complex set of groups fighting for power as Haiti moved toward another election.

The Sociology of Poverty

The extent of open sewage, people selling food on the streets, lack of infrastructure, omnipresent filth, people washing clothes in water that stinks of urine and feces, no running water in many places and an odd mixture of contradictions I have seen over and over again — a kid with torn up, worn out clothes talking on a pocket cell phone. Cars that don't work driving down the street next to a new Mercedes.

Haitians dress well when they work. Fantastically.

My being American is itself a trigger: people are proud to answer in English.

On the other hand, the crime problem in Haiti is serious. Money becomes God when it is not distributed fairly.

Over half the people I see are children.

I spoke with prostitutes in their young twenties who told us where the gay hangout is. They laughed at the thought of men going after other men. Poor gay people seemed confined to a neon lit place where you could sometimes hear jazz. It was interesting how often I heard that Rafael Bazin was a pedophile.

It was fascinating how my white skin and English automatically conveyed class status to Haitians who worked for or were in upper income enclaves as if replying in English was symbolic of status just as driving a white American around was symbolic of class. It is amazing how difficult it is to share the feeling, the nuances. There is no way to adequately describe the grinding poverty. It is beyond imagination. If we saw people, felons in jail living in conditions like these people, we would close the jail and arrest the jailers as violating basic tenets of decency and humanity. If a person intentionally caused humans to live like this we would call them evil, butchers, beyond redemption, monsters, sadists, criminally insane.

Yet the people in the poor parts of Haiti, which is most of the country, live in this jail.

No running water. Often no food for days. No shelter, or shelter that leaks, is dark, stinks of urine. Unpicked-up garbage that floats by your door during the rain and in which children play. Toilets that sump onto open paths in the streets and mix with wash water and drinking water. Agonizing dehydration, diarrhea, malaria, AIDS, tuberculosis. Virtually no medical care and the little there is unsophisticated. People crowd around for a chance to see a doctor. Superstitions and rumors substitute for medical information. Papers printed in languages like French, which most people cannot read. Babies begging for love and food and money, desperate for all three. Overcrowding, 10 or 12 people in a room. Depression and people crying. Fear and no electricity. Darkness, boredom and pain.

In short, hell.

Home

I eventually left and returned to Boston, full of the statements of hundreds that left me bewildered at the scale of the problems and the chaos. The lack of planning, the lack of resources.

I thought looking it all over that Aristide and his Lavalas organization would win the elections and I was right. But a new day for Haiti would be years away.

It is 2012 as I write these words, and Aristide has come and gone and come and gone and the country is still in chaos.

I deeply admired Paul Farmer and the many who spent years doing whatever they could to help alleviate pain and suffering.

Perhaps for now that is the best that those of us with smaller voices can do.

I did not know how to help.

I am just not rich enough.

134 /   1996 Vancouver: "One World One Hope"

In Washington at the 1995 annual retrovirus meeting we heard rumors about what had happened with an AIDS vaccine. In Vancouver at the International Conference on AIDS we learned why. The first brought hope. The second explained why we should have it. And incidentally gave a scientist from New York, Dr. David Ho, the front page of TIME magazine as its 'Man of the Year' for 1996.

The following section contains many excerpts from the March 17, 1996 articles by Huntly Collins and Shankar Vedantam in the *Philadelphia Inquirer* as well as many other sources.

Nancy Kohl and Irving Sigal

At 35 years old, Irving Sigal was the senior director of molecular biology at Merck. He was a spectacular scientist. He had been assigned to HIV research.

He believed that a step the virus needed to make copies of itself involving an enzyme called 'protease' could be crippled and that then HIV would die out. He had convinced Merck to let him study this and in February 1988 a young biochemist working under him got excited because she had showed Sigal was right — the AIDS virus she had disabled from using protease did not spread. It was no longer infectious.

She went to Sigal, showed him the data and after he studied it, he smiled. By this point in the epidemic 75,000 had died and another 5,000,000 were infected. What Nancy Kohl said that day was the start of an eight year fight to get a new type of drug developed. In only a few weeks Merck chemists had found several candidates. They had hundreds of possible drugs from experiments to block another protease inhibitor to lower blood pressure, but none of them were strong enough.

For eight months Sigal pushed his lab. By December they had built a three dimensional picture of the protease enzyme which would make it possible to design the new drug. Work was moving full speed ahead when Sigal had to go to London to a scientific meeting. He didn't want to go, the meeting took three days, and afterwards he rushed back to London's Heathrow Airport. He called his wife, Catherine, and told her he got an earlier plane than he thought possible, Pan American Flight 103.

The plane crashed over Lockerbie, Scotland; Irving Sigal was dead at 35 years old.

The company decided, after a lot of infighting, to continue to develop the drug. The first version led to resistance too quickly so they decided to increase the dose. It worked.

When it looked like Merck would abandon the drug before they tried out higher doses, the gay community raised millions of dollars and began studies to make the drug themselves. Merck got to the point of knowing the new drug would work but to prove it in a big test with many people would take a lot of money and time. Activists pleaded for a compassionate-use program to get the medicine to people before they died.

Merck gave out enough doses for 1,400 people chosen by lottery after getting 3,000 postcards, and thousands more faxes from people with HIV.

By 1995 Merck was testing the drug on humans. At the meeting of scientists in Washington that I attended, came the blockbuster news: after 6 months on a triple combination of Crixivan, AZT and 3TC, over 90 percent of patients had undetectable levels of virus — the combination was achieving more than a 100-fold drop in the virus.

It was the strongest data seen in the 15-year history of the AIDS epidemic. The FDA approved Crixivan on March 1. It was the fastest drug approval in the agency's history.

Vancouver, 1996

After the news spread at the national scientific conference in Washington, and the certainty that AIDS drugs would be a reality, it was not clear what news the international AIDS conference in Vancouver could add.

But in fact, it was important. It added an explanation of how to develop any drug cocktails that would work on AIDS and which the virus would not get resistant to.

It explained *WHY* the new drugs worked and provided a road map to many more.

First, an important experiment with another protease inhibitor called Ritonavir showed that those who took it lived and those who did not died. To the FDA this proved that a drug which reduced viral load would stop the disease and that meant a test for how much virus a person has could substitute for waiting years to see if people died or lived.

Second, Dr. Ho got up and with the help of the mathematics of David Perlman, explained a variety of things about the virus.

The key thing he showed was that when the amount of virus is low enough, the number of mutations would be too low for there to be a strong probability that the virus could develop resistance to the drug. He also showed that the drug was in compartments that were differentially impacted by the antivirals and that maybe with strong enough drugs we could cure the illness.

Robert and I left Vancouver feeling strange. We thought of many of our friends who had just recently died and missed the boat that was just now leaving with the new boats being built. We felt our grief. And we felt the enormous excitement — we were going to beat AIDS. I had this strangest feeling as I went to conferences in Europe, that the activists were shifting attention to making medicine and infrastructure available to the rest of the world in the name of humanity. I had no idea I would become a part of that effort.

135 / 1996: Another Gay Bashing

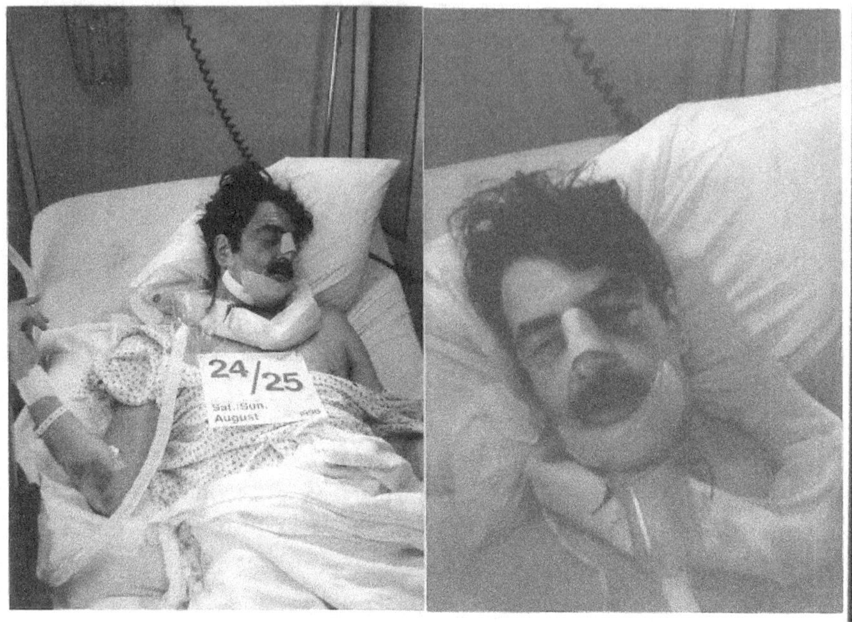

The picture above was taken while I was recovering from a beating I got at the Cheri Cinema in the Fenway, near my house. Jacob Dow, the young man who beat me up, and his father, and the police that got involved — they spent lots of time talking to the press and claimed that I had "no comment."

Lies come in many forms. One to watch out for is the "no comment" lie – the correct statement should have been: "Mr. Scondras was terribly beaten, and since his jaw was broken and he was in surgery, he was not able to explain to us what happened." But this does not make as good news as the imaginary story of me trying to have sex in a movie theater in front of 400 people — why not across the street in my house? A new fetish I assume. The actual accusation was that I had "touched" this young man "inappropriately." But that's not good enough copy so insinuations of "sexual assault" permeated the media.

I had to wait until the court dropped charges against me before I could say anything — part of our ridiculous rules that twist our legal system into a one-sided warped version of reality — when I could I put down in detail what my lawyers had found out, what the private investigator of the young man who had beaten me had found out, and to this day I have two questions for the Boston Police for whom I retain a degree of contempt. Why would you spend your time with Jacob Dow who committed assault and battery on me in front of 400 people, counseling him on how to file sexual assault charges against me, knowing full well I am a gay man and courts are predisposed to presume gay men are sexual predators, but not arrest him for trying to kill me?

Jacob Dow's Background

Jacob Dow publicly said to the press and police, while acting innocent, that he was "shocked, surprised" at my "touching him." But according to statements made by Dow in court documents from the State of Washington where he lived, he had been having sex with an older man who was his mother's lover for two years beginning in 1994. He never indicated at any time in the investigation in Washington that he was upset in any way having repeated sex with the man, a Darryl D. DeVore. This makes it somewhat incredible that he would voluntarily accompany an older man he knew to be gay to the movies alone, and then claim to be "shocked and surprised" by allegedly being "touched."

Interviews with over 100 people present at the theater that day watching the same movie could not find one person who saw sexual or inappropriate touching, but everyone said they saw me being beaten.

I decided to write an article for *In Newsweekly* under my own byline to explain to the public what had actually happened. It went like this:

In My Own Words

Now that the Kafka-esque drama of being potentially prosecuted for repeatedly bashing my head and kidneys on a young man's combat boots has finally ended (the prosecutors dropped the case on December 6th) I can finally explain what happened and tell you what I feel about the reactions and actions surrounding my gay bashing. As you may know, the District Attorney finally did the right thing, which should have been done in the first place, by dropping the ludicrous charges against me.

I think, in retrospect, the whole event sheds light on unpleasant realities about our society, our media, our justice system, and in a few instances on the dangers of our community trying to get freedom by adopting a "don't-ask-don't-tell" mentality in the struggle for sexual liberation. The latter carries with it the internalization and validation of heterosexist norms of behavior and moral codes which even straight people find intolerable, and which some grossly out of touch gay people suggest we adopt and support in order to appear 'normal' to mainstream culture.

What Happened?

On Saturday, August 24th, I went to the Cheri Cinema at the Prudential Center, to see a science fiction film, "Solo." I had a free ticket from the theater manager.

Unfortunately I am a smoker. I had tried to quit several times, growing more and more self-conscious as the no smoking movement (which I support) continued to conquer more and more public space. The mall area of the Prudential Center proudly announced in signs everywhere that it was a smoke free environment.

Before the film began, I was having a nicotine fit, but had no cigarettes and couldn't smoke in the mall anyway, so I headed for the smoking area, an island of refuge for the smoker minority. Given what happened later, I think the Surgeon General should put more warnings on the label — like "Danger, you could end up being beaten when you bum cigarettes from strangers."

As I approached and smelled the waft of smoke and there was a person who looked to me like any other of the 3,000 Berklee College of Music students I passed every day (the school is next to the Pru) and he was smoking up a storm. I went up to him and bummed a cigarette — which had to be smoked right there given the surrounding no-smokers land.

Some have asked me why I would talk to this stranger. Well, they probably don't smoke and they don't live in my old neighborhood where if you don't talk to students you don't talk to anyone — colleges ring my neighborhood with perhaps a hundred thousand students.

I also tend to talk to everybody, all the time. I gesticulate, talk, hug, emote, and wave my hands talking with them. I am a Greek. And meeting people is the thing I do most often and enjoy the most. I am not afraid of people of any age, sex, type or costume and I don't want to learn to be afraid. Also I taught students at Berklee and other colleges for over 25 years and it was a normal thing for me to do.

The young man and I started the ritual conversation of people forced together by circumstance. He seemed rather gentle, low key, and liked to talk. He told me about his twin brother, his home halfway between Seattle and Portland, and I told him about my trip to visit Mt. St. Helens and fly kites on the Pacific coast cliffs.

He talked about a job he had, mentioned getting us a drink which I told him was not for me unless it was soda pop, for I hadn't had a drink in years.

He asked me what I did, and as is my custom, I told him I had been the first openly gay city councilor Boston had ever had for ten years and that now I was working on the AIDS crisis.

Everyone who knows me knows that the first thing I tell people given any opportunity is that I'm gay. This is a long-standing habit of mine because it lets me see quickly whether a person is homophobic. While it clearly worked for me as a survival technique (I could back off from new acquaintances who might dislike gays) in this instance I am afraid it was part of what set off the whole chain of events.

It suddenly occurred to me that I might be late for the movie. I have never worn a watch (and this was before the advent of the cell phones and other modern communication contraptions) but Jacob, the young man I was talking with, turned his wrist over and I saw '3:20' and said, "Oh my God, I'm late, I've got to run..." and I explained I was late to a movie and if I rushed I could see it because there were a series of previews.

He asked me what movie I was going to see and I said "Solo." All of a sudden he got really excited, jumped up and down and said he had really wanted to see that movie.

I felt guilty. I had an extra free ticket and he seemed like a really nice person. He had spent time with me, given me two cigs, so I said, "You can come with me, I have a free ticket for you, but we have to rush because I'm late."

He said okay, and we rushed out of the Pru area and went to the Cheri. I waved hi to Chris who was at the theater at the time, a friend, signed in for the extra free ticket and rushed to the theater.

Anyway, as part of the team with Robert, the Ebert and Siskel of our local paper, I suffered lousy movies poorly. I'm a movie chatterer and usually people have to tell me to shut up. I leaned over to talk to Jacob who grabbed the seat next to mine, the only empty seats in sight, and acted like a movie expert pointing out that the android in the movie was a poor representation of the genre, in fact the whole movie was an effort to capitalize on better science fiction. To avoid being a nuisance, I was whispering this into Jacob's ear.

After watching for a while I got bored, decided to get some popcorn, leaned over and whispered to Jacob that I wanted to go buy some food when he got really quiet. I don't recall touching him, but given I had to lean over and whisper an inch from his ear so it's quite possible I touched him. He leaned away from me, and I heard him say "I gotcha." I don't know what that means, but the next thing I experienced was his fist hitting my mouth.

I didn't really feel pain. I was too shocked. Jacob kept hitting me and I remember trying to crawl over others to get out of the theater, calling for help.

I can't remember every detail that happened after this. I remember him kicking my face and my stomach and side and elbow and somehow I got out of the theater and into the bathroom. I leaned over the sink and a bunch of teeth with a section of my jaw fell out. There was blood all over me. My left eyebrow was hanging down and I couldn't see too well because blood covered it and my glasses were smashed. I needed to pee badly and when I did only blood poured out.

My hearing was confused as if everything was happening in a crazy dream. I had one thought in my mind... get to the hospital. I remember seeing flashing lights and wanting to yell out to them by my jaw had been fractured in three places and unhinged on one side so my mouth was just a floppy gelatinous thing. I don't know how I did it but I got to my house, which was very close to the theater, and drove to the hospital. I don't know how I managed this.

The next thing I remember was a discussion of whether or not I might have to have a kidney removed. I was lying in a hospital bed, being fed by one tube, painkillers and antibiotics in another, a catheter that seemed to drain more blood that urine from me, and a mouth that was wired shut.

People kept coming in and out of my room, but I don't really remember much of what happened. Between shock and morphine I was not living on the same planet as my friends, who apparently got me lawyers, and had been talking with the press.

While trying to recover from being nearly killed (the docs at the hospital, the Beth Israel in Boston who were dealing with me, said that if my smashed nose had been pushed a little differently it would have entered my brain) I finally realized that somehow I had been made into the perpetrator of some crime. I remember thinking this was crazy, like Alice in Wonderland.

I couldn't really figure it out. Here I was, lying in a hospital unable to raise an arm above my head with bruises on my elbow, unable to speak coherently with a mouth smashed to pulp, a nose broken, kidneys damaged, breathing with the help of oxygen and in constant pain and somehow I was being painted as the one who did something wrong.

As time went on, although I only was paying attention to getting better, I was slowly becoming aware that I was becoming a person who had been charged with a crime.

The one thing I remember the lawyers telling me was to say nothing. It was probably the hardest thing I have ever done in my life. I talk. That's what I do. That's who I am. To say nothing for three months while the press went into a frenzy fed by bits and pieces of speculation from haters, cynics and sickos drove me nuts.

Some people couldn't imagine a gay man with a young man unless there was some kind of sex involved. And somehow that possibility was used as a smokescreen, both by Jacob and many others, to justify a brutal beating. It intrigued me that the thought there might have been a 'sexual' approach (a hand on a thigh or genitals, depending on with whom you are speaking) became the issue, not the beating of a man who will live with pain and suffering for a very long time. As if somehow sex and violence was the same thing, one canceling out the other in the scales of justice and the minds of the public.

Innocent Until Proven Guilty

Our Constitution is something I have taken seriously. It means more than some paper on a shelf to me, and over the three months of silence I watched the media and the people who read it become the judge, jury and executioner in violation of everything they claim to hold sacred. I was treated as though I were a felon, guilty of some crime. The media has become the entertainment vehicle for our society and it distorts and titillates at will, creating havoc with our democracy and is a truly dangerous, distorted force in modern life (perhaps the advent of the internet will change this, I am not sure).

Had reporters or others taken fifteen minutes to think, the public and press would have been asking totally different questions instead of painting me as a molester.

To begin with, the young man is over the age of consent. If anything like a pass did happen (which it didn't) so what? Did he get dragged into a movie theater at gunpoint?

Secondly, I understand that the young man had been held by the theater's security guard who saw the beating, as did the manager who called the police, assuming Jacob would be arrested for assault. Instead of arresting Jacob, the police worked together with him and his father helping them draft and file a complaint against me!

In the dramatic "show cause" hearing at the Boston Municipal Court (all of which you can read for yourself as it is a public record) Jacob didn't come, as makes perfect sense, because he would have to publicly admit to beating me which means he would be admitting to a crime which would put him in jail a long time. When my lawyers Frank Jones and John Ward asked the police why they didn't arrest Jacob they said it was because I would not press charges. Then Ward asked them if they tried to reach me in order to ask me about pressing charges. They said yes. When asked where I was they said I was at Beth Israel Hospital. When asked where in Beth Israel they said the operating room. John Ward then asked whether my being unconscious and in surgery might have had anything to do with an inability to "press charges" the police said nothing. John then asked if I had died in the operating room whether or not some charge might be brought. There was no comment.

What we need to understand here is that it is not the job of a victim who is traumatized by a violent crime to arrest or to charge a thug. The police can and do arrest people when a crime happens and there is a lot of evidence that a particular person committed it. That's what the police are for and that's what should have happened. Had this happened, the press craziness would have been more balanced because the headline would have been "Youth Arrested for Attempted Murder," rather than "Scondras Charged with Sexual Assault."

During the three months of the charade, my legal bills went over $10,000. Had the case continued, would I have lost my home? A sick young man had bashed me, and then I was bashed further by a homophobic press, and then by a "system of justice." What hurt me the most though, was that some people in the gay community were also part of the chorus of anger at me, as if something I had done was wrong.

We hired American Investigative Services; they reported on September 11, 1996; I tell you this so you understand that everything I say can be verified. This is not a recollection; it is a reconstruction. For example, the police were not able to identify among the several hundred witnesses, even one witness who saw any untoward behavior toward Jacob on my part but dozens spoke in great detail how I was brutalized. In spite of this, the police supported Jacob and never arrested him for trying to kill me.

Incidentally, if I wanted sex with someone I wouldn't do it in a huge movie theater full of people. I would have walked across the street to my house.

One of the things I learned throughout the Cultural Revolution is how out of touch folks were with gay realities. Nobody would go to a movie and hold hands, because it was at that time extremely dangerous. This is why I was so stunned by the crazy media and public reaction and felt so completely betrayed by the organs of justice: apparently it's okay to beat up queers. Our private investigator found that the theater manager had to keep stopping Jacob from trying to beat me up more, that Jacob kept using the word 'faggot' and he chased after me intending to beat me more after I left the theater and theater people had to hold him back. He was clearly out of control.

This does not surprise me given that he was clearly struggling with being gay, hated older gay men with whom he had been having sex for the past two years, plus whatever confusion having that same man be his mother's lover must have created in him, given our cultural mores.

Another gay reality is that just because you're a guy does not mean a gay man is in any way automatically interested in having sex with you.

For example, I would never have sex with Jacob under any circumstances in any way – from my point of view he would be far too chunky and a top. I love skinny bottoms. A jury of my gay male friends would laugh if somebody told them I had shown any interest in someone who looks like Jacob. But in the warped minds of heterosexists, the notion that gay people have preferences just does not seem able to penetrate their assumption. The heterosexists have figured out that claiming a gay guy hit on a girl lacked some credibility but that's about as far as it has gotten.

I learned over time that Jacob was in his own way a victim of our society's homophobia. Sometimes we get a choice between suicide and murder when we are taught to hate ourselves. Jacob, who admitted to having sex with his mother's lover over a two year period, and who has been involved in several violent episodes, needed a doctor, not a jailer. I felt that Jacob was a volcano that would go off, and that there is nothing in our justice system that would actually help stop this from happening. He was taught to be disgusted with himself and sex and especially gay sexuality. He was a young gay man trying desperately to deal with self-hatred – as I had dealt with at seventeen for being a gay man – I did not have revenge or hate in me.

Of course I was angry, and if Jacob had one nickel I'd probably sue him for it. But to go through a traumatic reliving of what happened so that the Howie Carrs of the world could lick their chops and distort it for public titillation, and losing my home in the process that would result in Jacob getting 12 weeks in jail – that served nobody.

Had he been arrested in the first place, perhaps negotiations between his lawyers and mine would have resulted in some medical help for him. But given the time that has passed and the pain I would have to go through, I would not cooperate with any more of the pseudojustice that our ineffective judicial system dishes out.

One thing that had bothered me all along about this episode is that so many people cared so little about me or about Jacob. Except for the doctors and those progressives, friends and numbers of people in our community, the public at large saw the event as entertainment and rushed to judgment against all that they have been taught and swore to uphold as their values.

Ageism

I remember when Congressman Gerry Studds took a 17-year-old to Europe. He was condemned. It fascinates me that people who say they believe in love feel it must be age segregated, except of course for certain straight icons. Sidney Sheldon's 225 million novels each have a man "old enough to be her father" bedding down a young girl. Teenage nymphets who could be his grandchildren in James Bond movies surround Sean Connery. Romeo and Juliet are in their young teens. The widow of John F. Kennedy married a man nearly thirty years older than she. But for gay people, who in some ways have bought into the "Pepsi generation" obsession more than anyone else, an older man with a younger man is viewed as predatory. This is ridiculous and destructive for several reasons.

First, if we want people to support laws they don't necessarily like, we better start doing it ourselves. When a person is over the age of consent they are over the age of consent, period. Those who assumed I was trying to pick someone up who was over the age of consent and condemned it do our cause no service. Why just ignore gay rights laws if you don't like fags? And any other law we have. Why not just have anyone do anything they want based on any prejudice they have?

Freedom's price is to genuinely act upon and believe in and fight for people's rights even when they make you uncomfortable. Drag Queens have a right to dress up, period. And people have a legal right to approach anyone over the age of consent for sex, period. For our movement to start demanding that gay people act like straight people want them to act will more quickly drive us back into the straitjacket we have been trying to get out of than any other action on our part. And it reflects the knee-jerk reaction of those of us who mistakenly think that our freedom comes from the charity of friends who will put up with us if we 'behave' ourselves.

Those who understood all too clearly that freedom comes from power and power comes from unity with all people who are disliked and persecuted for prejudicial reasons won some freedom for gay people. To pretend that freedom is given to us by a benevolent power structure that somehow has come to its senses around gay sex is to completely misread power. They want our money and our votes. And to the extent we make those contingent upon our demands, and to the extent we keep a united front, to that extent we get our freedom.

Our greatest danger is not to understand the ways power accommodates demands when it has to juggle competing forces: it will always give you as little as possible and it will always attempt to get you to act and talk in ways that upset other forces pushing power in minimalist ways.

It is easy to misread assimilation as acceptance and power will always attempt to create the 'good' and 'bad' versions of a despised group so as to minimize the pressure from opposing forces and to create the best conditions for assimilation which is always the first choice and most stable end result for those in power.

From the day I walked into City Hall, Howie Carr called me a child molester and this reverberates in a culture which underneath its smiling faces still believes in this mythology. If there is a lesson to be taken from this event it is that the mythology surrounding molestation, in fact the very obsession with age cohorts and stratification by age with its attendant ageism trumps acts of murder and violence every time. It takes but a moment to check the statistics out on the amount of violence directed at gay people: what is not checked out so easily is how much of that violence is against gay people having sex in a park at midnight and how often violence against gay people is framed as gay people doing something illegal or violent against others.

This stems from the fundamental erotophobia that is one of the singular characterizations of Christian and Islamic culture and we need to be on guard for its many manifestations constantly. It is like that creature that grows two new heads every time you cut one off.

So many people came to my aid from the gay community it is impossible to thank them all in this book but you know who you are. Thank you.

To the few gays who were on the side of what we now call Fox News I can only say this: living your life and believing that it is a good one within the straitjacket of Christian culture guarantees that you will suffer your whole life from self-loathing because – get this through your thick head – they do not like you.

I have noticed another pattern among the preachers of assimilation: they never help anyone. They have never started a gay bowling league or fought for ending age discrimination in sex or tried to get a country like Iran or Uganda to stop killing gay people. Because assimilationism is a form of being closeted and you can't do much from a closet.

People kept trying to get me to hate Jacob Dow, but I repeated over and over that I would never use a system that has no ability to help anyone, like the courts and police, to try to help a person who is struggling with his identity crisis in all of its manifestations. Dow's behavior was determined by what our culture does to people who are gay, or some other form of being 'different.' I felt that Jacob was barely able to contain a rage that would take a long time for counseling and a very different family environment to resolve. Finding a way to stop the encouragement and congratulatory messages from his father and social group would be a more sensible way to get Jacob to start liking and accepting whoever and whatever he is.

It amazed me how often people were angry at me for not participating in the "punish the wicked" game that was indirectly at the heart of the beating that Jacob gave me.

I studied him and I forgave him. I did not forgive the media leeches and judicially robed fakes who acted as parasites and caused more damage to me ultimately than Jacob did. One reporter upon finding the material from the state of Washington said to me, "Oh my God you were telling the truth." It never, however, made the paper.

136a / An HIV textbook?

My body healed. I decided to move forward on our HIV projects — the most important one was the series of articles called "Reasons for Hope," a translation from public policy and scientific jargon into easy-to-understand English of the latest news in the fight to find a cure, so people affected by HIV had a chance to keep up with and participate in the ongoing decisions and experiments that impacted their lives. We had a team of key doctors who were HIV researchers as well as other activists review our articles before publishing them. We even gave companies the opportunity to clarify anything about their medicines that might have been confusing. It struck me as a bit ironic that we had to read a hundred pages of dense science, interview world-renowned researchers, and talk with people using the new therapy, before publishing half a page about it.

We got a contract with a book company, Chelsea House Publishers, to do a textbook for public schools on HIV but it turned out they really wanted an advertisement for the new drugs that had been invented to help stop HIV. We finally tore up our contract with them — by the time we published the material would be out of date anyway. Here was the first draft of our preface and introduction written in 1996.

Preface to the planned book

The disease called AIDS (Acquired Immune Deficiency Syndrome) has killed more than 25 million people – more than all the wars in modern history.

AIDS kills more people every day than were killed by terrorists who flew planes into the World Trade Center in New York City on September 11.

40 million people have HIV, the virus that causes AIDS. Every year 5 million more people become infected with the virus. Every year 3 million people die from the disease. Every year there are more people with HIV than the year before.

12 million children are orphans in Africa because their parents died of AIDS. Most of these children do not have HIV. Many of the children do not have adults to raise them.

Some of the AIDS orphans

How would you feel if you lived in Africa or some other poor part of the world and you learned rich countries had medicines that could have saved your mother and father? And that they decided not to give them out, even though it would cost the rich countries very little?

AIDS is a disease we know how to prevent. How to treat. How to beat.

Why do you think we have not yet done more to help?

Early in 2005 a coalition of Christian organizations and liberal organizations who ordinarily oppose each other, got together and succeeded in getting rich countries to forgive $40 billion worth of poor countries' debt to help them fight HIV.

This is nowhere near enough help to defeat AIDS, but it is a start.

The same coalition got President George Bush to commit $15 billion to fight AIDS and other horrible diseases around the world.

Unfortunately, there are many strings attached to some of this money and a lot of it has not yet reached the poor.

According to a study done at Harvard University directed by the world-renowned economist Jeffrey Sachs, the fight against AIDS, tuberculosis and malaria will cost $10 billion a year. Clearly Bush's $15 billion commitment over many years is nowhere near enough.

Fortunately, many other countries are helping as well. But again, not enough. Nations are dying.

Martin Luther King in his last speech on earth said, "Over the bleached bones and jumbled residues of numerous civilizations are written the pathetic words: 'Too late.'"

We hope we won't be "Too late".

Some people think the world has done little to stop the epidemic because AIDS mostly infects people who are devalued by societies. The poor. Gay people. Prostitutes. Drug addicts.

Some feel the lack of a big response is because one way AIDS is spread is by sexual contact and some religions oppose sex out of marriage.

What do you think?

Knowing about AIDS and supporting the work being done by thousands of activists, politicians, health care providers and researchers is the best way to put an end to AIDS. We can do it, because we did it before.

On May 8, 1980, the 33rd World Health Assembly declared smallpox had been eradicated globally. For the first time in history, humankind had vanquished a disease. It was not the first attempt to eradicate this disease from the whole world. It was the fifth.

Even when a vaccine for AIDS is created we will have to fight hard and long to succeed in eliminating the disease from the earth.

Knowing and learning about HIV and AIDS is the first step to ending the epidemic.

It can help keep you from getting infected.

It can teach you its symptoms and what to do if you think you may have caught it.

It can help you decide the kind of treatment that is best for you.

It can teach you what kinds of research you can help with, toward finding a cure and a vaccine. It can help you find research you can participate in, whether you are HIV positive or HIV negative.

It can help you get smart about what we need to do to put an end to the disease.

There is a lot at stake. Countries will collapse in Africa and maybe in time, India and Asia as well unless we stop the disease.

If HIV disease goes untreated it is possible for a worse version of HIV to evolve and infect people throughout the U.S., Europe and the rest of the world.

Why might this happen? Can you think of what kind of virus is being selected in terms of ease of transmission as this disease continues to spread?

World economies will be rocked if countries have to divert their attention from economic growth to stemming the ravages of death and dying.

According to Colin Powell, Chairman of the Joint Chiefs of Staff under President George H. W. Bush, AIDS is becoming a threat to national security as countries get desperate and civil unrest ensues because of the epidemic.

Thank you for reading this text. It is a step toward the solution.

And then we wrote a little story that became the center of our struggle to fight the illness because it incorporated all of the issues that were blocking our ability to end the disease at the time we were writing.

Introduction to the planned book:
An Alien visits Earth

An anthropologist from Mars came to Earth to study HIV disease. She quickly found an epidemiologist to interview.

"How serious is this disease?" she asked.

"Very. AIDS has already killed 22 million people. It has left us 15 million orphans and is threatening the survival of several countries."

"Oh my God!" said the anthropologist. "I guess you don't know what's causing this epidemic?"

"Actually we know more about the germ that causes AIDS than any other germ on Earth. Scientists found it in 1983. We understand how it's put together so well that we have three dimensional models of its parts."

"Oh," she said. "I guess you don't know how it's transmitted then?"

"We know exactly how it is transmitted. We know it's only transmitted by specific kinds of sexual contact or contaminated needles. It's not airborne and cannot be gotten from kissing or casual contact. "

"So, then you just don't know how to stop it from being transmitted?"

"No, actually we know exactly how to stop it from being transmitted. We have many methods to stop it outright – from not using drugs or having sex to something we call risk reduction. This means using sexual practices which we are sure have lower risks than other practices and using clean needles to reduce transmission in the context of IV drug use."

"So, these methods must not be very effective. All it takes to stop an epidemic is to reduce the transmission rate below one new infection per person who is infected, isn't that right?"

"Well, you're right. To end the epidemic, we only have to reduce the transmission rate a little. And the virus is not very good at infecting people. In fact, it's a virus that is rather difficult to transmit. We believe the sexual practice with the highest risk has about a one chance in 30 of transmitting HIV with each unsafe sex episode."

"So, then your methods of protecting yourself are not very effective?"

"No, no, condoms, safer sex, clean needles and using antiretroviral medicines to protect unborn babies and people who got accidentally stuck with contaminated needles are extremely effective at protecting people from getting the disease."

"Now I get it," said the anthropologist from Mars, "You don't have any way to treat the illness and before you knew how to protect yourself so many people got infected that even the small transmission rate resulted in a lot of people getting sick?"

"No. We have known how to treat the illness for 10 years. We have many powerful antiretroviral drugs that keep people healthy and reduce the amount of virus they have to extremely low levels. In fact, we have good reasons to believe treating people reduces transmission."

"OK, I understand, how foolish of me. You don't know how to test people for the illness yet and that's why you pass it on without knowing it?"

"Well, said the EPI doctor, "You're right about one thing. People are most infectious early in the disease, when people don't know they are infected. But we do have excellent tests which tell people if they have been infected, how long ago they were infected and even how infectious they are at the moment. Unfortunately, most people don't get tested. So we can't treat them early which we think would stop about 40% of transmission."

"OK," said the scientist from Mars. "Does it just cost too much to pay for all the tests and medicines needed to stop the epidemic?"

"No. Treating everyone in the whole world would cost people in rich countries the price of one box of popcorn and one movie each year."

The anthropologist from Mars looked confused.

"So, let me see if I understand this," she said. "You have this horrible disease worse than any other plague in the history of your planet. You know what is causing it. You know how to identify who is carrying the disease. You know how to treat those who are infected and if they are treated, they are less likely to pass it on. You have methods of stopping transmission like condoms and clean needles. And your world has plenty of money to pay for all of this.

"So how could this possibly be a problem for you? How could it possibly be an epidemic?"

The epi doc shook his head. "Because AIDS is not a medical problem. It's a political problem. And we haven't found a cure for that."

Then the epidemiologist took a big breath and made the following speech:

"Look, everything we could do about AIDS is limited by the politicians who only want to do what is popular, not educate and persuade.

"We should give out condoms and teach safer sex to children, but a lot of parents would rather let their kids die of AIDS than teach them how to use condoms. So politicians are afraid of funding this kind of program.

"We should distribute clean needles to stop the biggest way HIV is being spread. But enough people see this as supporting drug addiction that politicians run for cover.

"We should have treatment on demand for drug addicts. But a lot of people see this as rewarding drug addicts who they think are bad, not sick. They want to punish them and AIDS is a good punishment. So politicians are too scared of losing these voters to do the right thing.

"We should be testing antiretrovirals to see if they can be used as 'morning after pills' or even 'chemical condoms.' We are pretty sure they protect people from getting HIV right before or even right after an unsafe sexual experience. But so many religious groups think sex is sinful that politicians panic at funding the research. Anything, which helps people get sex safely, is equated with helping people be immoral.

"We should be studying safer sex and teaching ways to reduce risk by popularizing sexual techniques that are less risky like frottage and oral. But except for one President, politicians are terrified of being seen as supporting sex. And he really didn't have a choice. He was outed.

"Since so much about AIDS involves sex and it's a taboo, most people are pretty ignorant about it. And that means people are afraid of people with HIV. So that means lots of people who do not want to be identified as HIV positive are afraid to get tested.

"But being tested is the first step in a program to stop transmission In fact, in the U.S., people who get tested are punished by making them felons if they pass on the virus. If you don't know you have HIV you don't get punished for passing it on.

"In other words, everything that we could do to stop AIDS is blocked by politicians afraid of religious fanatics and the uneducated who together really run the world."

"Well," said the Martian scholar to the doctor, "Thank you for your time. And good luck with all this."

As her space ship took off you could hear her say, "Nice place to visit but I wouldn't want to live there."

136b / India and HIV

I was working one day in 1998 when I got a phone call from India. I didn't know anyone from India. I barely knew people from other cities in Massachusetts. A male voice with a singsong lilt said, "You must come to India."

He had a thousand questions about catching HIV, which didn't make sense given his monogamous heterosexual lifestyle. He said he was putting together a non-profit under the leadership of a doctor and ours was the first website he could understand so he wanted us to come to India to help him understand AIDS and to make sure the non-profit was doing things which made sense.

I said to him "Sir, I don't even travel to Cambridge, much less to India. It's too far away and besides I don't have the money to make a trip to India."

"Don't worry," he said, "I will pay for everything."

Hm. The first brushoff did not work. So I said, "I never travel alone."

He said, "We will pay for you to have a companion come with you."

I told him that I would have to first see if my friend who is an expert in AIDS in developing countries would come with me and that I would call him back. He said, "I will wait for you to call me." The phone service was iffy to India but his voice was clear and I had made an implicit bargain but I thought that the guy I had in mind, Stewart Landers, a gay lawyer who worked on HIV issues in developing countries, would never drop what he was up to go to India on a lark. So I called him and told him exactly what had happened.

"Wow," he said, "What an incredible coincidence you calling me right now."

I got nervous. "What coincidence?"

"It so happens," he said, "I have decided to take a month off and I would love to go with you to India."

The tickets arrived for Stew and myself. Stew was HIV positive, doing fine on his meds — I did not know the impact having a person completely healthy with HIV being with me would have on the medical community in Mumbai.

The Diary: 15 November 1998

My beautiful and thus unforgettable Robert drives me to Logan.
I love him all the more because of it. He is a magnificent
specimen of a man and I cannot forget that basic fact as I begin
on my journey... but I digress!

I didn't actually write that first sentence of my diary — it was there when I opened the otherwise empty notebook. Robert got to it first. I smiled.

I'm going to India with Stewart Landers (now a bit of a world traveler, having just returned from Kenya) ostensibly to see how to help the "Parkash Foundation" undertake an effort to stem the wave of AIDS, which threatens India like a tsunami.

Why India? Ravi Parkash, who made that call, has money. Trusts us. Stewart and I left for India with a theory: that we can get enough understanding of HIV illness while in India to design a proposal, then get Ravi to fund it, then convince scientists in the USA to agree — get a whole planeful of them to come over!

For me, the purpose of fighting AIDS was to make people not afraid of sex, not afraid of each other, to have fun, to improve the quality of life, to help the societies that had to shoulder the burdens of those who are ill have more energy. It was about quality of life, not duration. And that seemingly small difference from those who wanted to "save lives" was all the difference for me, for it led in every arena to fundamentally different decisions about how to live and how to die, what to study and when to accept, until the end of time.

Death was not the horrible thing about AIDS. For death is not horrible but rather the end of the little happiness that we enjoy for a few brief seconds in the clock of the cosmos. I did not fight AIDS to save lives but to push death back to where it belonged — a bookend perhaps, or a final chapter, but not the tyrant of the days we live ordering us to spend our time in fear instead of our fascinating follies and following our animal curiosities.

The land of Hindus

Actually, it is the land of Hindus and the Jain, Buddhists and Muslims and even a few Coptic Christians.

First word spoken on the Moon: "Houston."

First word spoken as we reached the airport from Stewart Landers: "Welcome to Bombay."

It was crowded in the airport, green painted walls, and crowds of Indians. There was a person sent by Mr. Parkash, thank God, to meet us with a sign, but there were many people with signs inside the rectangular space of the airport. The man stared at us and knew right away we were the ones. It had not occurred to me how we must have stood out looking so tall and white in the crowd.

By that evening, we were at Ravi Parkash's country home — a beautiful building of marble floors and giant beds. Sitting by the pool I wrote these notes. The dogs are sleeping by the blue water. In a small place of honor stood an elaborate stone elephant — Ganesh. There were bamboo and papaya and banyan and flowering trees whose names I cannot remember. The three wheeled motorized rickshaw left us here with Ravi's housekeepers who made us tea — they spoke little English, but English tea was more dependable a part of life here than it was in England.

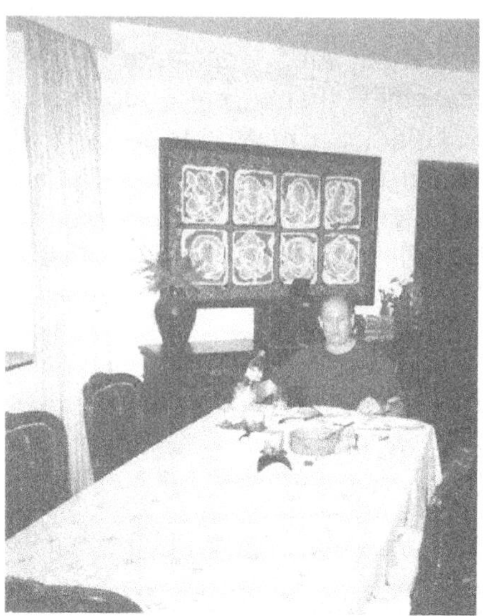

Stew and I made a plan: a memo of understanding so that Search For A Cure and the Parkash AIDS Foundation could be seen as partners. For the next few days, the main doctor Ravi hired will work with us to put together the elements of a realistic proposal, and we will then go to Pune for a party. I had to give an award named after Ravi's father to the winner of a horserace. Ravi is deeply into horseracing.

The air smells like curry and the servants are making breakfast. The roosters are crowing in the distance — and a parrot is imitating the sounds of the rooster. It's quite annoying.

I wondered how Robert was doing. Really my only regret was Robert not being there to share in this beauty. Yet I know what a struggle it would have been. I think he should move onto a new regimen to lessen the fatigue and side effects of the protease Inhibitors, the type of medicine for HIV that he was taking.

Our Work Begins

In search of a cure

By Shilpa Shet

IN AN one-of-its-kind endeavour an American social organisation will attempt to make treatment and medicines more accessible to HIV/AIDS patients in India. At the same time the organisation will also conduct probable clinical trials for AIDS vaccines in the country.

The Search For a Cure Foundation of the United States will tie up with Prakash AIDS Foundation in an attempt to universalise the AIDS problem. "It is one family, one world and one enemy (AIDS)," says David Scondras, president of the foundation during a visit to the city during the AIDS awareness week, "To reduce HIV infection in the world all of us have to work together."

People from the Search For a Cure feel that it's unfair that only a few people can afford treatment of the disease, which is already affecting millions all over the world.

The foundation has been meeting chief executive officers of big pharmaceutical companies trying to get the message across. The aim of the two foundations is to get pharmaceutical companies to reduce the cost of drugs.

According to Scondras, who spoke to **MID-DAY** at the Prakash AIDS Foundation office at Nariman Point,

pharmaceutical companies have a huge profit margin in every drug. "I feel that the market prices of the drugs are hiked by nearly 2,000 per cent, which makes it unaffordable to people in countries like India," he added.

The reason why the foundation wants to work in India is that they feel treatment of HIV/AIDS is not universal. "It's foolish that those in the US get the best drug therapy and most here do not get any," says Scondras.

One of the ways of reducing prices of the drugs would be by manufacturing them in India. "India has the infrastructure but there is no willingness to bring about a change," feels Scondras, "There could also be a tie-up between the US and the Indian government on this."

The foundation will conduct clinical trials on high-risk people in the country for the HIV/AIDS vaccine. The trials will be done on HIV negative volunteers.

A few vaccine trials are on in the US, but they are not effective, feels Scondras. "Because we do not have a large population. It will be more useful to have a faster study with a larger population. We have 14 vaccines to be tested and we do not have people for the tests," he adds.

He says the testing would be ethical because the vaccines are 'safe', but have to be tested for efficacy.

The Prakash AIDS Foundation will help in these endeavours and will also encourage research. "We will providing information on how traditional ayurvedic immuno-boosters can be used in the treatment of HIV/AIDS," says Ravi Prakash, chairperson of the Prakash AIDS Foundation.

The Prakash AIDS Foundation will have a clinic for providing information and counselling to any AIDS patient at their Nariman Point office.

"We are talking of condoms and awareness, but we not doing anything to help those infected. We have to start somewhere," says Ravi Prakash.

David Scondras and Ravi Prakash

From MID-DAY, Thursday, December 3, 1998 Mumbai

Stewart wrote an agreement between Ravi's foundation and Search For A Cure, which I signed. Our agreement and our efforts made it to the papers in Mumbai. *MID-DAY* wrote an article quoting me, "Pharmaceutical companies have a huge profit margin in every drug. I feel that the market prices of the drugs are hiked by thousands of percent above cost, which makes them unaffordable to people in countries like India."

Ravi Parkash and I signing our cooperation agreement

The article went on to say: The reason the foundation wants to work in India is that they feel treatment of HIV/AIDS is not universal. I said, "Those in the US get the best drug therapy, and most here do not get any."

It also went on to say that "one of the ways of reducing prices of the drugs would be by manufacturing them in India." That, in fact, would happen, but not in the way I imagined. Ravi went on to say that the Parkash AIDS Foundation would have a clinic for providing information and counseling to any AIDS patient at their Nariman Point office. "We are not doing anything to help those infected. We have to start somewhere," he said.

I was not aware how deep, complex and widespread the drug pricing issue had become. I was completely naïve about it the first time I went to India. As the CEO of DuPont Pharmaceuticals once told me when I asked about this idea of getting cheaper drugs made in India, "We already make our drugs in India (or China or Mexico or wherever we can do it cheaply)."

So I asked him, "Then why are the prices so high?"

"Because we set the prices to be the highest we can get from the people we sell to and are willing to buy them for. We don't set some arbitrary percent above cost — drugs already cost practically nothing to produce."

Years later I would be part of an ongoing fight with PhRMA (Pharmaceutical Research and Manufacturers of America), the pharmaceutical companies' joint lobbying arm, that would take me to Geneva and the World Trade Organization. And as it would happen, one of the people I met in India was finally responsible for taking actions that brought the prices of drugs way, way down in poor countries.

That day in India, after seeing all the press and reviewing what people were saying about us, we began a process of brainstorming how we could fulfill our mission.

Some of Ravi's interest in AIDS was from a fear of catching it — but why would that be of concern to him? We met a person who explained without words more of how Ravi became interested. One of the men who worked for Ravi was thin and emaciated; he was a friend of Ravi's family for many years and his HIV was why Ravi had decided to deal with AIDS.

The agreement with Ravi could be very important — it was a commitment to join forces on the people to people level. It could mean a great deal to the world. We devised a way in which we imagined patent holders could have big profits while poor countries could still afford the drugs, but our first take on this was wrong.

We knew that whatever solution we had we would have to fight for, because if it were an easy thing to do, it would have been done. But we understood that the obstacle to ending HIV on our planet was the cost of the drugs. Because by 1998 it had become clear to me that people who are treated for HIV would be less infectious.

We outlined a plan for meeting key industrialists, scientific investigators, NGO's, and 30 government ministers over the next week in order to assess the feasibility and lay the groundwork for a multipart proposal. We wanted preventive vaccines tested, get cheap antivirals made in India, do a teach-in of Indian clinicians, test herbal medicines, and establish an entire package for poor countries.

We spoke at some length with Ravi about "the plan," as we are now calling it — exciting. We decided to ask Ravi to orchestrate the production of antivirals here, use them to create a deeper, wider profit margin in the USA (e.g. this is how Viagra gets Pfizer rich, made in India for pennies and sold in America for tens of dollars a pill) and take a percentage of that profit to underwrite the cost of antivirals locally which could be sold on a cost plus basis. We also were aware that the India law, which does not allow for patents on products but rather on processes, allows for reverse engineering plus an alternative way to produce a molecule to bypass European and American patent laws. This might open the door to inexpensive medicines.

This plan would need the coordinated effort of local actors through the Parkash foundation and company actors in the USA. The plan by this time had reached quite a few pages, taking into account issues from compliance to availability of tests, multidrug resistant strains and how to avoid them, testing of vaccines, etc.

We met Monsud, the son of a wealthy Pune resident. He may have been the most beautiful man we had ever seen — and he had gay genes — he did the floral arrangements, flitted around checking "the artistic composition" of thousands of orchids, showed us his self-designed clothes — beautiful but, like all the people we've met so far, is out of touch with his gayness completely. Monsud said he wanted to learn about HIV. He has an MBA and we will try to involve him in two projects:

1. finding a place that could manufacture antivirals

2. arrange a teach-in of his peer group to form a rich kids organization to help with managing the Pune end of what we hoped would be a spring conference on HIV.

An observation changed our thinking about how to proceed:

The middle class in India, able to afford medicines, while small percentage-wise, is still comparable in number to America's because India's population is so huge. The middle class might be only 5% of the total people in India, but that means a middle class over 55 million people in 2005 and perhaps over 200 million by 2015. That would dwarf the middle class of the USA, which has about 50% or 170 million members in its "middle class."

This observation meant that an HIV program in India could be realized at the beginning pretty quickly, at least among the middle class — no small accomplishment given the numbers of people.

Ravi has security guards with guns, and always carries a gun himself, in order to 'protect' himself. It was uncomfortable being with so many guns.

Ravi is the in the middle of the election — which I'm advising him about — to be one of the 9 commissioners who run the race track, which he believe is full of corruption and is run down. He wants to save it as interest in it has waned. Ravi has two racehorses of his own. I have decided that Dauvgani, the daughter of Ravi, is the power behind the throne.

Stewart has written a speech for me to give for the 30 minute documentary on the Parkash AIDS Foundation. It will be fun. We met last night with the film folks who seem to know their stuff.

Are there places where there are tens of thousands of prostitutes, some female, others male? We must visit this site. One concept we came up with depends upon the social structure of prostitution, which, among the women, is a business with 'owners' and a special name for the managers. Targeting this group for testing, vaccines, and therapies are logical on three levels:

1. Best place to test efficiently;

2. Biggest bang on slowing the epidemic;

3. Easiest social structure to deal with centrally: convince the bosses and you've won.

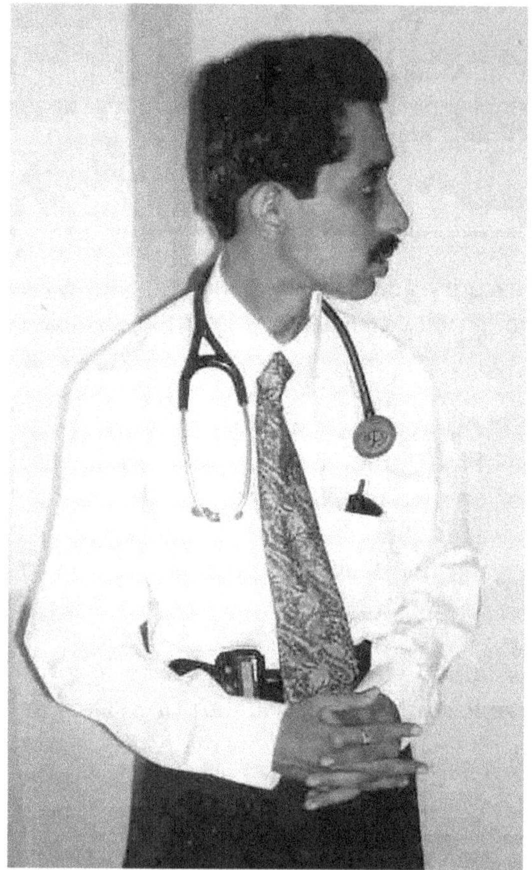

Shashank Joshi, M.D.

To make this real we need a solid long-term commitment to drug availability, assays for STD's and genotypic assays to avoid resistant strains overtaking the population, a lot of work.

I think we ought to check with our contacts at the NIH about testing vaccines in prostitutes — I doubt the NIH has the will to test the best candidates. Personally I wanted a test of all the vaccines and the prostitutes seems the right group to do this: we would get answers the fastest given the high rates of HIV transmission among them.

Dr. Joshi met with us: we redid the press release for World AIDS Day and are in the newspapers. Stewart wants us to get signatures on a letter of collaboration with us now. I think he's right. We also met Shaheen, a Vassar graduate. She worked for an organization going around the world in an airplane fitted out as an eye clinic. We're testing her skills by having her do the finished copy of the proposal.

It's Thursday. We are at Ravi's summer palace. Ravi, a member of the ruling class, is spending most of his energy at the moment getting ready for the election on the board that controls the race track — the English-created organization which has been adopted as many of English social institutions have been adopted by India's rich.

We're hoping that Shaheen will be able to make the Parkash AIDS Foundation actually work. Dr. Joshi is well meaning, full of energy and ideas, but desperately needs help. Shaheen showed up and Joshi too — along with a man who produces 20,000 tablets of an ayurvedic medicine made from 6 plants designed to fight HIV.

You would wonder why we were paying attention to things like this since the HIV antiviral cocktails were working. Answer: American and European antivirals were not available to most of India because most people could not afford them. In spite of the fact many were made in India. We had reached an ethical crisis — we knew how to control the disease but the people who lived in India could not afford the therapies. They could, however, afford ayurvedic medicines so we needed to know if those might work or delay the need for drugs that were too expensive.

Anyway, the tablets, according to data from Joshi, reduced the amount of virus and increased the CD4 cell count. I eventually would bring

Joshi and the data to the NIH. The tablets were an immunemodulator. So testing it for acute HIV activity *in vitro* will be difficult because it works by helping the immune system work well and it's hard to put an immune system in a Petri dish. The pills are a set of alkaloids, which allegedly are known to be immune boosters. Who knows? Anyway, we've got some, have access to many more and should be able to set up a trial checking RNA, CD4 counts and weight as outcome variables.

We tried to tell Joshi that the lack of structure at the Foundation was disastrous. He said he had a table of organization he would give us, and that he had authorization to hire six people for the Foundation. And he said to me, "I'm a doctor, not an MBA or economist."

Question: who supplies the HIV tests to India which they use to discriminate? In India an HIV test is given before an operation and if positive they won't operate. The blend of cowardice and the lack of compassion frustrates me, makes me angry.

I asked Shaheen for epidemiological data on India and a market analysis of retrovirals. Shashank Joshi is trying to help us set up meetings with doctors, NGO's, clinics and pharmaceutical firms, do a cost analysis and get epidemiological data. We also need data on any viral load/CD4 changes associated with the use of the ayurvedic medicines.

Voodoo, Mumbai's gay bar

We decided to spend Saturday night at a hotel in Mumbai so we can go to the only openly gay bar in the city, called Voodoo. I met a young man at the gay bar — a place that explodes to life for 30 minutes at night. He is a dancer. We went to the 'seamen' hotel. Little rooms. He was a wonderful lover — satin smooth skin, tattoos. He never asked for money, but I left him some anyway. I wondered if there was any meaning to the sex I had. He had a hard on and came, so on some level he had a good time. Or has he trained himself to perform no matter what? It's hard to say. I will write him and I hope he's for real. His writing is clear, he speaks English pretty well and his body is clean and well-kempt. It's obvious he works out a lot, so I believe is really the dancer he claims to be. A pretty boy. He is probably 25 years old.

In India, prostitution is legal but gays are not. Homeless dogs can be kicked out of the way, but even in the richest sections of the city of Mumbai, the homeless people are left alone to sleep and beg.

Ravi told Stewart and me we must stay in India and save the world. Ravi said that when he was 32 a woman who saw the future told him that when he was 45-50 he would meet an American with a first name starting with D that would make his name known around the world.

It's a country of myth and mystery. A truly different culture.

Anyway, Ravi's a mess. He is trying too hard. His big party at the racetrack is really a political event, although it will announce the Parkash AIDS Foundation. It is clear that Ravi — who called every voting member of the committee who ran the race track, some 800 people, inviting them all to the party at the track — is very concerned about appearances, from clothes to the image he is projecting. Given his history of drugs and prostitutes and his admissions of what he sees as an errant youth, he is trying to establish a kind of respect that I doubt he'll achieve or ever really need either.

It makes me wonder if the media's characterizations of me as a person who sexually abuses children is overcomeable — and makes me realize that, in the end, one only has the truth to contend with. What can you do? There are no ways that we can ever actually overcome the public's desire shaped by the media to believe what it wants to believe.

Anyway, I understand the kinds of anxiety provoking feelings Ravi is subjected to. And I feel for him.

Meanwhile, I'm hoping that we will get a call from the medical director of Pfizer to review the feasibility of vaccine trials in India.

Racetrack Party

The party involved tons of food, strange contraptions that blew air to cool the outdoors, food carved in the shapes of animals, the TV video of Ravi and myself showed on the race track video in between races.

When the award ceremony happened in the paddocks, to award the 3rd annual Parkash Memorial Mile Race awards to the top 3 finishers, I stood with Stewart next to Ravi.

Ravi said on loudspeakers to the whole race crowd that he felt doing something about AIDS was something that we should do 'seriously.' There were banners everywhere and flags, even jockey's uniforms, were labeled either "Parkash AIDS Foundation" or "Search For A Cure."

I held the mike in my hand and said in answer to a question about the state of vaccines:

In the US and Europe there are drugs that work and vaccines yet untested. Stew and I came 13 thousand miles to collaborate with the Parkash Foundation to see that India and the world gets access to these things.

Ravi always talks about his father and the SD Parkash Foundation as the creation of a great man, because he started the foundation and showed compassion by helping the sick and the poor.

I think Ravi is a great man for starting the Parkash AIDS Foundation to fight the number one killer in the world.

Party at Racetrack

Winner of Search For A Cure Race

Racetrack in Mumbai, the day of the fundraiser Search For A Cure Race

JJ Hospital

Shashank said to come to the hospital re: AIDS patients. A common expression across the nation is that servants would have no place to go and no way to live if they were not hired by the rich to serve the rich. (Reminiscent of the arguments in favor of slavery in the American South.) Ravi hires guards, cleaners, cooks, waiters, etc., full time.

We went to JJ Hospital, Sir J.J.'s Grant Medical College, named after a philanthropist who donated this huge complex to the people, and a series of similar hospitals across India. It is the government hospital for this state. Interesting to note that everyone can use it. MRI's, x-rays, etc. are available. Drugs too. But antivirals are not.

The woman who heads the Department of Internal Medicine is a lady of unsurpassed grace, quiet and firm. Her eyes are intense and sad. She is honest and clear. She said that government statistics on AIDS cases are in stark contradiction to the number of actual cases she alone has seen. We toured the wards with AIDS patients.

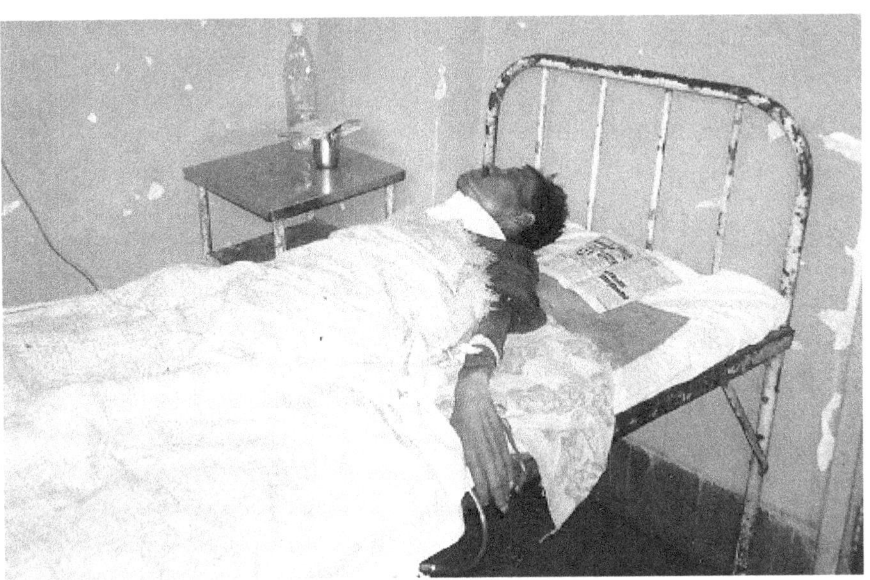

Man whose mother pleaded with me to save his life

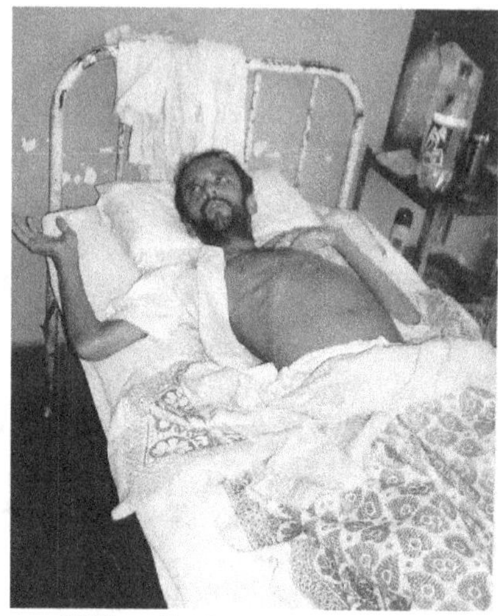

AIDS patient

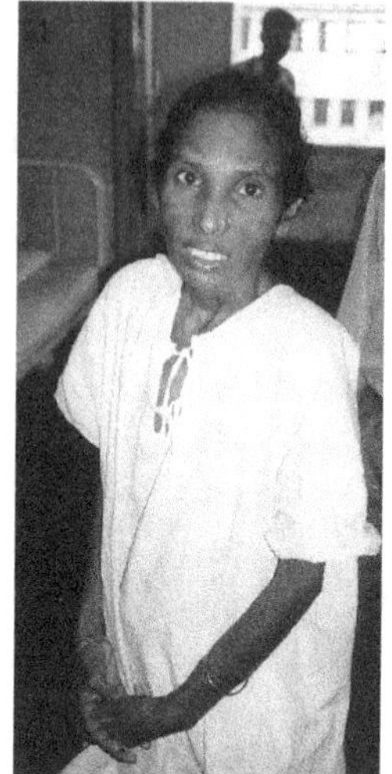

Asking for help

I watched a mother caring for her dying son who was having trouble breathing. A bag of bones with an IV attached. Her eyes turned to Stewart and me with a cross between a plea and hopelessness. Her head shook a little like 'no' or 'sad.' It broke our hearts.

The doctor says of herself that she suffers from depression every day watching people die and dying knowing there are medicines that can help but that it is too expensive for her patients so they must die. She needs journals, has no computer, is working with equipment and a physical plant that is run down and would not pass a building inspection here. The wards have cots of iron that are rotting, mats for bed mattresses, floors that are clean but run down, corridors lined with patients, patients flooding the waiting area. We watched as a husband and wife, both with HIV, came in to review their care.

The hospital cannot keep records of the patients with perhaps 200 new people a day coming in so people carry their medical papers with them.

The ELISA tests (used to determine if you have the antibodies to HIV) are faulty without being done twice, there are no viral load tests available. There is no in-house CD4 count done.

Alaka Deshpande, the head of the unit, says that a resident is paid $125 a month and that she is incredibly understaffed. They have the intelligence, will and need for everything and I felt overwhelmed. My eyes were wet. The great good we could do with so little effort.

When you look at the drugs you can buy at any pharmacy — what they cost compared with American costs — you realize what a ripoff the American products are. This might be OK in the USA, which can afford to be conned, but to allow millions to die and to allow millions to generate more infections and versions of HIV in order to hold onto a few more percentage points of profit is totally unacceptable. Completely unethical. We went to the Parkash Foundation and spoke with Joshi, made contact with the medical doctors of Pfizer, determined to move forward with the plans.

In addition we saw "Armageddon," the movie Parkash made about AIDS, and we also moved forward on an agreement. I did some email work and Stewart and I decided we needed to write an op-ed article to the Globe, perhaps from Mumbai. It was time to write and to fight.

I was also worried that so much time is passing. Why don't we try out ideas which might be better than what is happening vis-à-vis Robert's protocol. I'm frightened. If the virus gets through, I don't know what will remain for us to do. Il-2 and Remune might be the right answer. It seems a good guess but, maybe, just Remune? And if the window closes, who knows what this will mean? Anyway, we need to move on!

World AIDS Day

At a Forum Against Drugs and AIDS (FAD) a meeting in Mumbai with lots of TV cameras and news media, I gave a speech about what was on the horizon. We met a guy who built lots of factories for drug companies at the Indian Medical Association where we spoke. (I was specific there about the development of several new drugs including PMPA, ABT238 and T-20 along with the potential use of HU with DDI.) We ended up with a lot of press coverage.

Speaking at FAD in Mumbai about our efforts to get medicines

In the evening, we watched the burning of the AIDS monster by the Bay of Bombay.

The AIDS Monster

The next day, we met with an MLA (Member of the Legislative Assembly) of the BJP party – head health minister who is in charge of government medical offices in Maharashtra state. The state government offered to produce the drugs at cost if they got patent rights from the company. This is the basis for companies who really mean to help the world do so and the government of India would ensure protection of their American and European markets. This is crucial and we need to frame a public health agreement in the USA for this to become international policy around the HIV epidemic in countries that simply cannot afford the prices being charged by firms that are getting 5000% markups and up on their HIV drugs.

Two dailies in Mumbai covered our activities, one the picture of Ravi and I and an article on the objectives of the collaboration, the other detailing the agreement with the state government of Maharashtra with its 20-50 million people to provide red tape cutting and the use of the state pharmaceutical labs to create antivirals if an American firm would offer to share its patent.

We spent the day meeting with industrial experts such as the chief medical officer of CIPLA. CIPLA gave us some antivirals they were producing which we brought back home, some 95% cheaper than identical drugs sold in the USA. We met with the local head of Roche who agreed to giving 200 patients free fortovase (their early protease inhibitor).

We have made some progress. Each company we meet with is excited about the collaboration. Stewart and I had to plan carefully on how to make this extraordinary thing a reality, bringing a plan that would make HIV drugs in India affordable.

But it was time to go home. I miss home. I miss Robert. The only thing I am sad about is Robert not being with me.

It is clear we have a lot of real work to do… prepare for a microconference in the spring to set up a proposal on how to structure the big conference in the fall to get the smart team, our group that helps Search For A Cure decide on what to do, to provide input.

Before we left, Ravi cried and said that "HIV is everything."

GATT? Whazzat? A Glossary of Financial Terms

Compulsory licenses are licenses that are granted to governments under international trade law that allow them, under certain conditions such as a national emergency, to license domestic production of a patented product, copyrighted work, or other type of intellectual property without the permission of the patent holder. Compulsory licenses allow poor nations to manufacture generic medicines for public, noncommercial use at a fraction of their cost on the U.S. market.

The Food and Drug Administration (FDA) is the U.S. agency that oversees approval of medicines.

The Global Agreement on Tariffs and Trade (GATT) is an international trade treaty that regulates tariffs on traded goods. GATT includes the TRIPs (see definition).

A ***generic drug*** is a copy of a previously patented medicine that may no be freely copied. Generic drugs must still receive FDA approval.

Intellectual property rights refer to the rules that apply to patented or copyrighted products.

Off-label refers to using a patented medicine for a condition other that what has been FDA approved or is listed on the label.

Off-patent refers to production of a product whose patent has expired.

A ***package label*** on a patented medicine tells you exactly what the drug is supposed to be used for. The FDA oversees drug labeling.

Parallel importing is a trade practice that allows a government to import or buy a licensed product from a third party, without the permission of the patent holder, at a much cheaper price.

A ***patent*** is an official document that provides an inventor exclusive protection to make and market an invention, and the right to exclude others from making, using, offering for sale, or selling that invention. In the U.S., patents last 20 years for medicines.

The Pharmaceutical Research Manufacturers of America (PhRMA) is a lobby group representing the drug industry.

The Trade-Related aspects of Intellectual Property Rights (TRIPS) is a new piece of global legislation that applies to international trade of patented products. TRIPs is a provision of GATT.

A ***royalty*** is a payment made to a patent holder for the use of a patented product by another party. It represents a percentage or share of the profits made by the sale of the patented product.

The U.S. Federal Trade Commission (FTC) is the national body responsible for oversight in patent disputes in the United States.

The World Trade Organization (WTO) is an international body made up of member nations that, among other things, oversees trade-related aspects of international property rights.

137 /   Comeback

By 1999 I had become reincarnated, according to the magazine *The Improper Bostonian* (see cover photo). This placed me in the company of Isabella Stewart Gardner as she had spent her life shunned by those who did not feel that being who you are was more important than what the culture of the time commanded you to portray.

This led me to a freedom that those who navigate using their internal compass understand, and it has a price. You have to invent purpose and reality rather than inherit it from the nation-state that adopted you to participate in its dance for power and control. And you will need friends who travel with you to give help and solace, for you will be persecuted.

On the other hand, you will see what few get to see, feel what few can allow themselves to feel, and touch a reality that most never get close enough to reach. It's a price I thought was worth paying.

A Comeback?

Many news outlets asked about my planning a 'comeback,' which meant, in the jargon of politics, would I run for office again? I had already gotten one state law passed while out of office, creating bed-and-breakfast homes so that women whose husbands died unexpectedly could rent out their empty children's rooms to make enough cash to pay the mortgage without being charged hotel taxes and being reclassified as commercial property. After all writers, lawyers, shrinks, CEOs and others who worked out of their homes didn't get their homes charged commercial rates and lose their mortgages. Why should women who let folks use their kids' rooms to pick up some money for the mortgage have to do so?

I found that in many ways I could accomplish more not being in the limelight than constantly dealing with the glare of publicity, so I was not convinced it was a good idea even though I missed the fun parts of being 'elected.' I figured 'elected' or not, I would either go to heaven, or there wasn't any.

I had undergone a kind of personal transformation, learning how big the world really is, how complex, how tiny many of our grand issues actually are, how much the world suffers — and this changed my picture of what I should be doing. A gift of clothes from India gave a visual picture of the fact I had become something new.

The writer Joseph Mont wrote a clear article that detailed my trip to India writing among many other things:

As a Boston City Councilor David Scondras was a lightning rod for controversy. Openly gay and unrepentantly liberal all through the 1980's, he offered a voice, a loud and persistent one, that was normally unheard in a chamber dominated by the likes of "Dapper" O'Neil and Jim Kelly. But after losing a re-election bid in 1994 and undergoing a series of events that led to both personal and political meltdown, Scondras disappeared from the local spotlight…. He was gone. Toast. But move the dateline from Boston to India and Scondras has been anything but quiet or ignored. In what may be the oddest post-council career move in recent history, Scondras recently appeared alongside one of India's most popular television stars in a ground breaking soap opera episode dealing with that nation's AIDS epidemic. Where the Boston press has shown little interest, the India media clamored for details about their guest and newspapers including MID DAY, Bombay's largest daily newspaper, featured Scondras in front page stories. It is ironic perhaps that a country so steeped in the belief of reincarnation was witnessing what may be the rebirth of Scondras' once dead political career….

Throughout India, Scondras was warmly embraced by health officials and researchers everywhere he visited. When he speaks of visiting patients at MGH it is Mahatma Gandhi Hospital not the other one (Mass General Hospital). When he mentions a television appearance it isn't the public access airtime his former colleagues battle for. It was a small role, as himself, offering advice to a soap opera character who contracted AIDS as part of the plot line. Newspapers covering his visit focused on this expertise and reputation with not so much as a word about his personal life....His calm, almost meditative reflections on India gradually melt away when the topic turns to the current political climate in the United States.

"It pisses me off to watch the US Senate and the Congress behaving in such a frivolous way," he said, his quiet voice growing louder, more animated, more Scondras-like, with each new breath, "There ought to be a felony called criminal frivolity. These people have some nerve worrying about what Clinton does with his dick. That is nobody's business but Mrs. Clinton's. They have some nerve wasting my money and my time and our collective energy and dominating the damn media with this when we have a worldwide pandemic that needs attention....It isn't just disturbing because politicians are out of touch with the American people. We have known that for a long time. The question is now whether they are out of their minds. The fact that a handful of people in the United States can impose their agendas on the rest of society makes you wonder if it is time to blow the whistle and call all this into question. They have made us the laughing stock of the world."

He added that any return to active politics would allow people to see a much different person from the David Scondras they once knew.

"In an odd way it is nice being older," he said. "At the age of fifty-three I've moved into a different part of my life, and I no longer have the ego or motivations I once had." Those motivations in his early days, he said, "were all about personal power. It was about having a young gay man applauded by the very people who had once rejected him and all he stood for. It was all about personal acceptance and having your name carved in stone. It was about immortality. I'm in a different place now and all that is behind me. It is all about helping others now, and the only way to do that sometimes is through politics...the question is whether people will give me another chance and let me do what is best for our collective interest."

*   — from an article by Joseph Mont, portraits by Kathy Chapman , the* Improper Bostonian Magazine, *February, 1999.*

expensive and the mark-up much less dramatic, more affordable drugs would be available for AIDS patients in the United States.

India is also home to several herbal medicines that have shown promise in boosting immunity and reducing viral counts, Scondras said. Drug companies in the United States, with access to these herbal treatments, might be able to synthesize more effective drugs, he said.

The partnership will also involve clinical trials in India of an HIV/AIDS vaccine.

IF IT SEEMS THAT THIS ALL-CONSUMING work has lessened Scondras' appetite for politics, it hasn't. His calm, almost meditative, reflections on India gradually melt away when the topic turns to the current political climate in the United States.

"It pisses me off to watch the U.S. Senate and the Congress behaving in such a frivolous way," he said, his quiet voice growing louder, more animated— more Scondras-like, with each new breath. "There ought to be a felony called criminal frivolity. These people have

their availability and printed salacious sections of the transcript and broadcast the deluded ramblings. Portions of the phone calls are still available as online sound bites at Carr's page on the World Wide Web.

Scondras, further shaken by his long-time partner's AIDS diagnosis, went into isolation. As time passed, and Search For A Cure was established, it was a rested and ready man who once again dipped his toe into the political waters.

He began assembling a team of resi-

With India's much larger population as the study group, testing can progress at a much faster pace than in the United States, Scondras pointed out.

"To eradicate this disease in the United States, we are going to have to eradicate it worldwide," he said. "The only way to beat this virus is if there is less of it. Ninety percent of the world's AIDS cases are outside of North America, and if the disease remains unchecked in other countries, it will incubate around the world until it mutates into a version that is

some nerve worrying about what Clinton does with his dick. That is nobody's business but Mrs. Clinton's. They have some nerve wasting my money and my time and our collective energy and dominating the damn media with this when we have a worldwide pandemic that needs attention.

"On the list of the top five hundred pressing international and national problems, nowhere is Clinton's sex life," he added. "If it were in the list of the top one thousand problems, it won't matter

dents and political activists and crafting a "10 Point Agenda" that would serve as the blueprint for a 1997 run for an at-large seat on the council. A political fund raiser at The Harvard Club in May of 1996 proved that Scondras still had a large base of support and was capable of defying the prevailing conventional wisdom of analysts.

But it wasn't meant to be.

A political wag once remarked of a candidate that the only way his man could lose a particular election was by

The Nature of Comebacks

Long before and long after being an elected official I had written and passed laws and made the world a different place in many ways. Change was what I was about, and enjoying what does not change, the stability of the cosmos. Elections were positions on the public relations board of the company run by those who make sure the super rich maintain their positions of class and power, and while a great deal can be done from these positions, to see them as anything resembling running the show is to not know what the show is.

I wanted to change the show. You can't do that from an elected position alone. You have to build the three legs of the stool of change:

compassion, power, and wisdom, none of which come easily and all of which have imitators that are useless and distracting.

Travels

The NIH started a big meeting now called "CROI" (Conference on Retroviruses and Opportunistic Infections) at which all the country's scientists and HIV leaders attended once a year, some 15,000 people from across the country and around the world.

For some reason the people who ran the convention were not happy with us activists coming, but we did anyway. We figured out lots of ways to duplicate the entry tickets and got in pretty much everyone who needed to get in.

At a conference in San Francisco I got a call from someone named Dr. Ian Roberts, the senior medical advisor to the Ministry of Heath in South Africa, who was not allowed into the conference. He asked to come, claiming that there were 'dissidents' or 'denialists' who were gaining the ear of the president of South Africa, Thabo Mbeki. It was hard for me to believe the stupidity of both the denialists and the people running the convention, so we arranged for our friends to copy a registration card and got him in to show him that there was no question but that HIV cause AIDS. I introduced Ian to many scientists and leaders at the conference and he was deeply impressed. Not long after I would get an invitation to be a member of a special Presidential commission on AIDS in South Africa put together by President Mbeki.

One of the themes of the movement to get the world access to the new HIV meds was to make them affordable In poor countries. I had decided to analyze how medicines were made. It was a depressing analysis.

In summary, it became more and more clear that companies made meds that earned super profits, and not the kinds of meds that made the most sense. They were caught in a kind of paradigm paralysis that did not use what doctors and patients needed as their guides but rather how markets worked, a poor guide at best. Drugs invented by the NIH, like AZT, were taken over by companies like Glaxo Wellcome, now part of GlaxoSmithKline. It produced the drug compound in bulk in China and then put it into capsules, producing a product costing the company some 4 cents a pill and retailed in Boston at $5.89 a pill. Companies spend the vast majority of dollars in marketing and paying off stockholders and executives, with a teeny percent to the scientists. Almost no medicine was invented by any of the companies: they foraged the NIH-funded university labs and bought out patents, and foraged among teeny biotech's to find things that looked good. They took few risks, manufactured the drugs cheaply in India, Mexico, Canada and China, jacked prices up 3,000% to 7,000%, and then sold this stuff to rich countries to keep the longest-lasting highest average rate of return of any economic activity in the world, averaging some 40% on rates of return.

This was beyond sickening.

This is why in Europe ACT UP burned down the Merck pavilion, why South Africa went to court against companies, why Yusuf Hamied (the owner of Cipla in India) could make and sell a year's supply of AIDS medicines for $200 while big pharma sold the same for some $12,000-$20,000 a year.

I was determined to do something about it because it stopped most of the world and most people with HIV from getting medicine.

138 / Geneva

March 24th, 1999: The world is our community. We just boarded our flight en route to Geneva, then India again.

The international community had rules for when a country could produce drugs cheap by declaring a shortage or emergency — even the USA can do this but never has — and a world meeting of the World Trade Organization was taking place in Switzerland to talk about new rules that ACT UP was afraid would put an end to the generic inexpensive drugs being made by companies in places like Brazil and India and Mexico, which made it possible for poor people to afford medicines.

The companies claimed that these generics were inferior in quality (as interesting claim, since these big companies all got their drugs from cheap producers in the same countries and relabeled them, jacking up the prices) and we activists decided to go to the WTO and complain loudly about the scams.

Once again the invasion of those that allegedly 'protect' us — the continuation of payments for protection, not different in kind from any protection racket, is useful to those who made money on it. But who gets protected from what? What is the cost of that protection?

I realized what an extraordinary luxury in a world of poverty to speak of codon mutations and appropriate antiviral regimens as most of the world simply gets sick and dies. It is painful to reflect upon the reason for this trip – to convince the WTO and companies to support the right of developing countries to manufacture copies of our drugs to save their people. *OUR* people, if we really believe there is one world.

Anyway, like so many other matters in which the details are complicated, the underlying dynamics are quite simple. Many countries made copies of drugs which are a source accessible by a larger percentage of the world community than ours are. The WTO has moved under alleged pressure from the pharmaceutical firms through their lobby group called PhRMA, to stop this bootlegging of their medicines.

The result: horrible deaths. While fluconazole is unavailable, too expensive in the US version, it is no longer available in the cheap version. Fluconazole is a fungicide that treats cryptococcal meningitis, a terrible disease suffered by people with AIDS.

The irony is, as is so often the case in our 'modern' world, the companies make no money from stopping the cheap products because the expensive versions are simply not purchased in poor countries. People die. No one gains.

Anyway, I had a lot of work to do and I wondered if I was good enough. Yet in the last analysis, who is?

At the WTO

I spent time with *Médecins Sans Frontières* (Doctors Without Borders), and spent a lot of time with others to get a better background on the issues involved in international agreements about drug manufacturing, distribution, and sales.

At the meeting were 67 representatives from many countries. It was unusual for anyone from the USA to come to these meetings, but here were many leaders from Donna Shalala to Dr. Stuart Nightingale from the FDA. The lack of drugs in Thailand was one focus of the conversations. The meeting was lengthy and detailed about the legal status of patents and the way compulsory licenses can at times be used by countries to get around them in urgent situations.

A central idea at the meeting was that a patent really equals property but property is not an absolute right. For example your neighbor has a legal interest in how you use it. Burning down your house might not be your right even though you own it, for example. This is how the door got opened to ways to make drugs available in spite of patents — in effect the argument is that patents can be abused and result in people suffering as a result, requiring some remedy. The details on the legal issues were lengthy and hard to follow but interesting.

We heard from experts around the world the same story: the cornerstone of public health is the availability of medicines; they are priced out of reach for no good reason. In the USA the total sales were $112 billion, yet $4.2 billion was spent on advertising, larger than the AIDS research budget or any other research on any medicine. When you started to compare the costs of drugs, say between India and the USA, made by the same company, you got Lariam for malaria in the US costing $37 and in India $4; Prozac in the US costing $75 in India $1.50; Hytrin costing $78 per month in Boston but $1.07 per month in Bombay (in each case the *SAME* company brand). Yusuf Hamied, who owned Cipla, regularly made 200% profit margins selling FDA-approved drugs from GMC manufacturing facilities for some 90% or more reduction in cost from big PhRMA.

Countries like Australia pooled their procurements. Others relied on generic products (like Mexico and India). But everywhere there was a struggle to get access to medicine.

We heard stories of the continual warfare of an economic kind to force countries to adopt policies favorable to the profitability of whims of drug companies. It became clear that maximum profit does not mean highest price — there would soon be staggered pricing with lower pricing for poor countries — in part as the result of the years of pushing for them such as we were doing at this WTO meeting.

I Get The Mike

I was nervous to talk, but angry. I demanded that the reps from the big drug companies come forward and name a single drug that they spent the majority of dollars developing, because there weren't any. I demanded they name a single drug that a drug company invented, because I knew that there weren't any.

Every AIDS drug was made on a campus like Emory University or Yale, or at the National Cancer Institute, or was on a shelf somewhere invented years ago at public expense — like AZT, for example, invented at the NIH in 1965.

Some 70 percent of all medicines are supported, invented, tested by money from the US government on campuses, or in the Army — and the idea that a company that spends almost everything on advertising, big salaries for top execs of companies that never discovered anything, is something Americans need to know, understand and take action on.

We need a new law: that your patent lives as long as the amount of money you actually spent inventing and testing your drugs. For most companies that would mean patents that lasted an hour.

Companies mostly stop new drugs from coming to market that might compete with the ones they already have, hamper medical research that might impair their profits, buy patents to keep a medicine from being developed, or twist an old drug and call it a new name to give it a new expensive life. For example, Cubist Pharmaceuticals stopped daptomycin, the antibiotic that is so great on MDR, from getting one last twist to cure community acquired pneumonia (CAP) which kills a lot of people. They decided that it would cost about what it would make in new money to do the twist, so millions were deprived of a drug that cures CAP. The makers of Amoxycyllin knew years earlier that adding clavulanic acid would give it a bigger, harder punch and longer half life. They held off on doing this until the original drug patent ran out, then twisted it and we now have Augmentin. Of course millions of people could have benefited from this chemistry many years earlier if the company cared about people instead of profit.

The stories go on and on.

The conclusion: it is time to make a new model of inventing medicines and making them available, one that does not have as its main mission making millionaires of men with money. Most scientists want to see the world get better and we need to build a model that has science at the helm, not a bean counter.

139 / Africa

First trip to Malawi 1999, then serving on the Mbeki AIDS Panel South Africa May 2000, Working at AIDS Conference in South Africa in Durban where I meet Mandela July 2000, Meeting again in Malawi 2 October 2000, my heart attack, and finally 2001 Vice President Justin Malewezi of Malawi comes to Boston.

The First Trip to "the Warm Heart of Africa"

I spoke from the pulpit of the Arlington Street Church, to the followers of a faith that might be the only one I could consider embracing. I was inside the church where transcendentalism was taught from the mouths of masters like William Ellery Channing who were among the few who believed and taught the subjugation of theological ideas to the light of reason. I spoke about the worldwide AIDS crisis.

With some forty million people infected at that time and with more people having been killed by AIDS than all the wars of the 20th century combined, AIDS stood alongside malaria and tuberculosis as the three killers of humanity, dwarfing all others in size and yet paid far less attention than any of the conflicts whose enemies were human.

I remember looking over the crowded pews at familiar faces, in a church that reverberated with a rationality that is the hope of our future, for the rest of thinking is myth — the fog from which emerge the monsters of our minds. I was full of feeling about the quiet killer and tried to show people our possible destiny, for we were a people who had the medicines which the world needed and, like the Christian converts of old, could go on the new boats to the old world and spread the gospel of science and medicines.

Then Chatinkha got up.

She was seated in the middle of the church, but she had no problem making sure her voice was heard reverberating from the rafters. She was a big, black, African woman of energy and strength, with a loud voice that she knew how to use.

"If you care so much about people dying of AIDS, why don't you come to my country, to Malawi, in Africa and put your words in the ears of the people that can help stop this disease?" she said.

Chatinkha Nkhoma had HIV and was being treated at the NIH. She was apparently well-connected and had a huge roaring laugh. I liked her. I made a public commitment to come to Africa and help.

No one else at this time was going to Africa to deal with AIDS that I knew of and certainly no activists were.

It was Wednesday, October 27th, 1999 when I boarded British Airlines on my way to Johannesburg and then to Lilongwe, the capital of the former British colony that used to be called Nyasaland until its freedom. It was ruled by one man for a very long time. Then democracy broke out, and the power of the British embassy receded as the Americans took over the role of world ruler.

I am not sure why it has been my destiny to constantly travel to places thousands of miles away, given that I am so committed to so stationary an existence that I refused to go from Boston across the Back Bay to Cambridge, perhaps a two mile journey. But after City Hall, I traveled perhaps a hundred thousand miles in search of ways to help end the AIDS epidemic.

In this case, I was going to South Africa and then to Malawi. I went because Chatinkha convinced me from the power of her love for her people, many of whom were dying, that it was important to come and talk with the country's president. I felt I could help spread the news about the new medicines, organize efforts around their use and availability, and get a commitment to test vaccines.

I wanted to speak with the leaders in Malawi to learn what was going on in this country of ten million people.

I wanted to get a national meeting to frame a countrywide research agenda and action driven by patients and their doctors. It wouldn't be the research community nor the pharmaceutical companies, neither of whom had the mission, capacity, skills or, in many cases, desire to create functioning countrywide public health interventions.

I also wanted to get the leaders of this African country to come to Boston. It would mean attention, which empowered, for in this world communication is all powerful and heads of state from Africa coming to the USA would at this time bring attention to the fact that Africa was dying, that we had medicines that could stop it and that we need only give them the resources for a program to end disease in their country. Then the dominoes would fall and all of Africa would become involved.

I felt as I crossed the Atlantic again, more often than perhaps anyone I know and certainly more often than I would ever have guessed, that the life given to me after Rob's HIV got under control needed to be spent in an adventure of efforts to do whatever could be done to put an end to this disease. AIDS became my enemy. I became a foot soldier in a war that was not of my choosing. It is an odd truth that going in person is always more powerful than magazines, books, TV shows, Internet or letters. There is always more magic in being there yourself, a tribal connection that allocates credibility to those who go and see.

So I went and I saw.

On the long way across two continents I wrote pages on the issues I wanted to deal with in Malawi. I had no idea if any of this would get accomplished.

I got letters from Congressman Joseph Moakley, Barney Frank, and Senator John Kerry requesting I be given opportunity to speak with government officials and found later they were critical to my getting around the roadblocks created by the British and American officials in Malawi to my desire for direct communication with Malawian heads of state.

I also got a letter of support from Dr. Ian Roberts, the senior medical advisory to the South African Ministry of Health.

At this time there was a real fear that infectious disease could destroy enough of the world to end much of civilization.

What we would do over the next decade would determine in a way never true before whether this was the beginning of the end of our species or the beginning of a new era of collaboration.

Dinosaurs ruled the earth for over 200 million years. It would be so sad if a mere two million years was enough to move us on and off the stage.

Chad Womack, my friend now working at the NIH, made it clear that I would do well to get any agreements in writing, from any third world country. Accountability depended upon written agreements.

I felt so intimidated. It felt so strange to be just a little person in this vast world trying so hard to connect the people who together could help make the planet more hospitable to our species.

On October 28th the plane touched ground. I was in Africa.

Soon I was in Lilongwe. Betsy Chikapa, friend of Chatinkha, and others met me at the airport and I was ushered through the immigration process with lightning speed. I was carrying a huge suitcase filled with HIV drugs to give to people who needed them and to show that they exist to the many who did not believe in them.

A white van from the United Nations outpost picked me up and brought me to the office of MANET+, the countrywide people with AIDS organization where I met Victor Kamanga, my friend to this day. On the way I saw trees with purple flowers and a countryside where in the distance you could see volcanoes. It was magical.

The United Nations Country Programme Advisor Angela Trenton-Mbonde, a beautiful woman with long brown hair had arranged all the places I would stay, transportation and eventually orchestrated the key meetings over several trips to Africa which would result in the countrywide AIDS program in Malawi. This young lady was a key part of the team that eventually made Malawi the first and largest grant recipient from the Global AIDS Fund.

Chatinkha and I left soon for the industrial city of Blantyre for the launching of the National HIV awareness month and the strategic plan. It was inadequate.

We got a room at a hotel right out of Tennessee Williams's "Camino Real," surrealistic in Malawi. Bats flew everywhere making extraordinary sounds, a kind of gurgling whoop. We met people and instead of sleeping, as we should have, we stayed up talking all night. I knew many in Malawi were afraid and unfamiliar with gay people but they understood money. Walking by cars parked outside of a little bar, two boys asked me if I was a dick licker. It was a little confusing to me because men often held hands.

I went to a big tent in which were girls dancing, singing songs in English about ending AIDS, and met Dr. Bakili Muluzi, the President of Malawi who was energetic and clear about making sure people understood how to reduce their risks of getting AIDS.

I got pissed off because out of the mouth of Harold Varmus, the head of the NIH back in the US, were statements repeatedly broadcast that essentially said that Africans could not be expected to take their medicines with a level of compliance that did not lead to lots of HIV resistance. Harold did not understand places like Malawi: there were ATM machines, roads without potholes, bars and live music, a medical school, educated people, large extended families that took care of each other. My read was the opposite: that those destitute of hope and money in the streets of the central cities of the USA would be the hardest to expect compliance from. This was the big impediment to large-scale use of antivirals in Africa according to one of the most important government official in charge of AIDS.

And he was completely wrong.

After the show, I did two radio broadcasts to the nation, one on why I was in Africa and the other on how and why we needed to act to get medicines here. I said to take pills people need to count, swallow and have a mouth. I felt that Malawians qualified.

The next day the newspaper headline was "Rich to get medicines, poor to die." Here was a country with banks, auto tellers, payphones, brand new buildings, roads, cars, computer centers, radio, television, pharmacies, medical centers — clearly too primitive a place to figure out how to take a pill.

I sketched a Jacaranda tree with purple flowers. It is a beautiful part of the country I was visiting.

I went to a bar that night where music was fusion, dancing everywhere, strobe lights and laser lights, and it was clear that while gay might not be talked about, it was pretty obvious in many places as I watched men together in ways that were unmistakable. I ended up sleeping with a judge on the high court of Malawi in a beautiful building and realized that "we are everywhere" was not just about the USA.

I heard a lot about money being silly to send to the poor of Africa because it would be used by the powerful to enrich themselves and their friends. First, this was illegal, but frankly after decades of watching the politics of Massachusetts, I doubted there was more corruption than what I witnessed as a public official in Boston.

Chatinkha took a plane back from Blantyre to the capital, Lilongwe. I went with her and said, seeing the very small two propeller plane, "I'll never get comfortable in this plane unless I'm at least co-piloting." The pilot looked back and moved to the empty co-pilot seat and said, "Come on; let's go for it!" So I did.

"Courage," I said to the pilot who noticed my fear, "is doing what you want even though you are scared. And without it there is no adventure."

Victor Kamanga, head of MANET, the Malawian national organization of people with AIDS. He helped set up all the logistics for the several times I visited Malawi.

Lake Malawi

A man who owned the beautiful resort by Lake Malawi had a brother who was dying of AIDS. I decided to bring him antivirals to help for a little while, not knowing what else I could do at the time. We decided to take some time and spend it at the lake resort, me looking for monkeys and everyone else for some time off.

Malawi was a land of death, bodies every day filling the rooms that served as morgues. The leaders spent Saturdays at funerals. The country of some ten million had perhaps 300,000 AIDS orphans.

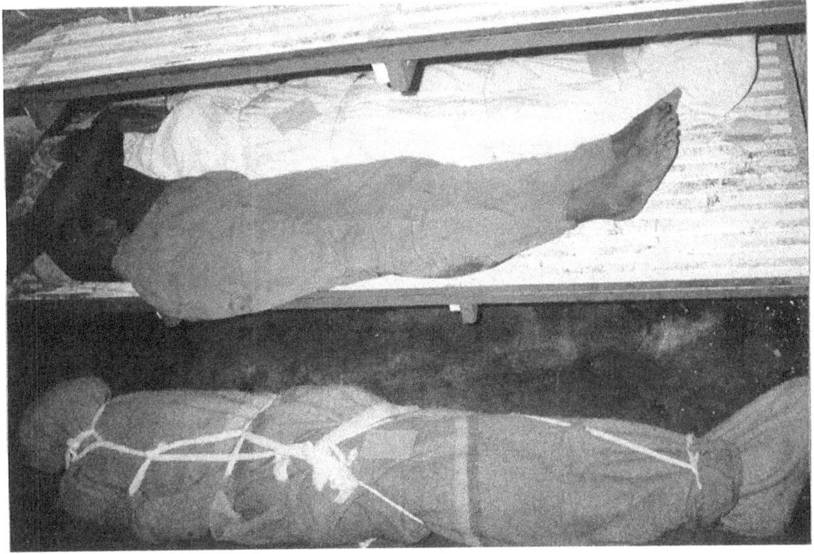

I visited the morgues seeing the bodies of the young women and men we were too late to help, too late in our efforts to get medicines and I cried. I would cry again when I had to leave and children would not let go of the van I was in because they knew I was leaving them to death.

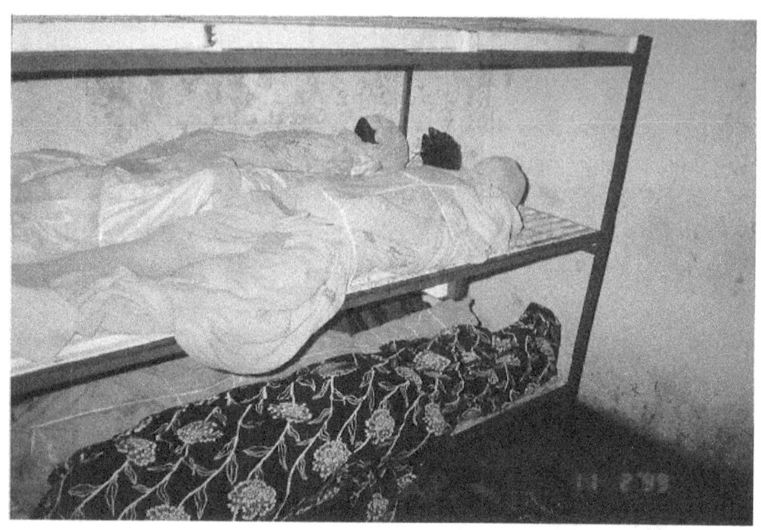

There was an image of a mother grieving that will stay with me all my life. I have a photo of it and will share it with you to help you understand how deeply I had become filled with the grief of the families. She wailed deeply, like the waves of a dark sea, from deep inside her, in a voice that stays with me forever. She was the voice of Malawi.

From the first movie we made about Malawi: see www.searchforacure.org

During the drive to Lake Malawi, I saw the baobab trees. They were awesome. Like giant people whose lower limbs had swollen, gigantic trunks and narrow truncated small branches. The looked like they had been pulled from the earth and planted upside down. There were women carrying containers on their heads walking by the road.

I saw a man who was not supposed to be approached. He was a "walking dead man."

The "walking dead man" protected his village from evil spirits, walking by the edges of the territory scaring the demons from harming the villagers. The "walking dead man" is everywhere in the world and equally effective. In some places we call them police. In others, soldiers. They all have their genesis in fear, and they all make it worse.

In the morning I taped a magazine article that will be broadcast in four segments on National Radio. Soon we would see how far I could get using the media to attract interest and attention. I had yet to be able to connect with anyone who was a leader in the government.

A woman who worked at the hotel died six months earlier. Her friend came to me and said that I should have come earlier and saved her life. Racha, who worked at the hotel, lost a 27-year-old son. The manager of the hotel had an orphan come to him whose father died. She has TB and AIDS and is 8 years old. He asked me to save her life.

I did not meet a person in Malawi who did not have a story of how AIDS had affected their lives. Chatinkha had a series of people in her room. I counseled one on her daily therapy.

I walked to the edge of the lake that night and was pulled back by a hotel worker who explained to me that the hippos killed tourists who wandered into their territory. They were not sweet big cuddly things; they were very aggressive about their land. I was told that when God made all the animals he put together all the left over parts which made the hippo. All the animals laughed at it. So the hippo went to God for relief. God said to live in the water. The water animals are more friendly so the hippo went to water. But God was afraid that the hippo was too big and would eat all the fish. Hippo opened his mouth and showed that he didn't eat the fish. This is why at night when the other animals are asleep the hippo comes out to avoid their laughter and eats. Which is why I should not walk by the lake at night.

The general manager of the hotel took me aside after dinner asking me lots of questions about medicines and AIDS and asked me to help his aunt who is sick of TB and pneumonia and is wasting at 38 years old. He is scared and sad for her and for himself. He is afraid he is sick.

We talked until late into the night. When we spoke about prevention, the manager of the hotel said, "From one president who gets blow jobs behind his wife's back to a president on his second wife reported to have spent much of her time in bed as entertainment to her bar's clientele, the messages about sticking with one woman comes from two hypocrites asking all of us to abstain from nature. It won't and has not worked."

I went to bed early in hopes of catching the sunrise. The hotel's CEO, who warned me again that hippos could kill, adamantly opposed all the efforts I made to walk by the beach.

I am awoken by a call at 5 a.m. to see the sun rise over Lake Malawi. I rushed to the water's edge. A red crescent appeared over the rock cone of Bird Island and slowly climbed, turning into a disk that reflected red onto the flat parts of the lake in between the waves. It is serene. Paradise.

Justin Malewezi

Vice President Justin Malewezi with Angela Trenton-Mbonde

I gave a speech to people with AIDS in Lilongwe at a meeting put together by Victor Kamanga, the leader of MANET. He is a very brave, dedicated man who would support me through thick and thin during the next thirteen years. The speech I gave was met with rounds of applause. A member of Parliament was there. A doctor who lives near the home of the Vice President Justin Malewezi was there, a Dr. Kayambo, who became friends of myself and Robert. He had saved Chatinkha's life and knew the vice president's driver because the VP's wife is Kayambo's niece. On the last day of my stay in Malawi he would convince the vice president to cancel appointments and meet with us. I grew determined to save the "Land of Fire, the Home of Human Life".

Malewezi graduated from Columbia University with a degree in biology, and was focused on the public policy implications of that science for Malawi. This country of ten million had 300,000 AIDS orphans and perhaps ten percent of its population had HIV. Perhaps more. So a voice of hope was sought after, and it turned out I was that voice. I walked into the halls of government and into the VP's office. He was far more formal than I would even be able to master, but he figured out that I had good connections because he had been given letters from Senator John Kerry, Congressman John Joseph Moakley, Congressman Barney Frank, members of our public health establishment such as Alfred DeMaria, the epidemiologist for the Commonwealth of Massachusetts, and many others. In part what I said and in part the letters from those in power convinced him to take me seriously.

I would work with Vice President Malewezi and many others over several years to make a treatment program in Malawi a reality.

An Open Letter

I had come to Africa before Bono and Madonna, before Bill Clinton and before President Bush's PEPFAR program for Africa, before the Global Fund on AIDS and before most of the world knew of the scale of the crisis in Africa. From Lilongwe I wrote the first of many articles trying to mobilize concern in the United States about the worldwide plague which would kill millions of people. The first was part of the series *Search For A Cure* would write for over 20 years. Here are copies of the documents:

Ref. No. ....

Telephone No. 782 655
Facsmile No.   781 521

THE OFFICE OF THE VICE PRESIDENT
P.O. BOX 30399
CAPITAL CITY
LILONGWE 3

THE VICE PRESIDENT

<u>Ref. No. VP/C/52</u>   30th November, 1999

Mr. David Scondras
34 Edgerly Road
Boston
Massachussets 02115
<u>UNITED STATES OF AMERICA</u>

Dear Mr. Scondras,

I write to thank you for briefing me on the work you are doing in the fight against HIV/AIDS.

On my part I have been making preliminary soundings among the donor community in Malawi on the use of anti-retroviral drugs as part of the attack on HIV/AIDS. The reaction has been mixed. I attach a reaction from the British High Commissioner which argues against the wide use of the drugs as "inappropriate use of precious development funds."

In order to counteract such arguments I would be grateful if you would submit a short paper putting the case for the use of these drugs. This will also enable me to properly brief the Government on your proposal.

Yours sincerely,

J.C. Malewezi
<u>VICE PRESIDENT</u>

cc: Dr. George Kayambo.
        Lilongwe

  :   Hon. Lilian Patel, MP
        Minister of Health and Population
        Lilongwe 3

  :   Dr. W. Chalamila Nkhoma,
        National AIDS Secretariat,
        Lilongwe

Africa is Dying

by former City Councilor David Scondras of the AIDS Writers Group of Search for a Cure-December of 1999

Lilongwe, Malawi.

I want to speak plainly, where each word is weighed on the scales of truth and relevance rather than money and votes. Africa is dying. To the lists of the endangered species that worldwide ecologists make, add tribes of Africa, for in the land of Bantu languages where I have spent some time, in the land of Fire,(the old name for Malawi), the tribes are dying. From HIV.

We can solve this problem if we have the will to do it. And because we have the power to stop HIV around the world, the fact we are not doing anything as the planet is in the grip of the greatest killer in human history, poses the greatest moral dilemma we have ever had to face. AIDS is not a medical problem. It is a political problem and an ethical catastrophy. As we do nothing, 8,000 Africans die every day of a disease we can stop with medicines that we won't give to anyone who is not rich.

Vice President Justin Malewezi of Malawi and I met for a morning a few weeks ago, talking about the hope of a plan to bring medicines that fight HIV to his beautiful country in Africa. He is a biologist and understands the impact of this disease. When I asked him what would happen if we could not get help for those suffering from this disease, he said "The impact of this disease is tremendous. I think we would lose not just a generation, but a nation". Yet, instead of action, I have heard excuses every day from drug companies and their apologists, governments including our own, and self annointed experts who rarely have spent five minutes in a developing country, on why we cannot give drugs to developing countries.

Some of the excuses have been brutally offensive--like the implication that developing countries have too much promisuous sex and deserve what they are getting. Well, first, Malawi has the best abstinence and condom program I have ever seen, with the President present as 4rth graders sing songs on AIDS and how to protect yourself from the disease. But there is more. American prostitutes and those who frequent the red light district of Amsterdam have a lot more promiscuous sex than I have ever seen in India or Africa. And yet, less HIV than among American IV drug users. HIV is not punishment for sin. It does not care about those of us who want to equate sex and sin. There are two big factors in predicting who will have HIV : lack of money and openness about sextalk. That is why Holland, where sex is viewed as a natural part of life rather than caught up in Christian and Muslim neuroses, has one third the amount of HIV passing from person than we do. It may even be that the type of virus in Africa and India, type

"C" is easier to catch that type "B" which is the American and European version.

The Vice President of Malawi sent me a letter very recently saying that the "British High Comissioner" (translation, 'the British Ambassador') replied to the Vice President's sounding on the use of antivirals drugs as part of the attack on HIV/AIDS by saying that the use of the drugs would be an "inappropriate use of precious development funds". This notwithstanding the report by Dr. Richard Stern in Costa Rica, which was ordered by its Supreme Court to give medicines to people with HIV, that a careful study in that country showed that the antivirals cost less than treating the opportunistic infections of HIV and losing the productivity of workers.

In the United States the Republicans want to give back 800 billion dollars in a tax rebate because the federal government has so much extra money. It would cost 18% of this to treat ALL of Africa. Such treatment is the only vaccine we have, for those treated are far less likely to transmit the illness to anyone else. If companies would donate drugs at the cost of production to help in this worldwide crisis, and if Europe would foot half the bill, the cost would be 1% of what the Congress *has voted to give away as surplus*. And American elderly and uninsured who cannot afford medicines could be added to the list of beneficiaries without changing that percent by anything worth mentioning.

I have asked the President of Malawi to come to the United States and the preliminary indications are that he and the Vice President will come in April. In my meeting with Vice President Malewezi, he said " I will be willing to come to New York probably in April to talk about Malawi, to talk about Southern Africa, and to talk about Africa, and to appeal to the United States to help." Search for a Cure has asked him to come here, to Boston, to speak on behalf of Africa.

I have heard that there is not enough "infrastructure" for medicines in developing countries. In Malawi, a country of 10 million people where at least 1 million have HIV and in which there are some 300,000 AIDS orphans already, there are roads and cars, a medical facility within 30 kilometers of each person, laboratories, doctors trained in the United States of America, medical programs which came so close to wiping out TB that in 1982 three of the four main TB wards in the biggest city were closed for lack of patients (a disease now back because HIV weakens the body's ability to contain TB), water and food and universal medical care, xray machines, internet, television, radio and the most important kinds of infrastructure that are needed for medicine: mouths and juice to drink the pills with. It is however not a country rich enough to afford HIV medicines *all of which were invented by scientists and laboratories paid by 100% by the U.S. taxpayer.*

Africa is not the land of Tarzan. Every part of the developing world is different, and the problems in each part are different, but nowhere are the problems of getting and using medicines for HIV as great as they are in the big cities of America among those in denial, or homeless or IV drug users. Yet we don't say that these

Americans should just die when there are medicines that save lives.

We need to push our government to save the world from a disease that is killing whole nations, mutating into new forms that may someday come back to attack us with a more lethal type unless we stop it now, from the enemy that has already killed over 300,000 Americans. If HIV had a seat at the U.N. and had declared biological war on the United States killing 400,000 people already, you can be sure this article would not be needed, for we can understand the old wars of people and guns. But germs are now at most one day away by jet plane, and this new enemy to our security has landed invasions of us and our allies without a whimper from our government because the enemy is not human. It is said that we are always fighting the last war which is why we often lose the one we are in. Well, the distances that protected us from foreign pathogens have disappeared and the global nation that stretches around the world has new security needs far different from those we have understood from our history. It is the germ that is the most dangerous of our new enemies. And it is public health that needs our military budget.

In the rift valley, where Malawi lies next to a large lake filled with hippopotami, the first humans built the first villages two million years ago. It would be sad if we let our birthplace become a cemetery because we would rather let our Congress spend the 50 dollars apiece we already gave them for some other idea that they have for us. How about paying for the medicines that our poor, our old and the world's sick need instead?

The new millenium begins with the biggest moral question we have ever faced. Will we let hundreds of millions of people die from a disease we know how to treat because we don't care about anyone but those of us with money and health insurance?

Basically the British High Commissioner said that Africans couldn't take their medicines on time and trying to save their lives would be a waste of money. It was a widespread opinion in the West. I disagreed.

Mbeki and AIDS

I got an invitation from Thabo Mbeki to be part of the special panel on AIDS he convened to advise him on HIV/AIDS policies in South Africa. I was warned that denialists (people who do not believe HIV causes AIDS) were in charge in South Africa and that the president had bought into their view. In Malawi it was about figuring how to pay for the AIDS drugs. In South Africa, it was figuring out how to convince Thabo Mbeki that HIV caused AIDS and that there were medicines that could arrest the disease.

Given that 25% of sub-Saharan Africa was HIV positive this was a critical job. I made a report on the trip on May 25th, 2000 and what follows is from that report.

South Africa and the Denialists

Following is a key section of Mbeki's letter to President Clinton regarding Mbeki's desire to hear out the claims of the denialists:

I make these comments because our search for these specific and targeted responses is being stridently condemned by some in our country and the rest of the world as constituting a criminal abandonment of the fight against HIV-AIDS.

Some elements of this orchestrated campaign of condemnation worry me very deeply. It is suggested, for instance, that there are some scientists who are "dangerous and discredited" with whom nobody, including ourselves, should communicate or interact. In an earlier period in human history, these would be heretics that would be burnt at the stake! Not long ago, in our own country, people were killed, tortured, imprisoned and prohibited from being quoted in private and in public because the established authority believed that their views were dangerous and discredited. We are now being asked to do precisely the same thing that the racist apartheid tyranny we opposed did, because, it is said, there exists a scientific view that is supported by the majority, against which dissent is prohibited. The scientists we are supposed to put into scientific quarantine include Nobel Prize Winners, Members of Academies of Science and Emeritus Professors of various disciplines of medicine! Scientists, in the name of science, are demanding that we should cooperate with them to freeze scientific discourse on HIV-AIDS at the specific point this discourse had reached in the West in 1984.

People who otherwise would fight very hard to defend the critically important rights of freedom of thought and speech occupy, with regard to the HIV-AIDS issue, the frontline in the campaign of intellectual intimidation and terrorism which

— THABO MBEKI

There had been a great deal of speculation on Mbeki's motivations and on the effects of his questioning our understanding of HIV illness. I was prepared for a grueling seven days.

On the way to South Africa, I met four other panelists and a reporter.

First was Joe Sonnabend, founder of AmFAR. Joe had been raised and trained in South Africa, was a pleasant guy, twinkle in his eyes, could be grouchy, and was cautious about what caused AIDS. He felt that there were probably co-factors in HIV that as of that time had not yet been identified. In point of fact the very extraordinary divergence in viral load and lifespans of people with HIV reflected the fact that people were all different and by definition would have differing responses to pretty much anything. This could easily mask a second or third co-factor precipitating AIDS. Many people believed the use of recreational drugs, for example, hastened or caused AIDS. However, Joe made it clear he understood that HIV was a necessary condition for AIDS to occur.

Next I met Harvey Bialy, a denialist who seemed full of anger. He made efforts to be friendly and controlled, but the frustration showed through. Tall, thin, bearded and aggressive. Bialy spoke of the 60's as if we were members of the same peer group and political movements of that decade.

Finally, I met Celia Farber, a reporter famous for her coverage of the O. J. Simpson trial, which ran in Esquire. She was pretty much in the camp of the denialists.

Dear Participant

Welcome to South Africa! We hope you will have a pleasant and productive stay.

We realise that this was very short notice but due to time constraints in preparing for the AIDS conference that is to take place in Durban later this year, a later date would not have been possible.

Your hotel account for bed and breakfast will be borne by the secretariat for the period of your stay. All additional costs will be for your own account.

On Saturday and Sunday during the lunch hour a representative from Reynolds Travel will be available for any questions regarding changes in travel arrangement that you wish to make.

Please do not hesitate to contact one of the secretariat should you have any requests or questions.

Hoping you have a pleasant stay.

Yours sincerely

ORGANISING COMMITTEE

Bialy came up to Joe Sonnabend and me, and proceeded to question Joe's morality for giving AZT to anyone and lectured me on the harmlessness of retroviruses. I told him that every decent vet knew that the visna virus and others affecting sheep, cows and horses were lentiviruses like HIV and killed animals with regularity. He ignored this, preferring to lecture on his concept that viruses which are "inactive" or passive in some way are harmless. I uncharitably called his thinking "rather shallow," pointing out that DNA was the most passive of molecules and that passivity in general was not the same as having no effects on the world. I pointed out that many passive things had significant effects — for example laws, relativity theory, a cookbook's directions, written language — among the many things that are passive but not impotent. Bialy took off angrily, and then returned to all smiles. He seemed determined to make sure we would become friends.

I was frightened to think I would have to cross the Atlantic Ocean with this set of characters.

Johannesburg (an area I had learned to fear) turned out to be an amazing, complex city with very different personalities. Among the first people I met were Malegapuru Makgopa, head of the Medical Research Council, the South African version of the NIH, and Salim "Slim" Karim, another South African scientist. Slim was fat and Malegapuru was thin. Slim was energetic and political, a mobilizer. Malegapuru was a friend of President Mbeki, a thoughtful scientist.

Malegapuru said he had spent some time with his friend Mbeki, trying to talk him out of the idea of taking seriously those who think that HIV does not cause AIDS. He claimed Mbeki is in fact concerned about his own feeling of certainty that HIV causes AIDS, and that his questioning is not just a political move.

When the panel had all arrived, we each shook Thabo Mbeki's hand who had come to underline the importance of the panel. I approached him, and after I shook hands, handed him the letter given to me by Bob Gallo. I said to Mbeki, "Dr. Gallo is one of our most famous scientists and would like you to please consider what he has to say as you deliberate what to do." The president looked at the envelope, handed it to a staff aide and assured me he would pay attention to Dr. Gallo's communication.

I am greeted by Thabo Mbeki in Pretoria, (the President of South Africa after Nelson Mandela) and give him the letter from Bob Gallo

That night a group gathered in my room. I passed around a note suggesting that "our side" meet, to figure out how to react to the other side.

Stefano Bertozzi began. He was an extraordinary man from Mexico with a clear mind. He initiated with an oft-repeated analogy that was elaborated upon throughout the meeting, saying that the denialists did more than simply yell "no fire" in a theater burning down filled with people — they accused the fire engines and rescue personnel of causing the fire.

Scientists from South Africa were seriously concerned about avoiding giving any credence through the respect for their presence to the position of denialists. We spent a lot of time talking through whether it would be best to boycott the meeting or to try to shape it.

The result of the evening meeting was an understanding from the South Africans that they would not walk out so long as something meaningful seemed to be happening. As a whole, we decided to not get caught in any emotional debate with the denialists and instead allow them to show themselves for what they were.

During the evening I got a call from Richard Knox of the Boston Globe, the medical reporter for the newspaper. It became clear quite early that there would be significant media attention on this panel discussion.

We were given a package of materials, which I reviewed the night before the first formal meeting of the panel. Among the materials were:

- A booklet entitled "HIV/AIDS Literature Review," a comprehensive guide to extant literature on every aspect of HIV illness in South Africa. It covered an extraordinary breadth of topics: a training manual for improving news coverage; Cape Town Sex Workers perceptions of the Female Condom, and so forth.

- A booklet on "HIV/AIDS in South Africa, the Impacts and Priorities".

- A document that summarized everything the Ministry of Health was doing and its views on various key issues.

Among numerous statements in these document, I summarize the following:

- A statement about the creation of the South African National AIDS Council (SANAC): It is a coordinating council representing government and civil society, consisting of voluntary represent-atives from business, labor, faith-based organizations, govern-ment departments, people with AIDS (PWAs), etc. The council was advised by a range of technical task teams of experts which developed detailed plans to address social, scientific and medical challenges associated with the epidemic.

- A statement about the government's stated objective of having an AIDS educator visit home in the country: This goal was extraordinary in its scope, and necessary given the scale of the crisis. At that time, perhaps one in four South Africans had HIV.

Here are a few direct quotes, which exemplify the government's commitment to fight AIDS, their concerns about Western medicine, and their contradictory beliefs about pathogenesis entertained by government actors:

- "The HIV/AIDS Strategic Plan for South Africa 2000-2005: major strategies are improved management of tuberculosis and sexually transmitted diseases and promotion of increased condom use to reduce STD and HIV transmission."

- "The Medical Control Council is awaiting the outcome of the South African Intrapartum nevirapine trial (SAINT) before considering the application by the drug manufacturers for the use of this drug on HIV positive mothers. [The South African Government is very concerned about toxicities of drugs and does not accept in general trials not done in South Africa]."

- "The widespread use of anti-retroviral drugs in the African setting is largely academic because of their very high cost. The pricing policies of the manufacturers are protected by patent laws."

- "Patients who are sometimes induced to sign up for the trials because of money or the prospect of free treatment are often not fully aware of all of the consequences. These include withdrawal of beneficial drugs when the trial ends."

- "Foreign drug companies are using South African HIV and AIDS patients as guinea pigs for drugs that will not be available for use in South Africa because of cost and patent protection."

- "The Government believes that only those clinical trials that will result in a direct benefit for all South African HIV/AIDS sufferers should be allowed in South Africa."

- With regard to prevention the materials stated: "The best vaccine is to avoid exposure to the HIV virus."

With regard to the expert panel on which I sat: "Some of the issues the panel will be asked to review include:"

- "Local evidence regarding the viral origin of HIV and other concerns regarding the pathogenesis and diagnosis of HIV/AIDS in Africa."

- "Medical interventions to prevent transmission of HIV/AIDS in Africa including mother to child transmission, HIV spread via injections, needle stick injuries or rape…"

- "Medical treatment of people living with HIV/AIDS and treatment of opportunistic infections in Africa."

- "The including on the expert panel of so called AIDS dissidents (i.e. those who believe that AIDS is caused by lifestyle factors such as poverty and malnutrition rather than the HIV virus) has caused uproar among the scientific and medical fraternity. It has been alleged that the Government is acting irresponsibly by forming a panel that might challenge orthodox views on the disease. Some have accused the government of encouraging 'voodoo science'."

- "Without pre-judging the issues, the government's view is that blind acceptance of conventional wisdom would be irresponsible. After all, orthodox understanding and responses have met with great success elsewhere in Africa."

These materials made it quite clear that many people had already decided that HIV caused AIDS and were working on a national program to intervene.

At 7:30 a.m. panelists listened to a press conference including the Minister of Health and President Mbeki. After a speech by the Minister of Health, which reiterated the material we read the night before, President Mbeki was introduced.

He spoke at some length, beginning with a poem now well known about his position on the cause of HIV, calling himself either a fool or a prophet. He reiterated the statements of the Health Minister, made it clear that he was concerned about the disease destroying his country, yet defensive about the invitation to dissidents — he reiterated what he said previously about the right for every view to be heard.

The closed session of the panel began at 9 a.m. One of the first people to speak lifted up the agenda, noting that Mbeki's first question was "What causes AIDS?"; he looked up at us and in a monotone said "HIV," then remained silent. Stefano Vella was eloquent and passionate. He pushed aside what he characterized as an accommodationist effort and basically said that if one thing needed to be made clear and crisp, it is that HIV causes AIDS and from this follows what needs to be done to manage it. As we went around the room, it became clear where people stood.

- Salim Abdool-Karim — South African leader: strongly in favor of finding a way to get antivirals into Africa in a meaningful way.

- Harvey Bialey — the Duesberg follower who was writing a biography of Peter Duesberg, clearly holding a great deal of respect and feelings of reverence toward the molecular biologist who was a leading denialist, made it clear he thought that it had never been shown that HIV causes the disease.

- Stefano Bertozzi — eloquent, sensible, cautious but firm. HIV causes AIDS. He worked in Mexico where he was an expert in health care economics.

- Étienne de Harven — a person who was unbelievable in having no problem denying the very existence of AIDS. I couldn't figure out what this person thought causes the weekly funerals around the country.

- Ann Duerr from the CDC. She was a person who spent years in Africa doing epidemiological work on HIV. Of course HIV causes AIDS.

- Peter Duesberg. Charming. Smart. Incredibly pig-headed.

- Roberto Giraldo — another denialist.

- Andrew Herxheimer — a person who, though a dissident, occasionally had contributions of a meaningful sort which amounted to doing trials to see what works and finding ways to test differences of opinion in the context of scientific data.

- E.T. Katabira — strong voice of reason.

- Klaus Koehnlein. This interesting man does not believe AIDS exists at all. He thinks there aren't any increases in deaths going on, just artifacts on how data is collected.

- Cliff Lane — number two on HIV at the NIH, who worked on a medicine that ultimately failed, the use of the cytokine IL-2, a growth factor for T-cells, in arresting the development of AIDS.

- Malegapuru Makgoba (William) — truly extraordinary thinker and a leader of the South African contingent.

- Sam Mhlongo — he was rather confusing and seemed to side with the dissidents.

- Wilfred Nkomo — an epidemiologist from Malawi with a sense of humor and absolutely no patience with denialists.

- George Perez — Cuban who wanted to focus on what could be done, not argue about HIV which he thinks is a waste of the guests' time.

- Walter Prozesky — head of vaccine development in South Africa and a very wise man.

- David Rasnick — thinks the drugs we used to fight HIV causes AIDS, not HIV.

- Keith Rawlings — head of the National Medical Association, representing most black doctors in the USA. He was exceptionally good on this issue.

- Joe Sonnabend: Believed in co-factors — other things not considered which contributed to the spread and severity of AIDS in Africa.

- Zena Stein — A woman concerned with mother-to-child transmission and determined to make us move onto what would work in South Africa.

- Gordon Stewart — He was quiet, polite, a dissident in name but believes that HIV causes AIDS or so he said at the meeting. He felt the HIV tests needed better validation as well as better record-keeping.

By my count (I omitted a few above), not counting the facilitators and observers, I counted 26 people with ten flat-earthers, more or less depending on where you put Stewart, and 16 definite round-earthers.

I was asked to give some interviews to the press — possibly to balance the many interviews with dissidents. I spoke with the press, who assembled as a group, and I doubt many ended up reporting much of what I said or who I was with any accuracy.

I met a very aggressive and interested reporter, Andrew Selsky, with the Associated Press, who did a story that appeared the next day in several papers in Africa. I would eventually end up on BBC radio, and doing several South African television shows. Apparently I was also quoted in the USA, and for some reason many of the articles misidentified who I was — Dr. Scondras. I repeatedly had to correct virtually everyone who wanted to give me credentials I do not possess.

I knew that my diary would end up in the news in South Africa. Especially the part in which I called the denialists "flat earthers."

The meeting of the panel reconvened and continued in an endless round table conversation, all taped, that basically got no where. Finally the day ended with a buffet reception with the Minister of Health Manto Tshabalala-Msimang and Deputy President Jacob Zuma (who was elected president in 2009). It appeared from his speech that Zuma didn't really take very seriously the idea that HIV does not cause AIDS. I spoke with him privately and he told me that he would make sure that the right thing would be done to get antivirals to the poor of South Africa.

Jacob Zuma (in 2013 President of South Africa) and
Dr, Manto Tshabalala-Msimang

The good guys met in Slim's room that night after the Zuma speech. We summarized the day's events, which seemed to be going better than anticipated, with the other side clearly outnumbered. Many strategic ideas were invented, debated and discarded and we all went to bed hopeful that something constructive might still come out of the sessions.

On Sunday the talks broke down, as was inevitable. The moderator's efforts to search for consensus was tagged by Cliff Lane as misleading. The group resisted getting pushed into consensus because everyone, including the denialists, agreed it was misleading. Looking only at consensus would lead to, for example, a consensus that AIDS drugs had toxicities, but no consensus that they helped with the illness. This would mean they should not be used, from a policy point of view, a very misleading conclusion. There was also the problem that consensus can lead to agreement on precisely the most irrelevant aspects of a problem.

One of the panel members, making an effort to get beyond the impasse, took the mike and asked, "Does AIDS exist and is there an epidemic?" in order to get everyone on the record. There was a lot of dancing around this from a few of the dissidents, but basically most of the panel agreed AIDS exists and there is an epidemic. As the meeting degenerated into political maneuvering to find ways to force a misleading consensus forward, there was constant resistance against getting results.

There were many interesting presentations of ideas from the panelists — in response to what data would show there is an epidemic, Katabira said it depended on where you are. In a house on fire you have direct access to the information. Outside you smell and see smoke and feel the flames. Far away you hear fire engines and perhaps can still smell the smoke. But aside from the entertainment value and perhaps some educational value, the meeting did not accomplish much.

There had been an effort to divide the group into three groups to deal with etiology, treatment and prevention. Members of the dissidents condemned this separating into small meetings, but the organizers got their way. The three groups had a recorder and a mix of dissidents and us and the results were chaotic and terribly misleading. We all decided to throw away the results of this effort.

A new effort to form separate groups based upon beliefs was pushed by several people including myself, and the organizers decided it was worthwhile and made it happen. It was decided that we would divide into two groups to which anyone could go, the one writing a list of suggestions starting from the premise that HIV causes AIDS and the other with the opposite premise. This idea led to two sets of suggestions to be reported back to the main group.

Everything said and done was filmed and recorded so eventually we would all have access to every word, but what I remember of the result is:

Herxheimer spoke for the denialists and their report said:

1.   HIV does not cause AIDS.

2. AIDS is not infectious or sexually transmitted.

3. Drugs are poisonous.

4. Treat the diseases called "O.I.'s" (opportunistic infections characteristic of the pathogens that take hold of a person when their immune system weakens).

5. Stop telling people AIDS invariably leads to death.

Our side (HIV causes AIDS) was represented by Slim and Bertozzi and included the following topics and ideas:

1. The need to create a positive social environment in which there is no discrimination.

2. The need to develop a meaningful and reliable surveillance model.

3. Move to reduce the incidence of this blood borne infections by:
    a. HIV screening, education and blood screening.
    b. Needlestick exposure policies.
    c. Precautions at workplaces.
    d. IV drug policies (e.g. clean needles).

4. Reduction of Mother to Child transmission through:
    a. Voluntary HIV testing.
    b. Contraceptive provision.
    c. Use of antivirals.
    d. Policy on breast feeding (it was discovered that HIV can pass in milk to a newborn).

5. Reduction of sexual transmission by:
    a. Safe sex.
    b. Promote condoms.
    c. Aggressively treat STD's.
    d. Post-exposure prophylaxis.
    e. Regulation of sex workers.

6. Treatment by:
    a. Building up the capacity of the health care system.
    b. Treatment of HIV cofactors if identified.

c.	Direct treatment of HIV with antivirals.
d.	Palliative care.

7.	Additional considerations regarding manifestations and co-factors by:
a.	STD's aggressively treated to determine the relationship to HIV transmission and rate of progression
b.	Prophylaxis.
c.	Develop local treatment guidelines.

8.	Additional considerations regarding treatment
a.	Monitoring of the present use of ART (antiretroviral treatment) in private hospitals among people with money.
b.	Acknowledge the need for South Africa to contextualize uses of ART.

Helen Gayle, of CDC and co-delegate to
Thabo Mbeki's "special panel on AIDS"

After these presentations were made. Helene Gayle announced that CDC would cooperate with the Medical Research Council (MRC) in South Africa to provide what data existed to show that the "Duesberg

Hypothesis" was wrong, i.e. left to no therapy, people with HIV get AIDS and die.

After the Sunday meeting there was a closing press conference. At this conference, the Health Minister (Dr. Manto Tshabalala-Msimang) said that for the very first time a group of eminent scientists holding such fiercely different views about HIV and AIDS met in one room to exchange views in a robust discussion in order to assist South Africa in framing a policy in the midst of the catastrophe. She said:

> *"I learned a lot. I am convinced there is a lot to do. I found this an unforgettable experience. It was an opportunity to exchange with each other, challenge, question, review knowledge. On a personal level it was an exercise in humility. To differ in a constructive context..."*

Lots of thank yous. She thanked the press. Reporters were charged with being accurate, responsible and true to spirit and substance. She announced that there would be an internet discussion for 6 weeks and a follow up meeting. A member of Mbeki's staff said:

> *"This is about millions of lives being lost. Despair of those who are ill from this infection...eyes of children who have lost parents. Duesberg and the CDC working together. Courageous effort by Helene Gayle to offer help in answering some epidemiological questions raised by Dr. Duesberg."*

Questions from the press to the Health Minister included:

What was the value of the meeting?

Answer: Very different scientists from all over the world agree there is real expertise in South Africa and in the developing world and that the value from elsewhere is to allow local experts to draw from others' experience.

AIDS had killed people, yes or no?

Answer: The purpose of the meeting is to get questions, a green paper of key questions about the cause of AIDS, its treatment and prevention. There are experiments which can deal with the issue of what causes AIDS. A subgroup of MRC, Drs. Bialy, Duesberg and the CDC will look at epidemiological data bases to resolve this issue.

Is there a domestic policy advantage to this exercise and questions about HIV and AIDS?

We already won the elections. If anything, we are getting more unpopular with these questions.

Did President Clinton send anyone and if so who?

Clinton and Mbeki talk among themselves. There were no panelists from the White House. South Africa did not talk to any other government in the world over the decision of who to bring to South Africa.

At Jo'burg airport I caught a flight back to Malawi, to Lilongue. I was worn out (no sleep for two days) and stressed out. Had a wonderful talk with Luc Montaigne at dinner the previous night.

Nobel Laureate Montagnier, co-discoverer with Robert Gallo of HIV, and I, discussing how to handle Thabo Mbeki's skepticisms about HIV and AIDS

I had made a promise to Epie, the boy who cleaned the room at the hotel, that I would get him some brochures on schools in Boston.

The last night in Pretoria an amazing thing happened with Epie. He brought me presents of wooden carving of animals I had told him I wanted to see. It was moving and my eyes teared up. He had reassured me the day before that it was okay to be gay in South Africa, that we were legally protected. He hugged me, and I had no trouble getting a crush on this man from Cameroon.

I would return to Africa to attend the world AIDS conference there in July, 2000.

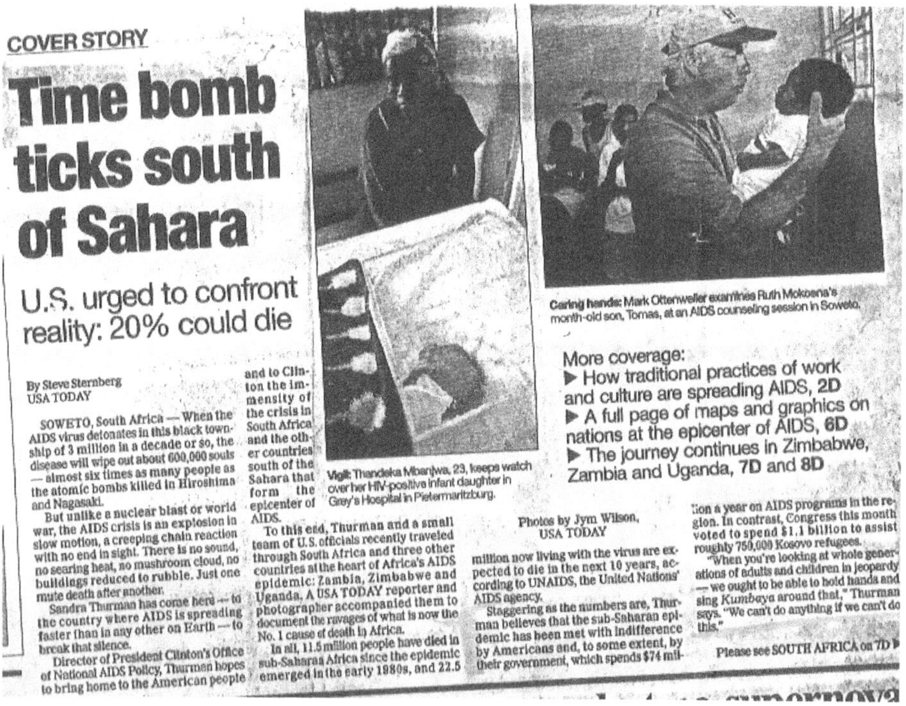

COVER STORY

Time bomb ticks south of Sahara

U.S. urged to confront reality: 20% could die

By Steve Sternberg
USA TODAY

SOWETO, South Africa — When the AIDS virus detonates in this black town- ship of 3 million in a decade or so, the disease will wipe out about 600,000 souls — almost six times as many people as the atomic bombs killed in Hiroshima and Nagasaki.

But unlike a nuclear blast or world war, the AIDS crisis is an explosion in slow motion, a creeping chain reaction with no end in sight. There is no sound, no searing heat, no mushroom cloud, no buildings reduced to rubble. Just one mute death after another.

Sandra Thurman has come here — to the country where AIDS is spreading faster than in any other on Earth — to break that silence.

Director of President Clinton's Office of National AIDS Policy, Thurman hopes to bring home to the American people and to Clinton the immensity of the crisis in South Africa and the other countries south of the Sahara that form the epicenter of AIDS.

To this end, Thurman and a small team of U.S. officials recently traveled through South Africa and three other countries at the heart of Africa's AIDS epidemic: Zambia, Zimbabwe and Uganda. A USA TODAY reporter and photographer accompanied them to document the ravages of what is now the No. 1 cause of death in Africa.

In all, 11.5 million people have died in sub-Saharan Africa since the epidemic emerged in the early 1980s, and 22.5 million now living with the virus are expected to die in the next 10 years, according to UNAIDS, the United Nations' AIDS agency.

Staggering as the numbers are, Thurman believes that the sub-Saharan epidemic has been met with indifference by Americans and, to some extent, by their government, which spends $74 million a year on AIDS programs in the region. In contrast, Congress this month voted to spend $1.1 billion to assist roughly 750,000 Kosovo refugees.

"When you're looking at whole generations of adults and children in jeopardy — we ought to be able to hold hands and sing *Kumbaya* around that," Thurman says. "We can't do anything if we can't do this."

Please see SOUTH AFRICA on 7D ▶

Vigil: Thandeka Mbanjwa, 23, keeps watch over her HIV-positive infant daughter in Grey's Hospital in Pietermaritzburg.

Caring hands: Mark Ottenweller examines Ruth Mokoena's month-old son, Tomas, at an AIDS counseling session in Soweto.

Photos by Jym Wilson, USA TODAY

More coverage:
- ▶ How traditional practices of work and culture are spreading AIDS, **2D**
- ▶ A full page of maps and graphics on nations at the epicenter of AIDS, **6D**
- ▶ The journey continues in Zimbabwe, Zambia and Uganda, **7D** and **8D**

Durban, South Africa: July, 2000

I waited for the bus which was arranged to get us to the Durban international conference on AIDS, where I met with people from *Search For A Cure* who came to Africa to see this amazing event, the first AIDS convention to be held in a "third world" country.

The convention center, across the street from a new Hilton Hotel, was beautiful. The media section was huge, and I met people from around the world and checked out press releases from hundreds of NGO's. The way into the conference was marked by little villages of people with special interests — disabled people with HIV, women with HIV, etc.

The day was spent in the chaotic assembly of thousands of scientists and activists and government officials from around the world. As evening came, the president of South Africa spoke from a platform erected near the convention center. Thousands attended.

Mbeki stood silent as applause broke out. We felt that the world coming together in this extraordinary country. Viewing the second freely-elected president of a country freed from apartheid was a statement in an of itself, a testament to the movement to share with the countries of southern Africa in which are the most poor of the earth while in a nation for whom hopes were high.

The president began with a formal greeting: "I am happy to welcome you to Durban and to our country...."

His voice was strong and clear with a sound that I have only heard in South African English molded by the Dutch and provincial Kwazulu Natal, by tribal languages and formal training, and the unmistakable impact of the people of England:

You are in Africa the first time in the history of the International
AIDS Conferences. The peoples of our continent expect that out
of this extraordinary gathering will come a message and a
programme of action that will assist them to disperse the

menacing and frightening clouds that hang over all of us as a
result of the AIDS epidemic...

He then turned to a statement from the World Health
Organization in 1995:

The world's biggest killer and the greatest cause of ill health and
suffering across the globe is extreme poverty. Poverty is the
main reason why babies are not vaccinated, why clean water
and sanitation are not provided, why curative drugs and other
treatments are unavailable and why mothers die in childbirth....
The gaps between rich and poor are widening. For most people
in the world today, every step of life from infancy to old age is
taken under the twin shadows of poverty and inequity. For
many the prospect of longer life may seem more like a
punishment than a gift."

I was stunned. The thought that life could be so painful that the
work I had done for so long to end AIDS might for so many seem a
punishment had never occurred to me. I came to see that for life to be
worth living was the first job, before even saving it. A person in one of the
least developed countries in the world has a life expectancy of 43 years. A
person in one of the most developed countries has a life expectancy of 78.
This means a rich healthy man can live twice as long as a poor, sick man.
That inequity along should stir the conscience of the world.

On behalf of our government and people...(we are) confident
that you have come to these African shores as messengers of
hope and hopeful that when you conclude your important work,
we as Africans will be able to say that you who came to this city,
which occupies a fond place in our hearts, came here because
you care.

We all stood up and applauded, feeling hopeful, feeling moved,
feeling a need to do something.

Winnie Mandela spoke, chastising drug companies for being an
obstacle to people getting medicines for HIV. She said:

(Phansi is a Urdu expression meaning hanging.) These were among the companies that fought to stop South Africa and other countries from making inexpensive copies of their drugs to save their people. At the time Winnie was talking, some 20% of South Africans had HIV, none of whom would survive without medicines and all of whom would suffer a lingering death.

I knew in Geneva how serious this fight between greed and grace was, but few leaders put it in such stark terms as Winnie Mandela. She called for South Africa to make the medicines no matter what the companies said and South Africa eventually did just that until the various drug companies lowered their prices.

Nelson Mandela closed the session in Durban. He came on stage inside the auditorium to a standing ovation, and smiled. After the applause died down, he began slowly and focused.

*This is not an academic conference. This is, as I understand it, a
gathering of human beings concerned about turning around one
of the greatest threats humankind has faced, and certainly the
greatest after the end of the great wars of the previous century.
It is never my custom to use words lightly. If twenty seven years
in prison have done anything to us, it was to use the silence of
solitude to make us understand how precious words are and
how real speech is in its impact upon the way people live or die.
In the face of the grave threat posed by HIV/AIDS we have to*

rise above our differences and combine our efforts to save our people. History will judge us harshly if we fail to do so now, and right now. Let us not equivocate: a tragedy of unprecedented proportions is unfolding in Africa. AIDS today in Africa is claiming more lives than the sum total of all wars, famines and floods, and the ravages of such deadly diseases as malaria. It is devastating families and communities. AIDS is clearly a disaster, effectively wiping out the development gains of the past decades and sabotaging the future. One in two – that is, half our young people – will die of AIDS. The most frightening thing is that all of these infections which statistics tell us about, and the attendant human suffering could have been, can be prevented.

Mandela spelled out use of condoms, destigmatization of the illness, testing and counseling, to move from rhetoric to action. He returned to his hotel where I was hanging out, giving me a chance to thank him. I felt a bit what Catholics must feel touching the pictures of a saint.

Over the years, thousands of people from rich countries joined their counterparts in poor countries to build the clinics and distribute the medicines needed to end these worldwide pandemics. I doubt any of us thought we would get so involved in an effort so huge so soon. But South Africa changed, and the drug companies changed. The CEO of Pfizer donated $100 million to Africa. Glaxo created a foundation to spend money on medicines in Africa. All companies changed their prices to make the drugs more affordable.

This happened in part because of compassion, in part because of the pressure from so many of us especially in the United States, but also because of what one man named Yusuf Hamied would do from India. The conference was an extraordinary event.

Before I left Durban, I met a young man who biked across South Africa as a way to say "do something," and we became intimate. It was a beautiful thing.

Return to Malawi: October, 2000

I had work to do. I asked Robert Redfield to come with me to Africa, and he said yes. I was moved by his willingness to come and help. He was a Republican, a devote Catholic, a believer in Christ and God, a former member of the U.S. Army, but more than anything else he was a doctor.

I asked Peter Salk to come, for his name alone would resonate among the people from many countries who would attend this meeting.

Peter Salk and myself, in Malawi at the conference to convince Malawi to develop a treatment plan

A group of people who wanted to make a movie came with me, eventually getting aerial views of Malawi in a military helicopter (how they managed this I have still to learn). For years you could still see this movie, and others, on the website of *Search For A Cure.*

I got Ann Duerr to agree to come, from the Centers for Disease Control. At the time, she was in the division of reproductive health.

Search For A Cure had no money. So each of the participants raised their own funds! And I went to Montreal and met with an old friend, so that Ian Roberts, the member of the health ministry of South Africa who wanted to attend the annual CROI conference on HIV held in San Francisco, could attend.

That friend was John Molson, whose grandfather founded Molson's Beer. He felt obliged to try to help the world in whatever way he could. He gave *Search* $5,000 to help out with this meeting in Malawi without which we could not have done it. I had dinner in Montreal with him, his wife, and kids, along with Robert, and was amazed at how caring, intelligent and supportive this Canadian was about our issues.

The vice president invited all the key actors in Malawi to the meeting and decided to open the meeting himself. This meant that in the end 43 people representing the health ministries of several countries, the United Nations staff, scientists, and others participated as formal members of the meeting.

The meeting in Malawi. Virtually all of the health sector leaders are in the picture.

Above is a picture taken during a break at the "Conference Investigating Options To Increase Access To Drugs For Treatment Of HIV/AIDS" and in the photo are virtually all of Malawi's leaders in health from hospital administrators to members of the UN delegation, from various ambassadors to the key hospital administrators in Malawi.

On the front row from right to left are Peter Salk, myself, Lisa Hirschhorn, and the gentleman on the left with a smile, balding head, red tie and white beard was Robert Redfield.

Vice President Malewezi entered the room, and spoke carefully, focused and clear. I realized that I had become a catalyst for a meeting that was needed and could potentially affect millions of lives:

No where has the impact of HIV/AIDS been more severe than in Sub-Saharan Africa. The impact of AIDS in southern Africa is devastating. Here is where a generation of children is now losing its parents to AIDS at an alarming rate.

The situation in Malawi is no less disturbing. AIDS is Malawi is devastating our economy. It is destroying the very fabric of our society. It is not only taking away our present, it is taking away our future and the future of our children. Apart from the almost immeasurable grief and trauma due to the illness and death of a loved one. The cost of funerals erodes savings at the household and national level.

The purpose of today's meeting is to address the feasibility of implementing a test and treatment program using anti-retroviral drugs.

The vice president went on in detail about empowerment of women, teaching the young how to protect themselves, analyzing the way Malawi's existing systems could be changed to help end the transmission of the illness from reducing multiple partners to ending stigma about the illness.

"My friend with AIDS is still my friend," said this African leader.

He went on to say that Durban taught us to break the silence, and that we needed to include people with AIDS in the design of programs to prevent transmission: "I appeal to religious leaders to show compassion and support to all those affected by HIV/AIDS. Promoting access to antiretroviral drugs lowers the viral load and thus contributes to preventing transmission of the virus."

This understanding was one of my contributions to His Excellency's understanding of the disease. It is an irony that in the United States it has taken thirteen years since the vice president said this fact about AIDS for the US to acknowledge this truth and incorporate it into the rationale and the urgency behind test and treat.

Justin Malewezi interviewed on film for our movie about Malawi. The couple behind me volunteered their time and effort to make a record of the meeting and turn it into a film which we would use to help focus attention on the crisis. Note the red ceremonial chair which Malawezi must sit in when he is formally representing the government of Malawi.

We convinced the vice president who, in turn, convinced the cabinet and president to allow him to represent Malawi in Boston and at the United Nations. Here is the first letter he sent formalizing the agreement:

Ref No. VP/C/20/1

Telephone No. 782655

Facsimile No. 781321

THE OFFICE OF THE VICE PRESIDENT
P.O. BOX 3090
CAPITAL CITY
LILONGWE 3

THE VICE PRESIDENT

8th May, 2000

Mr. David Scondras
Boston
United States of America

Dear Mr. Scondras,

<u>INVITATION TO VISIT THE UNITED STATES ON HIV/AIDS SEARCH FOR A CURE MISSION</u>

I accept your invitation to visit the United States of America in order to plead directly to the American people the case of my country, and other African countries which have been plagued by HIV/AIDs. If we do not find a way of managing HIV illness, it will not be a question of losing a generation but a nation.

It is our belief that people of your country are generous and compassionate, and if they are made aware of the grim HIV/AIDs situation in my country and Sub-Saharan Africa in general, they would respond with the help that we need.

Search For a Cure's role in asking us to visit the United States of America, and in facilitating meetings with key scientists and manufacturers of medicines, and in arranging for speaking engagements and media to allow us to deliver our message to the American public, is critical.

We applaud your efforts to help Malawi and the other Sub-Saharan Africa where public health has become the biggest impediment to development.

Thank you for the invitation. We look forward to meeting with you in Boston in September, 2000.

Yours, Sincerely,

J.C. Malewezi

**VICE PRESIDENT AND MINISTER
<u>RESPONSIBLE FOR PRIVATISATION</u>**

The campaign to get medicine for Africa was on its way. In Durban, Malewezi said, "AIDS in Malawi is devastating our economy. It is destroying the very fabric of our society. It is not only taking away our present, it is taking away our future and the future of our children"

I traveled across the country raising funds and awareness that there was a crisis in Africa. An example is the following from an article about a visit I made to Laguna Beach, California whose gay mayor was a friend of Robert and mine. We would visit Laguna many times to raise funds for many causes.

Laguna Hills, CA, 25 August 2000 –

The Ulysses Foundation today announced that David Scondras, member of South African President Mbeki's council on AIDS, enthusiastically supports their Costa Mesa fundraiser, Crusade for a Cure. Crusade for a Cure to be held at Costa Mesa, California, September 15-17, 2000 at the Doubletree, soon to be Hilton, Hotel is open to the public. "Malawi has 370,000 AIDS orphans and a fourth of its young people are infected. In the words of its Vice President, Justin Malewezi, stopping AIDS is not just about the "loss of a generation, but the loss of the nation," said international AIDS advocate David Scondras. "The Ulysses Foundation's event this fall is critical. Existing programs, while important, are not enough."

Malawi, a country with about ten million people, has an official HIV-infected population of around one million people, most of whom are young. Even though the president and vice president of Malawi have made repeated appeals, the antivirals that might help end this epidemic have not been forthcoming from the United States or elsewhere. Recent actions by the United States, including the signing of the African AIDS bill by President Clinton, and efforts by UNAIDS, are steps in the right direction, but real relief may not come soon enough to help Malawians.

Search For A Cure will use the donation from The Ulysses Foundation's Crusade for a Cure to bring some American participants to a critical meeting in Malawi this fall where nationwide test and treat programs will be laid out. "The Ulysses Foundation is making it possible for the government of

Malawi, a small African country with a big problem, to fight AIDS," Scondras continued. "Search For A Cure is in your debt. So are the people of Malawi." The Ulysses Foundation's Crusade for a Cure is a three-day multi-media convention with celebrity guests from genre fiction television shows, "Babylon 5," "Crusade," "Forever Knight," "Space: Above and Beyond," "Star Trek: Deep Space Nine," and "Xena/Hercules." It also features creative team members from best-selling Top Cow Comics' "Rising Stars" and brand new "Midnight Nation," a demonstration and tournament of the collectible card game, "Babylon 5," educational sessions hosted by OASIS, the LA Chapter of the National Space Society, and much more. ...

June 18, 2001

The City of Cambridge, Massachusetts notices and a head of state pays a visit
> *COUNCILLOR REEVES*
> *COUNCILLOR BORN*
> *COUNCILLOR BRAUDE*
> *COUNCILLOR DAVIS*
> *COUNCILLOR DECKER*
> *MAYOR GALLUCCIO*
> *VICE MAYOR MAHER*
> *COUNCILLOR SULLIVAN*
> *COUNCILLOR TOOMEY*

WHEREAS: It has come to the attention of the City Council that the Right Honourable Justin Malewezi, Vice President of the African Republic of Malawi, will be visiting the Boston area this week; and

WHEREAS: Vice President Malewezi and a Malawi Delegation are here on a mission to seek help in ending the AIDS pandemic in Sub-Saharan Africa; and

WHEREAS: The Right Honourable Justin Malewezi and the Malawi Delegation will be honored at a reception at the State House on June 22, 2001; and

WHEREAS: The reception is being hosted by the Massachusetts Black Legislative Caucus, the Office of Boston Mayor Thomas Menino, Search For A Cure, and the Africa Health Initiative; and

WHEREAS: The AIDS crisis in Africa is not an African crisis; it is a world crisis, and the health and well-being of all of humankind will be determined by our ability to stand together to end this pandemic; now therefore be it

RESOLVED: That the Cambridge City Council go on record welcoming the Right Honourable Justin Malewezi, Vice President of the African Republic of Malawi, and the Malawi Delegation, to the Boston area, and extending its best wishes for the success of their mission; and be it further

RESOLVED: That the City Clerk be and hereby is requested to forward a suitably engrossed copy of this resolution to the Right Honourable Justin Malewezi and the Malawi Delegation on behalf of the entire City Council.

In City Council June 18, 2001.
Adopted by the affirmative vote of eight members.
Attest:- D. Margaret Drury, City Clerk.

In   Barcelona   at   the   International   AIDS   Conference   in   2002, Malewezi said,

Malawi is one of the pioneering countries. An observation made by an eminent development specialist Jeffery Sachs, who is with us on this panel, noted that poor countries cannot afford expensive medicines while drug companies tend to focus their research on finding cures for the rich rather than the poor. It is important to acknowledge the vital role that civil society institutions have played in placing issues of HIV/AIDS onto the international agenda. Groups such as Search For A Cure and others have campaigned tirelessly for increased access to medicines.

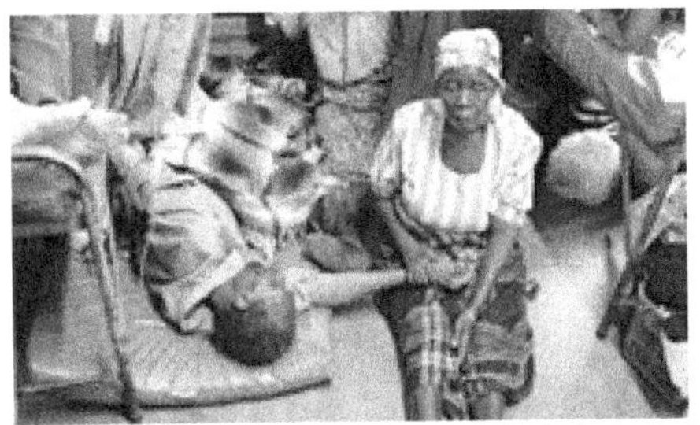

AIDS patient in Malawi, where 16% of adults are infected.
Credit: Denis Farrell/ AP

Seventeen years after HIV was identified, AIDS has finally seized the attention of the international community. The reason for the increase in attention to AIDS is clear. By 2002, 36 million people are HIV positive, and of those, 95 percent live in less developed countries. AIDS has taken 22 million lives and created 13 million orphans. AIDS has not only weakened the social, political and economic fabric of countries; it also threatens to undermine world stability. Nowhere has the impact of HIV/AIDS been more severe than in Sub-Saharan Africa. The region with less than 10 percent of the world's population is home to 70 percent of people living with HIV/AIDS. The HIV/AIDS pandemic will kill more people in Africa than all the casualties of all the wars of the 20th century combined. AIDS is devastating Africa — AIDS is destroying our hopes, our lives and our future. AIDS has a uniquely devastating impact on development and is at the centre of a global development crisis. AIDS kills young adults in their most productive years leaving grandparents to bring up their children. AIDS reduces life expectancy. Child mortality and poverty are projected to increase fueling a secondary pandemic of orphans throughout the region.

The HIV/AIDS pandemic in Africa has been described as a "catastrophe in slow motion" and as a "development and security crisis". While these descriptions capture the devastating impact of the epidemic, they do not bring out the urgency and immediacy of the danger facing Africa and, indeed the whole world. Nor do the statistics capture the tragedy of lives destroyed. Every day we are burying our children, our sisters and brothers, our workmates, our leaders, our teachers, doctors and other professionals. In the suffering and death of our brothers and sisters, we face grief beyond words and sorrow beyond tears. We cannot stand by and watch while our people are dying. The HIV/AIDS pandemic is the greatest threat to our future - it is an emergency and requires an emergency response by the international community.

Interview in *AIDS Treatment News*

Malawi Plan to Control AIDS Epidemic: Interview with David Scondras of Search For A Cure

By John S. James, AIDS Treatment News, September 21, 2001

In May 2001, when David Scondras was in Malawi, the headlines in the May 19-20 Weekend Nation newspaper read, "Few on the AIDS Drugs; Babies May Be Saved; No Hope for the Poor." Almost the whole front page was devoted to the epidemic.

Scondras was there working with health experts from Malawi and the U.S. trying to change that picture — by developing a plan to control the epidemic in Malawi, a plan that could become a model for other countries if it succeeds. While the number one goal is to reduce HIV transmission, this plan will also include medical treatment for those who need it — and extensive operations research to make sure that the program is working effectively. This September, officials from Malawi are coming to Boston for meetings to finalize the plan and begin steps toward implementation. [The meeting was postponed after the September 11 terrorist attacks, but is still scheduled for September, with a smaller delegation from Malawi.]

AIDS Treatment News asked David Scondras to explain this project to our readers. The interview took place on August 27, 2001.

ATN: Tell us what is happening now.

Scondras: *This will be the second trip that people from Malawi are making to the United States to get help. Experts and* *officials, including those responsible for Malawi's five-year plan to control AIDS, are coming to Boston to, among other things, meet with Jeffrey Sachs and others at Harvard's Center for International Development. They will continue a process begun several months ago in a previous trip, of having their country-wide plan reviewed by a group of scientists that Search For A Cure pulled together, and brought to Malawi as well as to Boston. Then, with the blessing of the scientific community that is reviewing the plan, they will seek funding from at least three different sources to implement that countrywide plan as soon as humanly possible.*

On this trip, Search For A Cure and Harvard are hosting them in Boston for about a week.

ATN: How did this project develop?

Scondras: *Two years ago when I first went to Malawi, the president of the country was on television and radio, explaining that there were some medicines that could help this disease, but unfortunately no one could afford them in Malawi, so they were going to have to do without them. This entire picture changed when we met with the vice president and explained how these drugs work. When it became clear that lowering viral load with these drugs might help reduce transmission, it became obvious that these drugs were a necessary part of the prevention program, not just help for people who are sick. In that context people became much more determined to see that there was access to them.*

Finally, when CIPLA (a drug manufacturer in India) and other generic producers offered generic drugs that were much, much less expensive, there was an increase in morale in Malawi. And when the Global AIDS Fund was announced, that morale reached the point that the vice president of Malawi accepted an invitation from Search For A Cure to come to the United States, and went to Harvard with me and met with Jeffrey Sachs and put this whole program in motion.

Malawi is determined to enact a countrywide treatment program that will stop the epidemic – that's the objective. This will be one of the tools.

ATN: Tell us about the country.

Scondras: *Malawi is a small country in Sub-Saharan Africa, one third of which is a giant lake. About 70% of the population of ten million are small farmers. It has two big cities, Lilongwe and Blantyre. It is one of the poorest countries in Africa, with a per capita income in U.S. dollars of around $250 per year. It has three main Bantu languages; a major one is called Chichewa. English is a second language for most people who are educated because Malawi was an English colony.*

It is a very new democracy; it emerged from a struggle to end a dictatorship only six years ago. The dictator had refused to allow the word "AIDS" to be used. The first thing the new government did was launch a prevention program across the country, with the president singing anti-AIDS and behavior change songs on television with schoolchildren to try to get people to understand that AIDS is a crisis and people had to change their behavior.

Development experts and economists came in to try to get the country going after the dictatorship ended. But they quickly realized that this country has about five years left to live. Malawi has ten million people, over one million HIV-infected. It has about 400,000 orphans who do not have HIV but whose parents are dead as a result of the epidemic. Up to a point, extended families and relatives can absorb orphans. But the ability to sustain life is being stretched to its limits as members of the extended families are now dying, as workers are dying and productivity is collapsing. The vice president compares the situation to an earthquake or other natural catastrophe, and asks why is the world so willing to help a country when there is a sudden disaster like an earthquake, but so slow when there is a crisis of equal magnitude that takes time to develop.

There has been a change. Malawi went from hopeless resignation to a sense of aggressive optimism. They decided they are going to live, and going to fight to live. This year Vice President Justin Malewezi said:

"Malawi has not been spared this worldwide epidemic. Sixteen percent of the population aged between 15 and 49 are HIV

positive. These people are commonly called People Living with HIV/AIDS. However, these are not the only people living with the disease. Every day we are burying our children, our sisters and brothers, our workmates, our neighbors, our leaders, our teachers, doctors and other professionals. In the suffering and death of our brothers and sisters we face grief beyond words, sorrow beyond tears. We will not stand by and watch while our people are dying."

A study by Hamoidi and Sachs looked at how the epidemic affects individuals and families:

"To take an individual case: a husband and father of young children, who earns a market income and who becomes HIV infected. He is likely to face years of declining market income due to absenteeism from work and reduced productivity before suffering a premature death. Household income will be diverted to pay for medical care, he is likely to sell assets and borrow at very high interest rates to get minimal access to palliative care. Upon his death, funeral costs will absorb savings from the extended family while his children may be sent away to live with relatives and their future education will be severely compromised. Tragically this scenario is repeated in Malawi every day."

Malawi's plan is a direct call for help, in human terms that are unmistakable and explicit. If we don't respond to it, then there's something wrong with us. We cannot say we didn't know about it.

ATN: Once the plan is ready, where does it go for funding?

Scondras: *Malawi already had a large and well-funded tuberculosis program, using directly observed therapy (DOT), with community workers who give medicine to individuals. Tuberculosis had been almost wiped out -- but AIDS brought it back. So the DOT people are willing to finance part of the program, as it affects their ability to control tuberculosis. (A recent South African study of people with HIV who use antiretrovirals vs. those who do not shows a dramatic difference of five times more tuberculosis among those who do not use the HIV drugs. So one can argue correctly that the antiretroviral* *program is an effective tuberculosis program, as 70% of tuberculosis patients in Malawi are co-infected with HIV.) The tuberculosis program is funded by the English contribution to the European Community.*

Malawi will have a DOT program for its HIV drugs, along the line of what Dr. Paul Farmer has done on a smaller scale in Haiti. But here it will be expanded to the whole country.

A second source of potential funding will be a request from the Global AIDS Fund. The World Bank will be asked to change the payments that Malawi is presently making on its debt, which are considerable, and returning them to Malawi as grants targeted specifically for this AIDS program.

In addition, Malawi is asking for a start-up grant from the World Bank -- which has been directed to make 50% of its future investments in developing countries in the form of grants instead of loans. Incidentally, the Bush Administration is supportive of this shift from loans to grants.

There is also an effort to organize an international concert to ask for support from the world community.

And in the U.S. Congress, Congresswoman Barbara Lee (D-California) is leading an effort to contribute an additional $150 million immediately to treatment.

ATN: How would Malawi purchase the drugs?

Scondras: *Malawi could use the International Dispensary Association (IDA) as a vehicle for drug purchases. The IDA (http://www.ida.nl) is a nonprofit organization based in Holland that has had a terrific reputation over the years for being the purchaser of the most inexpensive essential drugs for poor countries. They have decided to add HIV drugs to their list. They don't just buy the drug on behalf of the country; they also test the drugs on an ongoing basis to maintain their quality. Clearly for small developing countries, it is essential to have a dependable buyer who will get you the best price and guarantee the quality of the product. Malawi may choose to use the IDA* *for their HIV drugs, especially since they already use it for their tuberculosis drugs.*

Besides funding, other support comes from volunteers who are helping this effort and not getting paid, among them being quite a few U.S. scientists, including Peter Salk, M.D., from the Jonas Salk Foundation, and Robert Redfield, M.D., from the Institute of Human Virology, and people from the U.S. Public Health Service.

Several pharmaceutical companies are also going to try to help.

ATN: How is the AIDS program in Malawi organized?

Scondras: *Over a year and a half ago we helped put together a meeting in Malawi, under the leadership of UNAIDS, which helped create the Technical Working Group, a kind of committee with the sanction of the cabinet of Malawi. This committee was given the responsibility of developing a plan to use antiretrovirals in Malawi, and overseeing its implementation. It is the only committee I know of its kind that includes foreigners on it.*

The Technical Working Group includes all the major stakeholders in Malawi working with HIV, including the private hospitals and so forth. That organization is headed by the director of the AIDS program in Malawi. This is the organization that, if you are going to do anything with HIV in Malawi, you have to get approval from. Last week the Cabinet of Malawi gave the approval for moving forward.

ATN: Is there any opposition?

Scondras: *The government of Malawi is fighting hard for this plan, but not everyone is supportive. There is a lot of skepticism. Part of the donor community has been trying to get Malawi to not enact this plan, still saying it's unrealistic, you should do prevention only. Malawi is going forward anyway, because it does not see any choice. Malawi knows that even a perfect vaccine tomorrow would be too late to save the country. And besides that, it would be immoral not to try to save those* *already infected. This struggle has not been made public, but people have a right to know about it.*

ATN: What about foundation funding?

Scondras: *We will be seeking a planning grant to help finish putting the program together.*

Malawi wants to prove that you can stop an epidemic, and that antiretrovirals can be part of that program -- that it can be done. But the first target for this program is reduction in transmission of HIV.

ATN: Tell our readers about the research plans.

Scondras: *The plan itself makes a compromise between the demands of science and the demands of the economy, ethics, and politics. The scientific community wants to make sure through research on the ground that the choice of medicines is correct, that the delivery system is actually working, and so forth -- and that the type of therapy used is the right one, and wants to see which types of therapy might be better. Should we use interrupted therapy? Does nutrition have a role? What about use of immune-based therapies? You can imagine how many questions scientists have. But it would take years to answer them all. Meanwhile the country would collapse.*

So Malawi is starting the program by basically enrolling everyone into a best-guess approach -- using community-based directly observed therapy that can be taken once a day. But many people, in fact the majority, will be involved in a set of interlocking clinical trials, which the scientists refer to as operations research. These trials will test the different regimens and different styles of delivering them, to find out which work better. And as they learn what is best, they will phase out certain treatments and switch people to others.

Malawi will maintain the research component, so that Malawi will not only be a country that tries to stop the AIDS epidemic, but also will become the world's largest clinical trial system to find out the best way to reduce HIV transmission and improve on existing therapies across the world. For example, studies could test microbicides and see if they can reduce the rate of spread, or test vaccines. The research component, the ability to track data, analyze it, and feed it back to the working group and have the government make decisions about what to do, has to be much more advanced and larger than you would expect for a treatment program. The advantage is that this research will help everyone in the world, including people in the United States.

ATN: *Could you summarize what's happening now?*

Scondras: *In a few months Malawi will make history — as its leaders present this ambitious, countrywide program for stopping AIDS in an African country to funders at the World Bank and the Global AIDS Fund.*

Malawi will not survive unless this program succeeds. Today a million people are infected, there are 400,000 orphans, and the whole country has only ten million people. If this plan works in one of the poorest countries, then it can work elsewhere and will become a beacon of hope for Africa and the rest of the world.

This effort has been put together by a team of volunteers including some of the best medical minds in the world, students from Harvard Business School, politicians, ministers, people with HIV, people of good will from all walks of life, working together with leaders from Malawi. It is possible because activists from around the world have pushed for a worldwide AIDS fund, and for reduced prices of antiretrovirals. Malawi will come to the United States to work with some of this country's finest experts and activists, all committed to finishing the design of the program and finding the funds to put it into operation now.

Anyone interested in helping is welcome to call or write us and join this effort. Many of us feel that one measure of our civilization will be how the rich nations and people of the Earth behave during the most devastating epidemic in the history of the world.

Copyright 2001 by John S. James. Permission granted for noncommercial reproduction.

June 19, 2001

David Scondras
Search For A Cure
34 Edgerly Road #1
Boston, MA 02115

Dear Mr. Scondras:

On behalf of the entire Kennedy School community, we would like to extend our sincere thanks for your participation during Spring Exercise on the AIDS pandemic in Africa.

After your presentation, many students remarked to us and others that your perspective was insightful and inspiring. This year proved to be a high-water mark for the Spring Exercise and you should know that your participation played a large part in making this possible. For that, we are extremely grateful.

Thank you, again, for making time in your schedule to participate in this important endeavor. We hope that your experience was as meaningful for you as it was for our students.

Sincerely,

Sheila P. Burke

John D. Donahue

79 John F. Kennedy Street Cambridge, Massachusetts 02138

I know there is a lot to digest, but that is the nature of struggle. Details. Persuasion. It is now the 2017 and I still am in contact with my friend who runs MANET for whom I raised money to buy him a wheelchair, and Kayambo who still is treating the sick. Africa is no longer a place far away from my heart or my head.

Meeting To Discuss Options to increase access to antiretroviral drugs
For Treatment of HIV/AIDS in Malawi
(23-24) October, 2000)
Le Meridien Capital, Lilongwe, Malawi

His Honour, Justin Malewezi — Vice President and Chair of the cabinet Committee on HIV/AIDS Prevention and Care

Ms. Anne C. Conroy — Special Assistant – Office of the Vice President

INTERNATIONAL DELEGATES

Mr. David Scondras — Chairman, Search For A Cure

Dr. Robert Redfield — Professor and Associate Director- The Institute of Human Virology University of Maryland

Dr. Peter Salk — Jonas Salk Foundation

Dr. Ann Duerr — HIV Section Division of Reproductive Health CDC

Dr. Lisa Hirschhorn — Director HIV Medical Care & Research Dimock Community Health Center

MINISTRY OF HEALTH AND POPULATION

Dr. Michael O'Carrol — Ministry of Health and Population

Dr. R. Pendame — Secretary for Health and Population Ministry of Health and Population

Dr. Owen Kaluwa — Acting Programme Manager Ministry of Health and Population

Dr. Habibi Somanje — Controller Prevention Services Ministry of Health and Population

140 / Another old friend dies

Jack Powers

My friend Jack Powers died in 2010. From his *Boston Globe* obituary:

> *An activist who gave away everything from the coats he wore to uncounted hours helping the poor, he was a poet and publisher, a teacher and organizer, a man whose great height still seemed too small to contain his frenetic energy.*

I cared about him. He cared about me. So I am inclined to share the small work that remains of the efforts I once made to capture feeling in verse in the hopes it reveals something about the times and me that prose does not capture.

The City of Boston was better off with the artistic drama and caring of a man like Jack Powers. In a small purple store with paintings and sculptures hanging randomly from walls, seated in wooden folding chairs were people with poems like Nick Hattam, my friend, to the people whom Jack Powers brought together to form the group, the place, the event called "Stone Soup." I read these poems to this group at Jack's request years ago, and Nick read his poems to them many years later in 2008. I include both here as a testament to Jack, a goodbye to him and to share with you some of the poetry that came from the other side of reality which drives our lives.

Elegy — 1964

I

Waiting for the flower that bloomed fair
Beneath a Rockport Moon,
For the gulls that dived against the blue lagoon
And the horn of the lobster boat moaning at a copper sun

II

We climbed the mailbox then
Kicked the sand to watch the sparks fly white
Against that black,
And she ragged claw scuttled to the rock
Where the seaweed grew,
To wrap some in her hair,
For me.

III

For me, fair seaweed headed one,
Its sexes bobbing as she pirouettes
Bends low (the winds they blow) to
The city of the dead.

IV

The fallen stone reminded me of passing kings,
Of youth grown cold,
Of love long left,
Of time that lingered
Of those who carved Croatan
And laughed at a sinister snow

V

"As you are now so once was I"
the granite told me in the cemetery
But even stone washes clear,
"As I am now so will you be"
The triumph of a dead man
Illegible but smooth as rain washed rock
And sweet as forgotten sex.

What belongs to Nick Hattam — 2008

Teddy bear sitting
There with broken eye and ripped
Lips please burn for me.

Song of the last wind — 1967

I

Aeolius, penitence spent,
Windswept the sides of my mind,
And I
The purple narcissus,
Wilted over the bowl/

II

The fat judge himself cannot condemn the man
when the sky is blue
Beware the shadows and the cold wind
The reflections of a guilty mind./

III

Waiting for the snow, for the blue shadows,
For the cold wind,
Waiting for the eyes pane to grow frigid
For the subway
For the chariot
'Waitin' for to take me home'

IV

I know that black night
When eyes like chestnuts floating in milk
No longer wait.
I know the blue sky, when the good smile
Fades into the sound of an off-key guitar/

V

The zombie wind passes like the man who will not stop to pick you up
The emptiness you feel is the wind of promises that cannot be kept

VI

Madonna in purple
Black laced face blank as my check
Empty as my vault
Bends before the casket of the last wind
Smiles frigid at the thought of the rhodora
Waiting for Persephone
And the first flower of the winter snow/

VII

The song of the last wind wails wild,
Lays waste the phoenix and kills the dove,
Forgets the fire that warms white wings,
For the sake of a misplaced love//.

Love of Small Oranges/to jim

Suzanne played on
Wishing well while, mobile thinking,
He followed his mind to the river,
Making love of small oranges in greenhouse light,
Clouded Nepalese hills behind,
Thinking of yellow bulbs and
Sweet of Indian night.
Guitar lifted smiling bright,
Forgotten yesterday, tomorrow indigent,
He knew enough in a corner of his mind
To wait for himself/
Some day, where the wind blows azure and the sea,
Shining copper in morning light
Sways smooth,
He will touch the water and remember
The waiting sand.

Teeth

I am Hamlet
Waiting for the smiling man,
The man with the hidden bulge,
Waiting for the well dressed tooth to bite
Helpless in my weakness,
Weak in my indecision,
Indecisive in my helplessness
Waiting for the sound of silent guns

2010

The morning's sun, tinting buildings gold,
Peeled the great feather from the sky,
To reveal an impenetrable blue/
He would not tarry in the cold to remember other mornings,
Having forgotten perhaps the girls with azure eyes
And the old man with a black hat/
Time, a madman's leper,
Shuffled along,
Sapping the snap of forgotten twigs who once knew blue skies and sailed in seas
of aquamarine,
Hickory smell with sharp air,
Crunching snow and black branches with orange linings,
All left behind in the old man's shuffle,
To find themselves, perhaps,
Another happy eye/

— 2010

Jack Powers and Stone Soup: An elegy

On October 24th, 2010 Marc Goldfinger wrote a letter, *"For Jack Powers: This Should Have Been An Elegy."* It was published in *"Spare Change"* which makes total sense — *Spare Change* is a newspaper which homeless people sell for a dollar, and into which people like Howard Zinn and many of the intellectual and artistic leaders of our cities wrote. Here is what Marc Goldfinger said in his article, starting with a Jack Spicer poem, and continuing with a story about his wife:

Go mad. Commit suicide. There will be nothing left.
After you die or go mad.
But the calmness of poetry.
        — "A Poem Without A Single Bird In It," by Jack Spicer

My wife, Mary Esther, is a devout Catholic who goes to Mass
regularly even though she hates the patriarchy of the church.
When she could walk without a cane, she would go to Mass at
Arch Street in Boston, the noon Mass, and she would often see
Jack Powers there, on his knees, his lips moving.

She really didn't know Jack Powers. She did know that he was a
spiritual man. But the demons. She couldn't see the demons. I
knew Jack Powers from TT the Bears, a bar in Cambridge MA
where he hosted Stone Soup Poetry regularly. I started
attending there in 1994 every Monday night. I didn't know he
went to church regularly.

I didn't know that Jack Powers, in the late '60's and early '70's
founded a free school on Beacon Hill, Boston and started free
suppers for the elderly in the same neighborhood. I didn't know
that he taught Columbia Point Project kids remedial reading and
started a food co-op there too.

In 1987 Jack Powers told The Boston Globe, and I quote, "I'm
very solid on volunteerism because the extraordinary weight of
problems that visits the modern industrial society can't be met
with dollars alone."

I didn't know that Jack Powers, on a cold winter night, if he saw a homeless person who wasn't dressed for the cold, would take off his coat and gloves and give them to the person on the street.

I didn't know that he often volunteered at the North End Rehabilitation and Nursing Center, Boston, in earlier years. I know that he died there, a resident, of complications of dementia. I know that he ran poetry groups at McLean's Hospital, Belmont, where he sometimes was a patient.

I do know that he started Stone Soup Poetry Readings over 40 years ago and made everyone that I knew feel welcome there. I know that he was held in such high regard in the poetry community that poets such as Allen Ginsberg, Lawrence Ferlinghetti, Gregory Corso, and Robert Bly, among others, came to read for him and the poets who read regularly at Stone Soup.

It didn't matter what level your poetry was at – Jack would sign you up to read – and help you if you asked. He was there for so many. He was as non-judgmental as a man, as a poet can be. There are many poets who are quick to judge others. This is no secret in the poetry world. I wish I could say that I was as non-judgmental as Jack. I don't know.

Poet Gail Mazur, from the academic scene, said of Jack, "He wanted to gather everyone into the performance of poetry. In that way, he was a little ahead of his time."

Jack Powers was so much more than a poet. He was a man who gave so much to the world, a good man who reached out to those who didn't have. Jack wasn't money rich, not by any means. But he was possessed by a wealth that more of us should strive for, more of us should emulate.

But Jack was possessed by demons too. In the end, the demons took away all the gifts he had. It wasn't that Jack Powers didn't ask for help. He asked for help in more ways than many of us will ever know.

I know Jack Powers drank quite a bit. It can be said that he drank alcoholically. When I met him in '94, he was already putting the drinks down his gullet like they were water.

Jack Powers is gone now but his legacy will live on. There is much that many of us knew about Jack, but when it came down to it, no one knew the nature of the ticking clock within him that took him down. Jack Powers died at the age of 73. It was a sudden, slow death. Like Neil Cassady, Jack couldn't get off of the railroad tracks.

141 /   Thought Crime

"Upon the conduct of each relies the fate of all."
— Alexander the Great

Part One: War Crime and Sex Crime

I have always been a criminal.

Once my crime was refusing to kill brown-skinned people I never met in Vietnam. I was a sophomore at Harvard and 18 years old at the time.

I wrote a long letter to the draft board (which had informed me in 1967 or so, that I had to go and kill people). I explained in my letter that I had no intentions of doing any such thing. I remember saying that as far as I knew, no one had landed foreign troops in San Diego. Vietnam's military, without an air force or missiles, could hardly be called a threat to anyone 13,000 miles away.

I could not justify killing anyone just because someone told me to. I needed a good reason and had not heard one yet. I knew the explanation for going to war called the "domino theory," but had a very hard time believing that this hypothetical cascade of societies turning, one after another, into an evil socialist empire committed to the elimination of the United States held much danger to my family. It was hard to imagine a lot of power being built upon a foundation of rice paddies and Buddhism.

This position angered people at my draft board in Lowell, who warned me in writing that I would bring shame upon my family. In fact, it did make my family upset with me and they did become a target for nasty comments about their son being a Commie or a coward. But I have never regretted writing and sending my letter.

There is often no consistency between private and public acts. America, like many cultures, is a land of rationalized hypocrisy. It's okay to murder entire nations but heaven help you if you go crazy and shoot classmates.

The commandment now reads, "Thou shalt not kill unless the government puts you in a uniform and tells you who to shoot at."

I remember watching a plane lift off to Canada with precious cargo, more people escaping from the U.S.A., from murder and death. Hundreds of thousands of people fled from America, which in those days we spelled Amerika. About 100,000 settled in Canada, with the blessing of Canadian Prime Minister Pierre Trudeau. The FBI asked me if I knew certain people's names and whereabouts. I lied.

Among the escapees to Canada were Jim Green, who became a Vancouver city councilor; Dan Murphy, a political cartoonist; Andy Barrie, who was host of CBC Radio's "Metro Morning"; Jack Todd, award-winning sports columnist for the Montreal Gazette; Eric Nagler, the children's entertainer on "The Elephant Show" and "Eric's World"; and Mike Fisher, a founding member of *Heart*, a popular rock/pop band.

To some extent the Vietnam influx into Canada helped reverse the "brain drain," for the draft dodgers were among the brightest of Americans.

Jimmy Carter pardoned dodgers (but not deserters) in 1977. Some returned.

It is vogue these days among many to have been against the Vietnam War as Bill Clinton was. What most people don't remember or don't know is that until the end of the civil upheaval here in the U.S., those who stood up for ending the killing fields were despised, beaten, arrested, spied upon, and spat upon.

In 1970, I was giving a speech when a woman threw a chair at me, screaming that I was a bank burner.

About the same time, my friend John Pennington was told to stand still in a long line in Boston at the 'induction' center where people who were being drafted were supposed to get a medical exam. He had his girlfriend snuck in to take pictures of all of us who refused to line up, as we were American citizens, not members of the military.

Sergeant Brown screamed at us, and we yawned and sat on the floor. He made the mistake of touching John's girlfriend, at which point John swung at him and all hell broke out. We bolted the induction center shut; machinery was destroyed; the local Boston papers were informed that the induction center had been seized and that we were going to hold a sit-in until we were let free.

Or maybe something else happened less dramatic, like a vote on being against the Vietnam War. History has become blurred and the 60's were never well-recorded. One thing is clear however — Sergeant Brown's necktie, a fake one with plastic tabs to hold it on, ended up nailed to the door of a purple coffeehouse that was the home of the antiwar Boston Draft Resistance Group (BDRG) aptly named "Sergeant Brown's Memorial Necktie." John confirmed last year that he did have his girlfriend in the induction center taking pictures; he did punch Sgt. Brown and get his tie. The rest is fog.

Those who fought to stop the Vietnam War have some popularity or respect only in retrospect. In the 1960's we were criminals. The Quaker Meeting House at Harvard at Longfellow Park, where Joan Baez came as a girl (and where on occasion 'sanctuary' was given to those who refused to kill people) was a place I hung out a lot, and wrote poems of dubious worth during the long, long times we spent supporting those with the courage to just say no.

Sometimes my crimes were related to the struggles to end apartheid, or other international affairs.

As I related earlier, a group of us tried to stop the big company Deak-Perera from selling the Krugerrand, the South African coin that helped finance apartheid in South Africa.

I then met with the great black singer Harry Belafonte who came to try to help us make sure the state prosecuted us. Unfortunately the state dropped all charges no matter how hard we tried to get a trial.

Sometimes my crime was getting patented medicines to dying people while countries and courts fought over companies' intellectual property rights. I traveled the globe with others to get prohibited medicines across borders to places like San José Las Flores, a village in the mountains of El Salvador. Or I gave medicines to people who were sick on the streets of Malawi.

One of the many people I tried to get medicine for was the owner of a small hotel by Lake Malawi. I stayed at this man's hotel — it was beautiful. It's too bad I can't tell you the amazing way I managed to get him some antivirals — maybe after all the people involved are dead I could, but I probably wouldn't be around either. Anyway, it was not done fast enough to save him. He died. I am still sad about it, for I remember the long night with his brother by the lake promising him that I could help, talking about ways to save the owner who wanted to keep his sickness a secret.

Sometimes my crime was guilt by association. I was riding around the Central American country of Nicaragua in a jeep with Daniel Ortega keeping company with the Reagan-hating, allegedly illegal Sandinistas who ruled for awhile. I heard the sound of guns in the distance paid for by illegal Contra payments from Ollie North. I remember being buzzed by the American planes called bluebirds that Reagan said did not exist. I guess it was just a lot of earthquakes that shook the buildings I was in. I have tape recordings of meetings and you can hear the planes shaking the capital for yourself. Telling the world he was lying about the planes did not sit well with Reagan, the great communicator of lying gibberish who equated people that supported the real freedom fighters of Central America as traitors.

But the most sensational crimes nature ever commanded I perform are connected with bigoted police and psychotic laws interfering with my having sex. Most sex laws in the U.S. (and in most other countries with such bizarre rules) originate in religion and have no place in any law book in a country that says it does not infuse religion into its secular affairs. In reality, many American laws reek of punitive religiosity.

Sex not approved by the New Puritans is illegal in America. And to no one's surprise, by similar groups in countries where Muslim or Christian Fundamentalism rules.

Unless of course it is a prostitute giving a blowjob to a cop in a police wagon to avoid arrest. I watched this happening over the years with regularity in the Fenway part of Boston. It seemed a typical kind of police barter along with shaking down restaurants for food and shaking down gay bars for cash. A report from San Antonio mentioned in the 2007 report of Amnesty International called "Stonewalled" indicated this rape of prostitutes continues today.

I don't mean to imply all other countries are better. Around the world the age of consent varies from 13 in Spain to many complicated equations in other countries depending on the proximity of age of the partners. Different ages for gay and straight sex, different punishments for violating these totally arbitrary rules, contradictory sections of law. Now what exactly are these newlyweds doing on their honeymoon? Different rules for different sex acts.

There is no agreement on what is okay to do with whom when, where or how. But the transparent insanity of all of this has not made any difference to legislators, prosecutors, judges or other people who are supposed to be leaders. Nature marches on in spite of Islam, Pat Robertson and the pious, petty, powerful pinheads who dominate U.S. culture for the moment.

There are some six billion people in the world. Over half of them are under 15 years old. That means at least 3 billion people were born during the past 15 years. It took at least one heterosexual act to create each one of them. That means a minimum of 200 million unprotected sex acts a year. Or 547,794 acts of carnal intercourse per day. 22,824 per hour. And that is if every single sex act in the past 15 years led to a baby. Let's face it, the real number is ten times this, and this is the crime rate the guardians of our genitals are trying to fight probably because they are among the 10% that aren't getting any.

I remember meeting with Cardinal Law before he got his hands full dealing with blowback from his own anti-erotic crusades at his mansion in the Allston-Brighton part of Boston. I pointed out to him that his abstinence program was not doing so well in the parts of Boston dominated by the Catholic Church — wards 6 and 7.

In those wards where the clergy ruled supreme, our public health department's records showed that 10% of unmarried girls between the ages of 15 and 19 had a baby. And I do not believe that they were all virgin births. The Catholic potentate had nothing to say but repeat that abstinence was the cure for sin and the diseases of sinners.

America is about all sorts of contradictions. In matters of sex, the disconnect between what is culturally acceptable and what actually happens is a big one.

In a 2007 MSNBC poll of 77,000 heterosexual monogamous couples, 22% said they had had public sex during the previous year. Oops. Naughty naughty. But they are straight. Few of them were bothered.

We are meat fed to the voracious Christian right in exchange for their support of the Republican Party. Some of that meat is the infiltration into our society of religious laws, the key to understanding which is the equation of the new Christians that "sex = sin." America is turning increasingly into a country obsessed with stopping sex.

Part Two: The Columbus Day Massacre

It was October 8, 2006, Sunday night, the Columbus Day weekend. Monday would be a holiday.

Columbus is honored every year. He should not be. He was a Christian fanatic who condoned cutting off the arms of those natives who would not bring adequate gold to the Spaniards. Columbus brought natives as slaves to Europe and in return trips slaughtered people who would not submit to the foreign Spanish invaders. Why the Italians in the US cannot dump this genocidal me-too upstart in favor of a real explorer like Marco Polo is beyond me.

Another group of invaders, the Puritans, took control of northern parts of North America. Their influence still affects New England along with the Catholicism of the Jansenites that permeated Ireland and immigrated to New England. These religious fanatics had a very restrictive view of when and how and where sexual needs could be met. If you were a man it was to be in bed, at home, with your female wife. A woman was supposed to do what the man said.

This was not just true of the Puritans. England imposed the sexually repressive "Article 377" on virtually every colony in the world it possessed, replacing the virtually omnipresent support of same-sex relationships with its skewed view of the natural world. In the U.S., 135 tribes (according to *Living the Spirit*, 1988) had different sex and gender roles, inclusive of what we would call gay roles. This was true around the world in virtually every culture until the true believers came.

All conquered societies, which meant pretty much everyone in the world except for Thailand, were pushed to punish gays and repress sex.

Not that the conquerors didn't participate directly in creating a hell for gay men and women. They joined their surrogates with a vengeance:

- Thomas Jefferson suggested replacing death for gays with castration.

- The Spanish who invaded Louisiana killed men dressed as women.

- During the 17th and 18th centuries in the colonies, under the influence of religions that still provide the basis of our legal system, gays were considered 'unnatural' and whipped, castrated and drowned.

- Spanish colonial authorities in Cuba castrated those they considered gay and forced them to eat their own testicles covered with dirt.

Don't think this is a thing of the past. Two teenage boys were executed in Mashhad in northeastern Iran in 2007, after first being put in jail for 14 months, then lashed 228 times, then hanged. Altogether some 4,000 lesbian and gay men have been executed since the Ayatollahs took over in 1979.

In Iraq the new government, in Section 111 of the Iraq criminal code, exempts from punishment anyone who murders a gay man. So much for creating a "new society" in Iraq.

And do not assume the United States is an exception.

In a 2007 report Amnesty International said there is a serious problem of police brutality in the USA including abuses that amount to torture, selective enforcement of laws, inappropriate searches and a lack of any accountability.

I know a lot about this. Both professionally, when I helped put together and testified before the St. Clair Commission about the rampant homophobia in the Boston Police Department, and throughout my life as I have been the victim many, many times of police deciding to do a little bashing. Such as....

Thought Crimes: Threatened with death by a police officer for having imaginary sex with an imaginary person of an imaginary age

So, getting back to Columbus Day:

I refuse to march in the Columbus Day parade, like most elected officials do, because I will not honor a Christian fanatic that killed innocent people. So for me, the Columbus Day holiday weekend has always been a time of loneliness, and this particular Sunday I stayed home alone a bit bored.

Monday was a holiday, of course. I decided to spend some time talking on the net, which I have done for years.

I signed in around 10 o'clock and checked my emails on AOL. There were none that I recall. Then I went to the AOL gay men's chat room, called BostonM4M. Going to the chatroom requires my agreeing to the terms of service (called TOS in the lingo), the agreement with AOL that everyone must sign before being able to enter a chatroom of this kind. This is similar to being age-checked when entering a bar.

My screen-name was Topdadd. Good screen-names in gay dating areas do several things: they tell a reader what kind of person you are dealing with, what they probably would be sexually interested in, and often how old the person is. My name told whoever saw it that I was an older man that liked to nurture and play the 'top' role in sex. The 'top' role means insertive sex but also means nurturing, taking care of, doing the 'work' whether that means having lube or having a clean bathroom and towels. It also often means the person is aggressive but would tend to support the partner who would be a 'bottom.' 'Top' and 'bottom' are roughly the equivalent to male and female in the gender role differentiation common in most European and American cultures.

Since screen-names are the first thing a person usually sees of another person in the chatroom, it is useful to choose names that select out people who would not be interested in you. Given the hundreds or thousands of viewers, this is important or you could spend weeks talking to people inappropriate to your niche. In gay culture there are so many niches that it would take forever to connect with a partner without some selection mechanisms. I suppose calling the handle you are known by as a 'screen' name makes sense given its role in screening.

Before going any further, it's important to explain that gay male culture is fundamentally different from heterosexual culture in many ways that make the common rules for heterosexuals fundamentally inapplicable to gay men.

For example, gay men cannot have children so the pressure to use sex to procreate, and the fear of it, or desire for it, are not part of the mating dance. Gay sex is for fun, not to preserve the race. Also, gay men socialize as men, understanding each other's needs very quickly. Their counterparts are socialized differently with different objectives in dating.

A good example is that you can tell gay bars in a city from straight bars with a simple test. If the police are never called to a bar, it's a gay bar. Everyone in a gay bar is a potential mate, which makes the dynamic completely different. A gay man beating up a gay man in a gay bar would be about as common as a straight man beating up a woman in a straight bar. It does not happen with enough frequency to be of any note. This does not mean that gay men have wonderful private lives free from abuse. It means that in dating settings, expectations and behaviors are fundamentally different between gay and straight settings.

Another fundamental difference is that gay men have all experienced violence at the hands of heterosexuals and police, or heard of it. So gay men are nervous about connecting.

I am often asked that given the dangers why do you try to connect? This is a little like asking why, in a previous world where food was often contaminated, why did people decide to eat?

Gay men, like myself, have lived in a world of danger from childhood. We have decided to either stay closeted (the majority) and lead lives in secrecy which can be protected at a high price, or alternatively to come out and risk physical and verbal abuse. I chose the latter, perhaps because I'm a terribly bad actor.

IM Topdadd

Well, nature continues to rule, and I continued to talk in the internet gay bar, when I got an instant message (IM) that said nothing but "18 m." Now, no one can IM you unless they are also in or watching the chatroom, i.e. in the dating bar with the TOS age-check. So you would assume that when you receive an IM, that the sender is looking for a connection, probably sexual, so I decided to check this out.

It was obvious that the person who IM'ed me was over 18. First, in general gay guys often tell you they are younger than they really are; he said he was 18 so he was likely 5-10 years older. This lying probably is the result of the youth culture pushed by constant Pepsi ads that after all are appealing to the biggest spenders in the USA, the young. Also his screen-name was cubscout4master86 which meant he was saying he was 20 years old (born in 1986) looking for an older dominant (Master) to be a bottom to.

In any event, I was trying to figure out why this guy was IM'ing me — there were contradictions. The 'cub' didn't fit well, as it implied he wanted a 'bear' which is a large, hairy guy. I'm tall and thin without a lot of body hair. But I did have facial hair. I would never have IM'ed him given his screen-name and not being a bear, but he started it, so I played along.

When I replied to his IM, he began to tell me how turned on he was for me, that he had read my profile (a part of AOL that describes the person in more detail; you can find it through his screen-name). My profile indicated an interest in guys around 30, and also spelled out what I was interested in as a top, and that I was an older gay man.)

Anyway this guy told me he was very interested in having sex with me, that he had had sex early that night which had been unsatisfying, that he wanted to connect with me right away, that he had had four lovers not counting 'hookups' (a 'hookup' is a quick rendezvous not intended to lead to a relationship but rather to satisfy an urge). Again, this meant he was over almost certainly over 18 as lovers usually last a year and there is usually some time between them. If he had had four already that is 4 years plus some months in between each. If he started at 14 years old he would still be over 19 years old. Unless his 'lovers' lasted two weeks apiece separated by a grieving period of 24 hours.

I almost never connect over internet. It's a place for fantasies, and in general you have to assume that whatever anyone tells you is not entirely true.

When I do connect, I prefer people coming to my house. During the past ten years, prior to this night of 2006, I had gone out to a hookup perhaps four times. When you go to a hookup you assume that who you meet will differ in many respects from what you are told. There are two reasons for this: it is very difficult to communicate the 'chemistry' of a person — much less his looks, personality and interests — via pictures and words. The second is that people tell you a blend of what they think you want to hear and what they wish they were like (not the same things) which is rarely what they really are. So you go to a liaison with an open mind and a grain of salt.

On the other hand, I had never been approached with this level of enthusiasm as far as I can remember.

I asked him where he was.

He said, as part of the long conversation, that he lived near Lawrence General Hospital. This made me feel a little better because I'm terrible at directions and I knew that Lawrence was on the same road, route 93, that I took to visit my 86-year-old mother.

I insisted that he send me a pic of himself.

He sent one of a naked guy on his back wearing a hat, who looked about 30 years old given the wrinkles etc.

I told him to come by my house if he wanted.

He said he did not have a car. This worried me, because although lots of gays are unemployed and live at home, I didn't usually like driving. Makes me nervous. But for some reason I felt like getting out of the house that night.

After we spoke for awhile, he said something unexpected. He sent me an IM that said "I lied to you before." I replied, "about what?" "I'm really only 15."

Yeah. Sure. I counted the number of times halfway through a conversation a connection of mine would mention that he was really a woman, that he wore bras and panties. I remember one person from Northeastern whom I never met as a guy. He/she came over as a woman, never allowed me to touch her genitals, and I never knew her (after the required beginning of our first conversation during which time he was of course a he) as a guy.

This does not mean I like girls, panties, or bras or that I ever thought I was actually speaking with a woman. It meant that I would put up with these people's desire to fantasize for whatever reason it happens. They put up with mine.

I figured that this guy was about 28. Ten years off your age is about right for the usual lying, and this guy lied.

I decided that his "I'm 15" was a fetish given my screen-name (playing son to daddy in other words, a common fetish). He might be assuming I liked young guys. (I don't. Nothing wrong with them, just not personally interested in the exhausting way young people explore the world.)

He called me "daddy" once which convinced me I was right about my guess.

I was not sure I wanted to go to Lawrence, and I wasn't 100% sure why he was pretending to be 15. So I told him to call me up right away. It is very, very hard for a 30-year-old to sound like a 15-year-old. Previous efforts to get him to call me had failed, and this time I insisted.

And he called.

And his voice was certainly not that of a 15-year-old.

I said to him, "Stop playing; stop the game for a second. I need to ask you something. Are you a cop? Is this some kind of thing with police trying to catch gay guys? People have told me that in Boston gay men were being attacked, arrested by cops like never before."

He said, sarcastically, "Yeah, look out your window, your house has cop cars all around it."

I actually got up and walked while talking on my cell phone and checked out the window because the stories had scared me. There was nothing.

Then I said, "Look, I'm serious. Are you a cop?"

He got serious for a moment. "No, I'm not a cop."

I suffered from the common belief that cops have to identify themselves if you asked them to, so this confirmed my belief that he was a fetishist who liked pretending that he was young.

As an aside that becomes important later, note that no one who believes a person to be, say, 15, would ever ask them if they were a cop. During the lengthy conversation that ensued, which was interrupted a few times because he needed to 'call me right back' (no explanations) he told me a good deal about his past. I decided after listening to him that he was somewhere between 23 and 28.

I felt he had to have had a lot of experience with gay subcultures to know how to frame a screen-name so specific, knowing what cubs and bears were, knowing that a master would fit that scene and be occasionally a bear, and this in turn meant he had been involved for a long time in gay chatrooms.

He wanted me to come to a gay cruising area near the Lawrence General Hospital. It made sense he would know where the cruising areas were given his depth of experience.

I was nervous about this because gay men are sometimes assaulted by thugs and homophobes, lured to places and then beaten. I decided that if we met, we would go get a coffee and if anything happened it would be in a motel. Hookups were successful maybe 50% of the time. Usually one or the other person turns out not to be interested. During the conversation he asked me to bring him some alcohol.

I apologized, saying that I didn't have any (and if I did I wouldn't bring it, the last thing I wanted was someone high when I was trying to talk to him and maybe have sex. I hated mixing sex and alcohol). I also reminded him it was past eleven p.m., and in Massachusetts, all liquor stores were shut after eleven so there was no way to get any. He seemed to take this news without protest.

I grabbed a bottle of pomegranate juice for the ride, and, as I usually did, I put some condoms in my sock so I wouldn't have to look around for them, and a few packs of lube on me, just in case. My decision to go to Lawrence even though I virtually never go out to anyone had more to do with wanting to break the monotony of a long empty weekend than anything else.

I got worried about getting to this park he talked about as I am notoriously bad at driving directions. I get lost a lot. He said he would call me periodically on the phone to make sure I was not lost.

It seemed a little odd he would not give me his phone number, but not uncommon in chatroom etiquette. He called and gave me explicit directions over the phone on how to get to the park. He stayed on the phone most of the time. He was amazingly knowledgeable about street directions, proper exits off the highway, how to get back onto it when I got off at the wrong place, what turns to take to get to the park. I recall thinking that he must drive a lot or be a taxi driver to know all these details.

As I drove up a street by the Lawrence General Hospital, he told me to take a right into a big parking lot behind which there was a lot of darkness. It seemed to be a park. There was no lighting so it was very, very dark.

I was told where to park, but somehow the person talking to me seemed more harsh, more pushy. I started to like him a lot less.

I opened my door and looked to where the darkness was, by the side and behind what appeared to be a small ornate relic of a building. But I couldn't see anyone. Why was he hiding from me?

He asked me if I was alone, but I was not sure why he asked.

I heard a loud voice tell me to come over here, this way.

I panicked because it was a very different voice than I had heard earlier. I felt I had to do what it said. It sounded as if I would be punished if I did not obey. At this moment, I decided that this was all a trick for a group to bash me. I got cold and felt I couldn't do anything about it at this point. I walked toward the darkness, where the voice said to come. It was difficult as I was terrified and my feet hurt from gout.

Lawrence Cops

Suddenly I was blinded by two incredibly bright lights which bombarded my eyes, and assaulted by people yelling, more than one, all at the same time. I could not understand what they were saying and realized I was being attacked by a group of haters. They asked me if I had a gun. What a weird question. Then they tried to pull my arms out of my sockets, behind my back and I pushed back saying, "What are you doing?" They made me get on the ground.

I pleaded with them not to hurt me. I had had a heart attack before and it was very hard to lie on my stomach on the hard asphalt. One of them came over and bashed my head even though I said not to, that I had had a concussion, that I could die, stop it. My heart doc said stress could kill me too.

One of them, sounding incredibly angry, came over and put a gun to my head, which was twisted against the hard asphalt surface and hurt, and screamed in my ear, "You fucking pervert, I should kill you right now! I'm gonna kill you right now! I'm gonna shoot you right in the head!"

I said, "Go ahead, do it. Just do it." I wanted this over with. I didn't know who these people were exactly, but I was convinced that I was going to be killed right then, shot in the head.

Someone yelled, "We'll teach you to come to Lawrence." I managed to struggle up, eyes not seeing clearly because my glasses were gone and blood was in the way. I saw my cellphone on the ground and bent down to get it. Someone said, "Yeah, now you're stealing my stuff." and took it from me. I mumbled something like, "I'm sorry; I thought it's my phone."

They pushed me into a car, and drove me to what turned out to be a police station across from the hospital.

When I came in, the fat cop at the desk with a ruddy complexion shook his head, not at me and said to one of the others something like "You gotta stop doing this." I was photographed.

They had me take off my shoes and they put me into a cell — bars, small, smelly — and they ran in and out of the cell yelling at me at the top of their lungs, "Where is the alcohol?" I kept telling them there isn't any alcohol, I don't have any, and that I wanted to make a phone call and get some medical help. I was bleeding and couldn't see out of one eye. The man at the desk said that if I called and if the bailman decided not to come I would have wasted the call or something like that. It meant that if I called I could end up staying with these creatures for two days. He asked me if my damage was life threatening.

How the hell would I know? I did not want to stay where people who beat me up hung out. I kept asking, "What did I do?" No one answered.

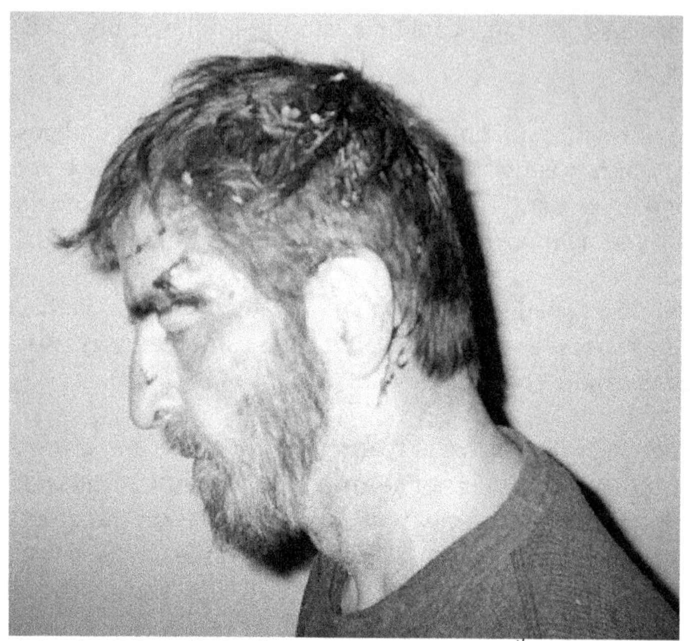

Pictures taken by Robert Krebs the morning of October 9th, 2006, Columbus Day.

Eventually I paid the bailman $40, got a cab to my car, and drove home, swaying on every side of the road, until I got to Cambridge. How I got there without an accident is a miracle. When I got home, my partner Robert was all business. He is amazing. He took me straight to Cambridge City Hospital. A Sergeant Lashley from the Cambridge Police Department showed up at 6:55 a.m. at our request. When he saw me he said, "No matter what, no one should be treated like this."

The hospital had a person who took official pictures of me. Robert had already taken a bunch. The hospital kept the results of their exam in a special place to preserve a "chain of evidence." Among the tests, they did blood screens showing that though I drank some pomegranate juice which they thought was alcoholic, there was no alcohol or drugs in my system.

We called my lawyer, David Duncan, and told him what happened. And we met him the next day to decide what to do. It had not been a very good day.

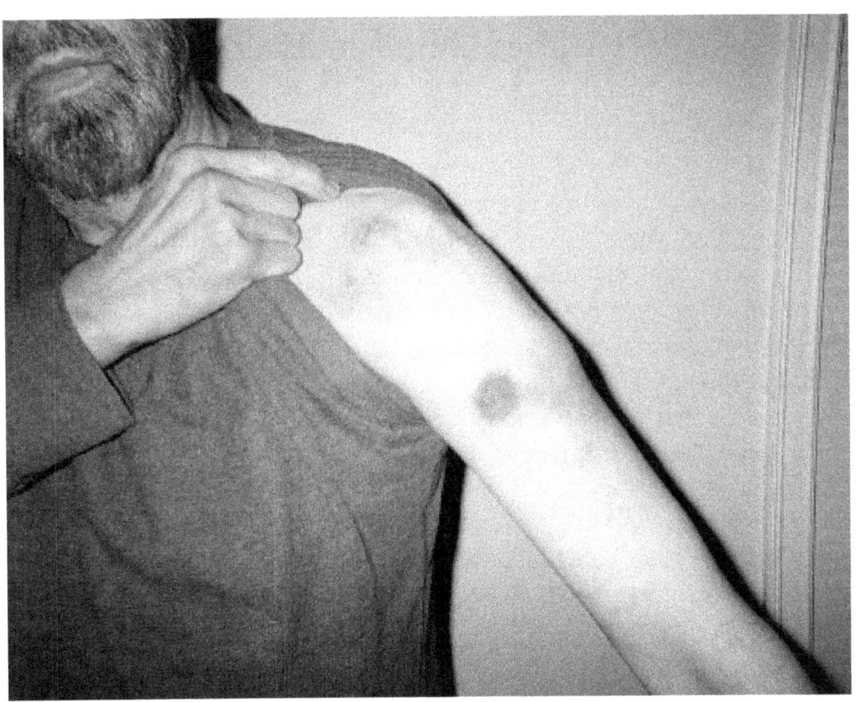

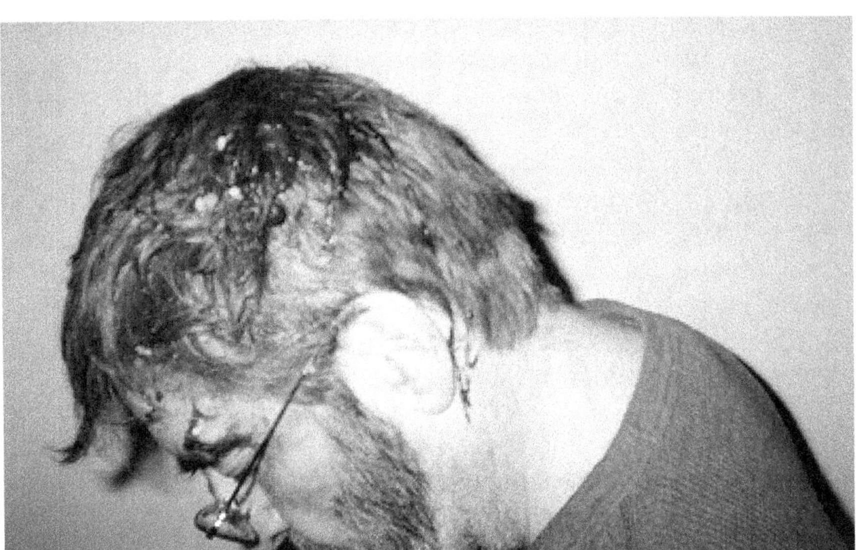

Pictures taken by Robert Krebs the morning of October 9th, 2006, Columbus Day.

Part Three: Child Molester

The people who are supposed to be objective who are in charge of public safety claim I am a child molester. This makes better news than dropping a case that has no substance. And news, not truth, is the master of our society. It does not matter to them that I am beaten and threatened with death by a Lawrence police officer for having imaginary sex with an imaginary person of an imaginary age. Or that they are breaking the wiretap statutes of both the state and federal government to even look at the police report much less create one from illegally obtained information. Or that nobody who isn't a moron would think the imaginary person involved in this scam was a 'minor.'

It was October 10th, a Tuesday, the day after that Columbus holiday. At the district court in Lawrence were my lawyer David Duncan, adorned with his great hat that kept sun from his eyes, Robert looking stoical, and me, a bit dazed.

The courthouse is new and architecturally quite good. And huge. Tall ceilings, meant to impress, with gigantic lobbies where a lot of Hispanics and African Americans assemble along with a handful of poor whites to get ripped off along with taxpayers who pay for the not-as-advertised 'judicial' system.

Judges, prosecutors, hangers-on, and court staff, whose jobs range from calling out "Hear ye, hear ye, the honorable xyz is gracing us with her presence," to other equally irrelevant nepotistic jobs filled from the local politician's "do a favor for a friend" list of the unemployed. This fills up the building with alleged caretakers of truth – a commodity in short supply, mainly because it is rarely sought.

And they all, with the possible exception of some relatively new probation officers, feel privileged, superior, self-important and actually put their noses up into the air, from time to time.

As Robert and I sat on the wooden benches where the untouchables waited, fenced off from the lawyers, judges and "hear ye" callers by thick wooden posts and beams, we noticed that virtually nobody had a lawyer. Those who did not were told to pay a $65 witness fee (which everyone pays irrespective of whether or not there are any witnesses) and to do community service to pay off the cost of the 'free' lawyers. There were five such overworked 'free' lawyer people in the courtroom, with perhaps 30-50 people assigned to each on this one day. I hope that was it for that month. And it becomes rather clear that whatever 'justice' is, it probably needs more than 1/30th of a lawyer's time to achieve. However, as we shall see, justice is not the objective of the judicial system at all. It is a self-delusion, or rationalization for an entirely different set of incentives, agendas and motivations.

I noted a TV camera in the courtroom. This means that someone knew I was there and I would make the news big time that night.

So much for innocent till proven guilty. You see, the damage done by the media already exceeds much of what a court metes out. This does not count the distortion of incentives the media creates among those prosecutors wanting to advance themselves by getting mentioned in a newspaper and those district attorneys who, in Massachusetts, have to be elected and are very sensitive about what the press says about them. Prosecutors are supposed to be about finding truth, not press coverage.

So the prosecutor, a woman who seemed pretty in tune with the compulsively irrational state Attorney General who got her seat by prosecuting alleged sex offenders who didn't do much offending, was not interested in my mug shots of blood and gore. She did nothing to investigate and prosecute those who assaulted me, and threatened my life. But she would spend a year or so making sure that the world would believe I was a child molester.

Turns out in real life, I have actually never had sex or tried to have sex with anyone under 18 years old even when I was under 18 years old. Not my thing. But facts have never stopped demagogues from pushing fear, and demagogues need not be loud, male or mean to destroy societies and individuals.

So this woman, this assistant D.A., Jana DiNatale, with a hook nose, a desultory manner and an overly serious stare, walked up to the judge when my case came up and basically said that the state had little to comment. But then she saw the TV camera. Robert and I saw her stop in her tracks, and return to the judge saying that she wanted ten minutes to prepare some remarks, she had changed her mind about having nothing to say.

You bet.

When she returned, a few minutes later, she violated every rule of common decency and the Massachusetts bar, by publically calling me a child molester in front of TV cameras and the press. Now I am not a child molester, I have not been convicted of being a child molester and moreover I was not charged with molesting anyone. In fact I couldn't be since there was no one to molest in the first place.

Specifically I had been charged with the somewhat odd 'crime' of "enticing a person believed to be a minor." Meaning, believed by me. And I certainly had no doubts this guy was over 20.

It is illegal for a member of the court to prejudge a defendant, especially if it might lead either a jury to become prejudiced or, in my case, if it could be expected to cause the public to be angry at me and threaten my safety.

Specifically, rules of ethics upheld by the Massachusetts Supreme Judicial Court says a prosecutor cannot give any opinion as to the guilt or innocence of a defendant or suspect in a criminal case. Also, Rule 3.6 says that a lawyer shall not make an extrajudicial statement that a reasonable person would expect to be disseminated by means of public communication (like a TV set for example) if the lawyer knows that it will have a substantial likelihood of materially prejudicing an adjudicative proceeding in the matter, or increasing public condemnation of the accused.

Well, this made-for-TV performance, in addition to breaking all of the above sections of law specifically passed to ensure the professional behavior of these public servants, illegally quoted what she knew were private conversations between me and the man I never met, breaking the state and federal wiretap statutes. (See Chapter 272, Section 99, General Laws of Massachusetts which specifically prohibits police from looking at private communications on the internet without first getting a court order unless they had begun a police investigation *BEFORE* checking out private emails, IMs, phone calls and so forth. No police investigation had been ongoing, it turns out.)

Oh, and she also broke the laws of common decency.

Bottom line: a prosecutor is supposed to be careful to make sure that the evidence against the defendant is adequate to convict (more about this later) and not supposed to publicly charge the defendant with being guilty of a crime he is not even being charged with and of which he has never been convicted.

The judge was quiet the whole time, and notwithstanding pictures given to him of the damage done to me, did not ask the prosecutor (who is legally responsible for the police), if she made any inquiries as to the circumstances of the bodily damage the pictures revealed.

Bad times for people caught in a witch hunt.

That evening the TV news all carried pictures of me with quotes from the woman saying I was a child molester. The headlines in the Cambridge paper where I live said essentially the same thing and for a week the news was about my being a sexual predator of children. I could not go home through my driveway because too many TV trucks blocked the way. When the press saw my car, reporters rushed to me with mikes in hand asking, "How does it feel to be a child molester?" They are not stupid; they knew perfectly well I could not comment until after a trial on much of anything. My lawyer and every good lawyer will explain that talking to the press is a bad idea before a trial because whatever you say can be entered into the court case. You end up with trial by newspaper reporters. But by asking me to comment reporters can then say "Mr. Scondras refused to answer questions," not explaining why, of course.

Motivated by who-knows-what, the prosecutor decided she needed to have my laptop. Whatever was said between me and whoever the twisted man was that started this mess was on that man's computer, so the prosecutor already had everything she could possibly need concerning what was said on the computer. Not that she used all of it, because if she did there would have been no case at all, heaven forbid. You see, the computer exchange makes it clear that the man I was speaking with was not a minor, which makes him legal to have sex with, much less just talk about having sex with.

Now it turns out that my house does not contain my laptop, as Robert brought it when we saw my lawyer the day after I was beaten, and gave it to him. But I rented parts of my house out to other people: my roommate Brian's computer, and Robert's computer, disappeared with the gendarmes.

It did absolutely no good to explain to the police that the machine that they were looking for wasn't at the house. Because the prosecutor wanted more than my computer. She wanted to check out to see if I had 'access' to children's pictures. If she knew me a bit more she would know that there isn't a single picture of a child anywhere near me, much less a child. I don't like pictures of them. They remind me of their noise, interminably boring conversations, demands for constant attention, perpetual ADHD, saliva, self-obsession, messiness, and they are by definition unsocialized. A child of mine would think his name was "Shut up and get out." But the hunt for tiny buttocks went on interminably, raping my house and tenant's property.

Reporter Erin Smith from the *Cambridge Chronicle* took an old conversation she had with me about a hundred things and twisted it. I told her a long time ago in the context of a very long talk about many different things that it was sad that young people say a 17-year-old that had consensual sex with a 15-year-old would end up in jail, that we needed a better way to manage emergent sexuality. So after this farce of an arrest her article was headlined, "Scondras says ok to have sex with teens."

So the agents of the state, by violating my constitutional rights in reading my mail and listening to my phone calls, tampering with the evidence so it sounded bad, ignoring and state and federal laws that protect privacy and communication, violating the rules that prescribe what is and is not permissible in a court, and by ignoring a lot of common sense, turned my life into a mess. Just the way Boston's right wing radio announcer and *Boston Herald* writer Howie Carr has wanted it from the first day he came to Boston City Hall, the day I got elected, and made it clear to me and my mother that he, in his publicly spoken words, thinks: "Gays are sick."

Part Four: Computer War

The war over who gets my computer. Who really was behind this effort to get me in jail. The price of the closet.

The prosecutor wanted my computer. In an America that foolishly thinks prosecutors and police are somehow immune to politics, personal issues, and are neutral parties in disputes, the police get to keep the evidence. To trust the police is to trust the neutrality of a trained guard dog. It is simply stupid. Do you really think that there are no manipulations of evidence through selection, tampering and disappearances? That evidence is fairly kept and presented?

In any event, why in the world did the prosecutor want my computer? Well to go on a fishing expedition and look for kiddyporn of course.

Not that anyone is exactly clear where the line between a sixteen-year-old and a fifteen-year-old begins or where the line between kiddyporn and pictures of your kids playing in the pool should be drawn. Nevertheless, the one consistent observation in the U.S. Senate's voluminous internet predator committee report on child molesters, is that they invariably collect a ton of pictures of children. I am not sure if the report says naked or not.

I have no pictures of children of any kind, anywhere, period. But let's spend months debating who gets my computer. This in spite of the fact the law in Massachusetts says that the prosecutor can't have stuff that is the hands of my lawyer. My money and time — as well as the taxpayers' money and time — were wasted to win their ridiculous jousting matches. The prosecutor never actually got my computer, but this effort to get my computer took over ten months to deal with and actually never did get resolved. It cost me $10,000 to litigate what a ten-year-old would understand: you can't have stuff given by someone to their lawyer.

I suppose one could say, "Well, if you don't have any kiddyporn then why fight over who has the computer?"

Because it is none of the prosecutor's or any government's or for that matter any non-government person's business what I have on my computer. Or in my diary. Or in my mind. Threatening a person with reprisals if they don't share what they think is the road to totalitarianism. The road does not start with Hitler, it starts with little concessions to fairness and principle like who gets to look at communications between me and my lawyer. It ends with judges and police out of control.

On my computer were letters to my mother, poems, things written about Africa where I spent a good deal of time. All of these things and many more were on my computer which are private communications. This concept of 'private' is dying in an age of cell phone interceptions, opening of email by hostile strangers, national identity cards tied to medical records and on and on. I believe that freedom is about privacy more than any other single thing.

So my lawyer fought and succeeded in keeping a computer that had nothing illegal on it from a prosecutor determined to break the law and engage in specifically prohibited fishing expeditions. In her mind and in many people's minds, the end justifies the means.

The end *NEVER* justifies the means.

So we went to the court in Lawrence, the expensive building that houses the judicial part of the empire, and succeeded in getting a judge to agree that the phrase in state law "no search warrant shall issue for any documentary evidence in possession of a lawyer" meant that "no search warrant shall issue for any documentary evidence on my computer in the possession of my lawyer." For $10,000 of mine, not counting what the taxpayers spent on this enlightening exchange.

While all of this high priced enlightenment was going on, I was slowly getting enlightened myself to what actually happened that Columbus Day weekend.

It turns out that an off duty Lawrence cop, one Sergeant Ryan E. Shafer, either ran into or was approached by a guy who was later described as his "closest friend," a Michael Fornesi, who said he was 20 years old. This Fornesi, a security officer was at work at the Lawrence General Hospital where, I guess, security guards spend their time in gay chat rooms while working. Apparently Fornesi is a policeman wannabe. Anyway, he claims he got a message from me (denying that he started the IM conversation).

This off-duty cop Shafer says he told Mr. Fornesi to tell me that he was 15 years old to which, he says I replied, "Call me right away." Actually I demanded he call me earlier lots of times because I didn't trust he was who he said he was. I wanted to hear him on a phone which is more revealing and harder to fake than the fantasyland communications of the internet. But the prosecutor used the remark out of context to mean, "See? He got interested right away in Fornesi the minute Fornesi told him he was 15." Actually that's when I had to decide why Fornesi was lying about his age, fetishist or gay-basher, and talking to him on the phone and asking him if he was a cop was part of that investigation.

The prosecutor described my language toward Fornesi as 'vulgar.' The prosecutor's recitation to the court also fails to mention the earlier conversations with Mr. Fornesi, in which equally 'vulgar' ideas and language was used by Mr. Fornesi toward me. In other words, we were talking dirty like you do with your wife before having sex. For the education of the prosecutor, this is called 'foreplay.' It's a concept with which the prosecutor was perhaps unfamiliar.

Incidentally, I got this information directly from the documents the prosecutor filed with the court so you can look at them yourself. The prosecutor to build up her case of me as a child molester, quoting me as saying on the phone to Mr. Fornesi, whom I know by now is in his 20's, "You know, a lot of people have prejudices against guys who like to have sex with children." Of course the prosecutor left out the entire context of the conversation, which was lengthy, during which Fornesi complained that he was not talked to by anyone on the internet, and my explaining to him that his choice of being 15 was not o.k. with most people, that they had legitimate concerns about guys who like to have sex with children because there is an issue about children being able to really give consent. I then explained that there were good reasons for having an age of consent, even though there might be legitimate debate on what that age was and who should determine it.

So it was clear that the police and prosecutor were happy to delete whatever they wanted from statements and trust in the lack of curiosity of decision-makers about what any average person would see were missing statements, what those statements were, who said them, and why they were deleted from the presentation to the court.

Incidentally, the prosecutor changed Mr. Fornesi's actual phrase which was "I lied before" to "I am only 15." I asked, when he said he lied, "About what?" Then he said he was 15. The same way my bra and panty guys tell me about this fantasy halfway through a deal for a hookup.

Why did the prosecutor, who had all the evidence, every word written on the computer available to her, choose to delete this critical phrase "I lied before?" Because it leads to the obvious questions, "What did Fornesi tell him before?" and it implies Fornesi told me a different age before, which would not help the prosecutor get me in jail. After all, my crime was *BELIEVING* Fornesi was 15, which only a moron could do after all he said to me prior to and after this "I am 15" lie.

It is a fair question why I didn't end the conversation with Fornesi since I understood on some level how crazy the police and prosecutors are. Unfortunately the answer is simple. I was stupid. I put myself in harm's way in part because I tend to live in the world the way I feel it should be, not the way it is. Or maybe some of the stupidity came from genetics. The old Greeks observed that a man has two heads, a big one and a little one, and once in awhile the little one runs the show.

I am guilty of stupidity and being human. But certainly not molesting anyone, or 'believing' this incredibly screwed up security guard was 15, or capable of enticing anyone. I'm too poor to offer anything as enticement that a guy can't get a lot easier without me.

Well Sgt. Shafer, though off duty, breaks the state and federal wiretap statutes by intercepting my private communications even though there is no court order to do so, nor is there an ongoing investigation or me or what I do going on. He sets up a group of thugs from the Lawrence Police Department to beat me up, (claiming of course that I was "resisting arrest"), steal my cellphone (claiming of course that I was trying to steal one of their cellphones, the first thing I think of doing after being beaten), and enticing a person whom I believed to be a minor (Fornesi, the over 20-year-old security guard).

There are many unanswered questions about Shafer and Fornesi. Why was Fornesi in a gay men's chat room? He claims he would not have done anything but go home except that Shafer pushed him to do what he did (lie about his age and so forth after talking with me for an hour about how much he wanted sex with me, and being clear that he was over age).

My own therapist and others have a simpler explanation of what went down. Fornesi, the wannabe, was caught by his insane cop friend Shafer playing in a gay men's chatroom. Shafer was making an unscheduled visit to his friend during his time off. To find some excuse for being in a queer room, Fornesi says he is trying to catch this guy who is hunting for children.

The rest is my broken head, twisted arm, endless courtroom craziness, and demoralized spirit.

Part Five: Guilty Until Proven Innocent

Like the prosecutor in my case, the Media makes sure that whether you are guilty or innocent of anything makes no substantial difference, to the extent public perception affects you.

I remember a mentor of mine, one Neil McGee, saying "What is perceived of as real is real, insofar as its effects on politics."

In my case, the city manager of Cambridge, an Irish pol from Lowell where my mother lives and where I grew up, couldn't wait to get a letter to me telling me that I was fired from my organizing job in Cambridge. However, the contract I had with the city required that the Area 4 neighborhood board approve such things, so I wrote a polite letter of resignation.

The *Cambridge Chronicle* incorrectly implied that I was trying to cover up being fired by resigning. Of course so-called reporter Erin Smith, who could never write a line that resembled accuracy, never bothered reading my contract with the city, or worse, did read it and didn't get it. Or didn't care.

It amazed me how little respect for our Constitution the media, pols and courts ever seemed to have. It was as if the Magna Carta never happened.

I lost about $30,000 the first few days, by losing jobs and paying for bail and other expenses, long before a hearing would happen.

This was mostly because the newspapers didn't bother to print anything except a sensationalized version of the police report written by the drunken lying homophobic thug who wore a badge. And everybody is afraid of the Media.

Keep in mind that the whole point of "innocent till proven guilty" is that you are supposed to treat people the same way you did the day before they were arrested, at least until after the trial. But these guys, both in the media and those who were reacting to the media, could not wait to act as judge and executioner, and it's wrong. It is so terribly wrong, yet nobody does a damn thing about it.

If you think about it, everybody is afraid of the media, and everyone uses the media as a weapon. The media rules. The media, like big companies, has no religion, nor integrity to sets of complex ideals or stuff like that. Its real commitment is to getting the biggest market share it can get, because the people who make money in the media business sell themselves to those who need to manipulate Americans into buying stuff nobody really needs.

Anyway, to add insult to injury, the mayor of Cambridge (a ceremonial post held at that time by Ken Reeves, a black gay man for whom I spent a lot of time helping in his first run as an openly gay person of color to the City Council of Cambridge), sent me a letter by way of a personal courier. I knew something was up when I saw the mayor's magnificent gas guzzler parked near my house and the short, smart but obeisant white guy leap out to give me the envelope from Mayor Reeves. It was written on official stationery, "The office of the Mayor of Cambridge," and read:

Dear David:

As the Mayor of Cambridge, and your friend, I am asking you to immediately resign your position as Community Organizer for Area Four. I am also urging you to immediately seek psychiatric help, as well as alcohol and drug abuse treatment. I will not be able to speak with you or have any contact with you until after your court case is finalized.

You have to meet and know Ken before you realize what a joke telling me to get a shrink is coming from him. He thinks the role of mayor is to cut pretty ribbons, repeat "I feel your pain" as often as possible without actually doing anything about it, and put flowers in pots on lampposts. He enjoys the pomp but does not use the circumstance to advance our many causes.

It's interesting that the Progressive Democrats of Cambridge, a small group of people who actually pay attention to local politics, for the first time dumped Reeves from their slate as a direct result of how he treated me. Given the small size of the PDC, there was little practical effect on the election results. But the fact so many people were outraged at Ken's lack of loyalty surprised me.

The silence from some former "friends" was deafening. People were afraid, but those who were not had a few things in common. They were smart, had had experiences with the police, or they were young and had little respect for the institutions of government.

Many of my friends told me to get out of the United States to avoid the witch hunt. This witch hunt is very serious. But so is leaving the country for good. I considered the possibilities. My real nationality is Hellenic — I am a citizen of Greece because my grandparents all were born in Greece. I have only to claim it. My mother sent me the birth papers of a grandparent, and marriage licenses for Dad and her and so forth, all of which went to the Greek consulate to get my citizenship. I could go to Greece where the constitution forbids a Greek citizen to be extradited. I could disappear in places throughout the world where my friends live.

But I was not sure it was the best way to proceed. Surely a Jew needs to think about leaving Nazi Germany, but when? How do you know when what you lose by staying is greater than what you lose by leaving?

Well, during this painful time the Harvard Gay Alumnae came over for brunch; Jesse Gordon, a politician who ran for City Council in Cambridge, visited me often (he co-founded the Progressive Democrats of Cambridge and was instrumental in removing Mayor Reeves from their slate); Gary Dotterman, our resident Communist paid his respects; my mother, family and many, many of my neighbors supported me, including the Bishop of the local Pentecostal church!

Jesse Gordon later summarized the witch hunt situation from that painful time: "The gay community abandoned Scondras because they wanted to make sure that defending homosexuality was separated from defending pederasty; the progressive community avoided Scondras because they believed the police and the media reports; the African-

American community stuck with Scondras because they disbelieved the police and the media reports." When I asked him why he was willing to come knock on my door instead of believing the police and media reports (he is a progressive but not gay and not black), Gordon responded, "When I was a kid, there was a guy who was shunned in our small community because several neighbors saw him shooting up with drug paraphernalia. So one day my parents knocked on the guy's door and asked for his side of the story. He had epilepsy, and had to shoot up daily, but was so shunned that he couldn't tell anyone. That taught me there's always another side to the story, so I knocked on your door, expecting the same."

I have taught over 5,000 students, among them 4th and 5th graders. You would think after being one of the most well-known public figures in local history, who is openly gay, that someone might mention being molested if it had happened over the past 40 years. But no one did. Because nothing has ever happened. That's my side of the story.

Part Six: Thought Crimes and Plea Bargains

I'll detail here how the judge made it clear he is not interested in my side of the story; Sgt. Shafer is fired; I decide to accept a plea bargain; I am given a GPS system that does not work well; and I am placed on the sex register as a sex offender.

It is the night of Halloween, October 31st, 2007, the thirteenth month since the Columbus Day massacre. It's fitting to be writing about Salem, Massachusetts, a city that gives only lip service about regret for old witch hunts. It is the home of the Sex Offender Registry Board (SORB), which manages the new list of witches that the born-again Puritans persecute. It took a previous governor having his wife accused to put an end to the earlier Salem trials. At the time Deval Patrick was governor of Massachusetts. I voted for him, but he seems uninterested, uninformed, unwilling or unable to do much about this new witch hunt.

Tonight, Halloween 2007, a U.S. state rounded up its list of sex offenders, the majority of whom were children caught kissing, or guys caught peeing by the side of the road, and put them all in a concentration camp.

The justification — there always is a justification — was to protect the children, of course — an old rallying cry from the murder of Socrates to the eternal slander against gay men that they are child molesters.

This notwithstanding the evidence: no child has ever been sexually approached by a convicted sex offender during Halloween, but facts mean little to those driven by fear. And as a matter of record, the vast majority of sexual molestations are from daddy to his kids.

It is simply a fact of life that the Constitution's common sense is violated whenever wretched God-fearing true believers panic over the latest demon they invent.

In our society, we have defined danger in a way that makes having both freedom and security impossible.

In the religious model of crime and punishment, safety from demons requires us to give up our freedom. We were upset about the trashing of our freedoms by judges in the exact same way when Joe McCarthy trashed them; when the religiously insane trashed them in Salem witchcraft trials; and when the government of the United States trashed them by ignoring the Constitution in Vietnam.

And those of us who understand tyranny continue to fight for freedom which we are farther from today than we were fifty years ago.

The history of the United States is a history of mobs scared to death by one media inflamed panic after another, put at ease by a binge of persecutions by politicians and prosecutors who invariably invoke protecting the public from imaginary dangers as justifying their unilateral stripping of constitutionally protected freedoms.

So I found myself once again in the depressed city of Lawrence, in the courtroom of Judge Gaffney. It is always frustrating to attend sessions of judges and lawyers conducted in their private language at which your fate is decided by dicing and parsing the rulings of men and women on different cases decided at different times about different issues that usually have little if anything to do with your case. What is even more frustrating is the obedience to form devoid of function that characterizes courts. For example, as defendant I have to be in court. This in part is to make sure that I am aware of what is going on. But in fact, the language of court has evolved so far from ordinary English as to be a variant of Sanskrit, and my presence is merely to 'prove' that a vestige of justice, my right to hear what is going on, has been preserved. In fact, from time to time you have to tell the court that you agree that you understand what no one in their right mind could possibly really understand. But to say that you do not would bring you punishment.

Any good reporter knows that getting two sides to a story, and pitting two people who are spokespeople for each side, two 'experts,' is a lousy way to find out what actually happened. There can be few processes destined to make more mistakes and be driven by myth and fancy rather than fact than the process used to arrive at the simulation of truth put before judges.

For this reason, in theory but not practice, district attorneys and law enforcement are supposed to be tirelessly checking out facts to make sure that what is prosecuted actually happened. The government is supposed to be the safeguard of justice, not an advocate for a side or driven by political frenzies.

But in practice the latter is what justice in America has become.

Nearly a year has passed since the massacre of October 2006, and the judge still has not heard any information except the police report, full of distortions, irrelevancies, outright lies and checkable allegations that are not checked. So I was faced with the reality that the judicial system itself was decidedly not interested in figuring out what happened or seeking justice. If there was the slightest interest in justice, the judge and prosecutor would have shown some interest in how I happened to need brain surgery after this arrest, for example.

Judge Gaffney was prepared to talk about the computer today, but the prosecutor, Jana DiNatale, had a problem A story from the media helps explain the difficulty....

Police Sergeant fired after drunken-driving arrest

Lawrence Eagle-Tribune, July 21, 2007, by Zach Church

Police Sgt. Ryan Shafer was fired yesterday by Mayor Michael Sullivan one month after fellow officers arrested him on charges of drunken driving and leading police on a high-speed chase. Sullivan, in a July 18th letter to Shafer, cited that the arrest as well as a February restraining order and a 2002 assault arrest was "conduct that calls into question your ability to comport yourself in accordance with the laws you have been sworn to enforce."

Lawrence Police arrested Shafer around 3.a.m. June 21 after Methuen Police tried to pull him over for erratic driving. Shafer led Methuen Police onto Interstate-495 south, pushing the truck he was driving to about 90 mph, police said.

That arrest saw Shafer serve a stint at a state detox center before returning to Lawrence where he was released on $500 bail.

Shafer had been on administrative leave from the Police Department since February when a Lawrence woman obtained a restraining order against him. In asking for the order, the woman said that on February 25th, Shafter slashed tires on her Mercedes-Benz while screaming profanities at her.

The woman also accused Shafer of looking at her phone bill history and recent text messages and driving by her house and the homes of her friends. The article concluded:

In 2002 Shafer was charged with assault and battery. Police said he assaulted his girlfriend during an argument with his sister.

One would hope that Ms. DiNatale would belatedly realize that her case against me was based upon the testimony of a person hardly to be trusted. But Ms. DiNatale was more interested in preserving her sense of dignity and winning a case against me than the truth. So rather than tell the judge that she felt the case should be dropped, she framed a plea bargain which would offer me probation and require me to be on a sex offender list in exchange for me in essence dropping my claim to innocence.

This was a very, very hard decision for me. It was virtually impossible for me to lie about myself, and to say that I was guilty of enticing a non-existent minor made me feel like puking.

David Duncan, Ms. DiNatale and the judge went into a conference. In essence the judge said he wanted the case prosecuted and would not let it be dropped. Why, only God knows, as the judge gave no reasons. It seemed that the judge was patently uninterested in any information except for what was in the police report which was written by a drunk fired by the mayor.

My lawyer handed the judge a report on me written by Carol J. Ball, Ph.D. who was a founder of New England Forensic Associates, an organization that specializes in the evaluation and treatment of sex offenders. I had a comprehensive psychological and sexual evaluation conducted which took several weeks, including diagnostic interviews, and psychological tests (Millon Clinical Multiaxial Inventory-III, the Abel Assessment of Sexual Interest, and the Posttraumatic Stress Diagnostic Scale).

The report handed to the judge on the front page summarized the results of this comprehensive examination. It reads in part:

In summary, my report concludes that there is nothing in Mr. Scondras' character to suggest that he would cause harm to anyone, particularly children. Furthermore, results from the objective sexual and personality tests indicate that Mr. Scondras' sexual interest is only toward adults, and his history is consistent with those findings.

The judge casually looked at the report, pushed it aside to his left, and continued talking, making it very clear he was not interested in the opinions of people who actually professionally deal with sex offenders on a regular basis.

He said, "I want to see this prosecuted," in effect dismissing serious questions about the credibility of the sole source of information, the police officer fired by the mayor, and the only relevant information from someone who actually knows about child molesters.

After talking it over with Robert, I decided that given the lawyers lack of confidence that he could convince a jury to set aside prejudices and given the fact the jury in this case would be chosen by a judge not particularly interested in truth and clearly driven by fear and preconceptions, that the plea bargain was the lesser of two evils.

The free justice system would not pay for a lawyer unless I were broke and the for-fee system already cost me over $20,000. If I continued to fight, we would go bankrupt between court costs, lawyer fees, and lost revenues resulting from the media's name-calling.

Also, I had had a massive heart attack several years ago. I know that I could not survive much more stress. And if I ended up in jail, I would not survive. It seemed that the death penalty was a high price to pay for the dubious opportunity of talking to a jury that most certainly would not be my peers, would not be free from Christian prejudices about sex, and would not be free from the panic about child molestation.

Given this reality, I very reluctantly decided to go along with this monster's plea bargain that preserved her ego and notched her belt.

Later, every one of the people I complained to about the $1,200 fee from probation, the $300 a month fee from a GPS monitoring system that does not work and which operates as an electronic leash less efficient than those used for tracking animals 20 years ago and far less efficient than the GPS systems you get in any modern car, the insults to my dignity, the limitations to my freedom which makes it hard to do my work because it limits my ability to travel which I need to do to survive, the damage done to my mental health etc. every one of the people in the system essentially said, "Well, it's better than if you were in jail." Yup. Better to lose a couple of legs and arms than be murdered.

On February 20th, 2009, Justin Brennen, my probation officer, cut away the strap that for 18 months monitored the whereabouts of dangerous people like me.

Part Seven: The fires of San Diego

Feel the night
The cool wind rushing against your face
The machinations of a mad God
The turbulence of ecstasies

His pain reveals he knows
He hurt you.
Forgive him
For your freedom's sake

Don't wait for regret,
For the well dressed tooth to bite
For the morning you remember who you forgot to touch
Who waits for you in silence on the sea

To save him from the water of his home
You are like both the earth and sun
Blinded by light but forever caught in paradox
Giving to the world and being the world that receives it.

— David Scondras, October, 2007, to Nathan

It is the beginning of winter. I find it hard to sleep with this piece of plastic strapped to my leg. A monitoring device is in my home, and a cellphone that loses charge after about six hours. I have no idea how people who need to be out of the house at work for eight hours cope with an electronic leash that keeps them, in effect, under a kind of house arrest no matter what the courts pretend it is.

The state legislature, as is their custom, passed a law requiring that sex offenders – no matter what the offense assuming there even was one – have to have a monitoring device. And pay for it. As is our custom, we not only have a system that oppresses us, we have to pay for it. There is no purpose served by this monitoring system. Not one person has been made safer by it.

I had to meet with my probation officer every two weeks. There is little to say, and it is not clear what the point actually is, other than this incessant desire on the part of the system to constantly make you behave in an obedient fashion.

Sex has become a human behavior subject to the most cruel, irrational and desperate kinds of rules, laws and interventions. Behind all of this craziness is fear. And what people fear is always used by power brokers to elect people, un-elect people, make money, and every other kind of distorted action that fear inevitably feeds.

Sex scares people. They have been taught by virtually all religions to place more importance to it than it is due, and to equate it with violence. The residue of cultural mores surrounding sex and procreation, the transition from matriarchal societies to patriarchal structures has led to a chaotic disaster of sex rules, laws, and customs that mitigate against anybody growing up happy with their sex life or comfortable with sex itself.

What is even more fascinating than the new Puritanism is the fascistic mentality of the solutions it offers: jails are about punishment and mandatory jail sentences being pushed in most states across the USA are about revenge, not protecting anyone.

It turns out that sexual behavior toward children are almost always by a parent, friend, someone known to the child and the family, and more importantly less than 5% of the offenses in any year are the result of someone on the sex offender list committing them. 95% and more of new offenses are done by people not on the list. So the list does not help *ANYONE* protect children from *ANYTHING*. In fact it diverts resources that could be spent actually figuring out how to protect children and adults from real dangers, but this is just not happening.

The list is about the illusion of control, like a lucky rabbit's foot is about the illusion of control. An illusion which keeps the public from ever finding a real answer to the issues of exploitation of people. In addition the laws have been written in a way that allows zealots and fanatics to successfully lobby for laws which punish those who are the cause of new problems extremely rarely, except in very unusual circumstances. The problem is that these laws are not written by people with any expertise in child development.

If we really cared about children, we would want them to have a healthy, happy sex life. It's a big part of life. And we would put a commission together with people who actually *KNOW* about sexual development, psychologists who have studied this their whole lives, students of gay life who can contribute an understanding of the unique elements of this lifestyle which do not conform to any norms established by familiarity with heterosexual behavior, and lawyers who care and understand civil rights and our Constitution. Such a commission would review all the sex laws and redo them to make them a way to have healthy, happy sex instead of a way of encouraging the sick and the angry to target and be predators on gay men and others whose sexuality, while normal, is hated and feared by this loudmouthed minority.

Such a commission reviewing all of our sex laws is long, long overdue.

Anyway, to return to the story, I had to go before the sex offense registry board to be classified in terms of how 'dangerous' I was to others.

Mind you I have never had sex with anyone underage, nor have I ever enticed anyone at all to do anything sexual with money or alcohol or anything else.

But that doesn't matter.

I was with Duncan, my lawyer, and Dr. Carol Ball, a famous psychologist who had analyzed me for pedophilia for a good deal of time.

The people at the hearing represented a board that was illegally constituted from its inception. State law in Massachusetts (Mass General Laws Chapter 6, Section 178/k) specified that the board had to have 7 members with credentials like PhD's and MD's , psychologists and others with expertise. However, it does not, and did not, and what it has decided in terms of classifying sex offenders for the past decade is illegal, a stretch, beyond its mandate.

But I went into the room with an order to keep my mouth shut. I suppose given my inability to suffer fools in silence, that this was a good idea. In any event, there was a woman who was the "decision maker" clearly talking to the prosecutor who represented the board that had already tried to classify me as a moderate risk.

I have not done anything wrong and felt I should not be on the list, in fact I don't think lists are good things at all. The police already have everyone's records, and nobody else should have them because nobody else can actually do anything except target sex offenders for violent attacks. And many have been killed.

The prosecutor was amazingly hostile and irrational. He said to Dr. Ball, "How would you feel if Mr. Scondras *had* sexually approached a 15-year-old?"

She pointed out to him, "But he didn't."

"Yes, but what if he had?" said the prosecutor.

"But *HE DIDN'T*," said Dr. Ball.

This is the kind of exchange that characterized the entire session. A waste of time because the system was polluted with people who were mentally aberrant to begin with — why would they be taking on the issue of classifying sex offenders anyway?

The group was presented with a variety of letters and documents. One was from Dr. Ball, the result of the many tests I had taken. The end of her detailed and lengthy report said

> *Test data indicated that Scondras' sexual interest is solely toward adults. In the clinical interviews Mr. Scondras became distraught at the thought that he would be accused of sexual misconduct but most directly that he would exploit a young person. Furthermore there is nothing in his history to suggest that he has ever engaged in sexual misconduct with an underage person. In summary it is my professional opinion that Mr. Scondras is not at risk to sexually abuse a minor and does nor present any danger to society.*
>
> *— Carol J. Ball, Ph.D. New England Forensic Associates.*

Dr. Ball is one of the country's most respected experts in sexual offenders. She knows I am not one.

It makes no difference because those who make decisions about people like me have no respect for and do not need to pay attention to doctors or psychologists or any other evidence from experts.

Part Eight: Whining

Before you get the idea I am whining about myself, trying to just ventilate about a personal injustice, check out some stories from the 650,000 people now on our national sex registries, which destroy a person's chances of getting work; force her or him to live away from churches and schools, and often out-of-state; deny him the chance to interact with young people; and taint his entire life.

Here is one typical example of a person in Massachusetts. I changed the name to help protect him, but it's been circulated widely by the police:

From xxxxxxxxxxxxxxxx
Sent: Monday, April 07, 2008 3:09 PM
To: xxxxxxxxxxxxxxxxx
Subject: Re: Help for a sex offender in Mass.

I live in Hyannis on the Cape. Many things like this have gone on here, 3 times they have placed information on TV, in flyers as well as on the internet. Misrepresenting the charge that I was charged with as on a child. The charge that I had put on me 21 years ago by my ex-wife who recanted it in court and went on to marry me and have 3 more children with me.

The registration board has classified me a level 3 sex offender. My life is ruined! I can't get a job, a house, or even stay in a homeless shelter. The town of Yarmouth doesn't allow you to be classified as homeless. I can't do any thing. I have lost all hope in even living.

If you have any advice its welcome.

In discussions to clarify this email asking for help, this man explained to me that he was convicted of non-consensual sex with a girlfriend (they were both adults, mid-twenties), because of a dispute they had. He finally plea-bargained because he thought it would just go away after parole. That was years ago. He and the woman made up and are now married with children. He must still register. But the worst problem is that a local police department has circulated an incorrect flyer stating that he was convicted of indecent assault on a child. He has no other arrests or convictions than the one described above.

To continue examples (from "Out of control," by the organization "Ethical Treatment for All Youth"):

- *Mary's son age 16, Oklahoma*

"He admitted he had sex with her twice back when they first met before he learned she was 14. My son was arrested on two counts of sexual abuse, third degree felonies. He was facing charges as an adult and a twenty year prison sentence."

- *Pam's son, age 12, Pennsylvania*

My son was charged in Michigan with a "felony 1 criminal sexual conduct child under 13." He in fact did indecently touch a boy of 6 years old. He was 12 when this happened. He performed oral sex on him. He has to register for life. Now we have the fear the new Jessica's Law will make it so he cannot go to school any more.

- *Shannon, age 13, California*

The reasons for placement were a sexual offense done when I was 13 in California. Basically I engaged in consensual sexual acts with three neighborhood boys ages 13, 11 and 8. Treatment involved putting a rubber band-appearing contraption held up through a computer around your penis while you sat in a dark room with your pants to your ankles listening to various audio recording stories.

- *Garrett Daly, age 13, Arizona*

Our daughter Devon came to us and said Garret had been touching her. The night our son was to be awarded his Eagle court award he was arrested and put in jail. The next day, Saturday, the county attorney decided to change his charges to the adult court. On Sunday our daughter Devon came to us and told us she had lied. We again went to the authorities but no one would listen.

- *Matt, age 14, West Virginia*

He paid with ten months of his life locked up, then was involuntarily committed to a psychiatric hospital. He was forbidden to have any contact with his family. Our son had gone through compete psychological testing at the National Institute, Johns Hopkins, giving completely opposite results and recommendations than these experts.

- *Tony Fillingame, age 17, Texas*

My son was a registered sex offender because of an encounter he had with a 13-year-old girl who misrepresented her age. Tony was literally kicked out of a sex offender's treatment program because he chose to confront the leaders about trying to force him to lie.

- *Asa Morton, age 19, Texas*

She stated she had just tuned 17 we had no idea that my son could be charged with sexual assault of a child. Asa was given 8-year deferred adjudication with lifetime registration as sex offender. He cannot find work. He cannot live with anyone in his family because of minors.

- *Carolyn's son, age 18*

My son was convicted of sexual assault on a minor for consensual teenage sex. He had to sign a contract when he entered treatment agreeing to aversion therapy, penile plethysmograph, and lie detector tests. It also stipulated the therapy would involve masturbation.

These are a handful of cases that involve young people exploring sex and how our systems treat them. Adults like myself are treated far worse, especially if we have sex with younger people whether or not they exist or are legally above the age of consent. There are 650,000 so-called sex offenders on the sex registry which does nothing but make them targets for irrational hatred.

Police create sting operations in which bait-and-switch is a time honored tradition, one which caught me in their net. And there will be no help until enough people grow up and realize that those who are truly demons in our culture have grabbed child molestation as a cause that allows them to continue the same anti-erotic hate campaigns that characterized how gay men were treated for centuries.

Anyway, besides Carol Ball, others sent letters to the board of incompetents and fanatics who judge my fate and the fate of all the so called offenders – the new witches. Letters include the following:

From Alfred DeMaria, M.D., Director, Bureau of Communicable Diseases:

Over these past 15 years that I have known David Scondras I have never observed any indication that he has presented or does present a danger to others.

From Bishop Brian C. Greene of the Pentecostal Tabernacle Churches in Cambridge:

I am writing this letter on behalf of David Scondras with whom I've had the distinct pleasure to serve in our community on the Board of Directors at the Margaret Fuller House. I have found him to be a tireless community advocate for what has been considered the poorest area in the City of Cambridge. I certainly do not believe him to be a threat to our community. I do not believe his conviction warrants that he should be classified in any way shape or form.

From Debra Wise, an actress who lives across the street in Cambridge:

As a mother — I have two teenaged daughters ages 16 and 17 — and educator — I currently teach playwriting in the Cambridge Public Schools and have worked with children for 30 years — I honestly do not believe that David presents a danger to children or to others. I want to submit my unqualified assessment that David poses no threat to young people. I hope we see him often on his porch and having him as part of this community.

Similar letters we sent from Peter Salk (the son of Jonas Salk, the inventor of the Salk vaccine), the country of Malawi, roommates, other neighbors, family members....

It made no difference.

We need to totally revamp our sex laws. They have become tools to gain power, destroy lives, act out revenge fantasies, create a new class of people who can be hated, and make money.

I got depression and negative feelings during this horrible experience. But I also got love. My artist friend Michael wrote me the following:

Baggy Clothes

*A dedication to my friend David
by Michael Altamari*

*I kissed you on the forehead
I kissed you as you lay sleeping
And then I left you there
Feeling like a proud father leaving his son*

*I kissed David the giant slayer of an era gone by
David a lover of men
Yes it was I who was chosen to witness the awkward teen
of such powerful intellect and character
As he lay slumbering toward the evening of our time*

*A time when in his youth he spoke up against injustice
guided by a love so strong that it soaked him right to the very core of his being*

*A love he could not deny
and trusted to guide him
In all his dealings with the world*

And now he sleeps and waits
Aging, wondering, dreaming

Sleep David, and rest
But still love and remember
You have lived well and proud
And done great things in your time
Sleep and rest as we slip into the dreams of tomorrow
Which fit us like the baggy clothes we now find ourselves in

I can now reach across this great distance of time and space and say
I love you David,
I always have
And I always will

The painting is by Michael Altamari in 2016

142 / God Bless America, by Big Brother

A blessing is for the most part something you work hard at getting. It is not winning the intergalactic lottery engineered by some imaginary creature that doles out luck. The very phrase "God Bless America" is an implied supplication giving power to a fake deity and removing power from the person uttering the phrase. Invoked by Presidents and priests, it simultaneously removes responsibility for each others' welfare from each other to this God creature, implies that a lack of blessing reflects our undeserving nature or bad behavior, reinforces the notion that obedience to power is the way to blessings presumably comprised of long life, freedom from pain, and a Maserati in the driveway. It indirectly reinforces obedience to our rulers who throughout history have adorned the mystique and affectations of gods.

Yet nothing but science and its attendant hard work has ever delivered the goods, and God never had anything to do with any of it. I have no patience with those who insist on this idiotic myth and suggest a careful reading of *The God Delusion* by Richard Dawkins and *The End Of Faith* by Sam Harris for mildly toxified brains, and a switch to Buddhism for the truly addicted.

Gods are supported by rulers precisely because they teach people to blindly obey invisible rulers more powerful than ordinary people, and this obedience to authority is the lynchpin to the power of the rulers of our societies.

And yet only by vaccinating people to protect them from the mental virus of religion and fundamentalist thought can we hope to reach the stars or cure diseases, for the very obedience and acceptance of divine truths or the whimsical decisions of mortal rulers guarantees our development of scientific knowledge will limp along cautiously sneaking around the obstacle course created by the various true believers of our world.

As I said earlier, I have always been a criminal.

I am a gay man. So for the first 40 years of my life I lived hidden from "the law." At the 1270, a gay bar in Boston, I was protected by the money paid to the Boston police who shook the bar down, as they did to all the gay bars, to not raid and arrest the people who danced, talked, drank and networked within.

And this was the improved version of life: the old Punchbowl flashed lights on and off when the police were coming so that gay boys could switch partners with their lesbian beards to make their dancing legal.

My life is no more about sex than Bill Clinton's presidency was about a blow job in the White House. But in a society driven by demons that invent sin and equate it with sex, there is no room for the heretics who are born every day in every place there is a birth, for sex is as normal and wonderful and inevitable as all of nature's commandments.

So Bill Clinton gets impeached for a blow job in spite of the best time economically the USA had in over a hundred years, while George W. Bush never got impeached in spite of the fact he lied about weapons of mass destruction, killed thousands of Americans in a war whose justification was those lies, destroyed the best economy in our history giving us an additional debt of $9 trillion, created the conditions that led to the biggest successful recruitment drive for Al Qaeda in its history, led even friends like the British to condemn his support for torture in secret prisons, destroyed the freedom that has been the central principle upon which America was based through the Patriot Act and hundreds of other small encouragements to those who would use fear to replace it with a punitive religiosity in laws ranging from sex offenses to criminalizing various kinds of freedom of speech.

I have always been a criminal to those who pray to the gods of the past and are ever ready to condemn and punish anyone who does not believe in their mythologies which cannot be proven or even debated.

Epilogue / Notes to the Survivors on What We Learned

"There are two struggles: for the land and for the mind."
— *Mel King*

We have been asked to explain what the past has taught us—what understanding Robert and I got from the experiences of our life. This epilogue represents our opinion about the present world power situation and our speculation about lessons learned for the future. These four volumes are organized as a chronological story; except that this epilogue is instead organized conceptually.

I / The Heart of the Problem

Most people think of work as something you have to do to get enough money to live. As a negative thing, something you want to get free from. Does it have to be this way? It does not. In the 1938 *Homage to Catalonia*, George Orwell recounts his time with the Anarcho-Syndicalists who ran Barcelona during the Spanish Civil War before the Americans, Russians, and Franco's Fascists collaborated to destroy the farm collectives. I'm no anarcho-syndicalist, but let me go back to explain how these ideas came about and are still relevant.

The experience of work as a necessary evil was the result of a bizarre and very bad idea which began perhaps 20,000 years ago with the invention of large scale farming. That idea was the idea of "owning." The idea of owning lets us makes sense of the world but also obscures it, causing us to see it through an ideological lens. "Owning" as opposed to "using" became a lens through which we now see much of the world — but "owning" is a construct, not the result of immutable genetic predisposition. As such it can be modified.

If someone could "own" enough land, then the landless would have to become workers on the "owner's" land — peasants, serfs, slaves, tenants or migrant workers — and the relationship they had with the land morphed into a relationship with the owner of the land. The tenants could not pass the land on to their kids. They never knew how long they could use it. The food it produced did not belong to them. Their relationship with other people who worked on the land became competitive: tenants became scared of anyone who might be willing to work for that landlord cheaper than they could, because their jobs did not belong to them.

All of this was very different from working a community-run farm in Catalonia with other volunteers. Everything else we are going to talk about was shaped by this original sin, ownership itself.

It all begins with a simple question: Whose land is this? Whose body is this? Whose ideas are these?

Lots of thinkers have warned us over the centuries that our trajectory based upon the unlimited "ownership" of capital by individuals (and later corporations) was unsustainable. Adam Smith, Jeremy Bentham, David Ricardo, and Thomas Malthus all, in different ways, tried to spell out the problems with the nascent capitalism of 18th and early 19th century Europe. A few very recent examples of such thinkers are:

- Al Gore, who wrote *An Inconvenient Truth,* summarizing the consensus among virtually all scientists that we are destroying our environment.

- Rachel Carson, who with *Silent Spring* warned of a coming end to our planet's friendliness toward our species.

- Noam Chomsky taught us the role of propaganda in maintaining the security state and state Capitalism.

- More recently there has been Thomas Piketty in *Capital in the Twenty First Century*, Nobel Laureate Paul Krugman in many *New York Times* articles, Joseph Stiglitz in *The Price of Inequality* and many others who have shown the persistence and damage done by the huge inequality of wealth and income in capitalist societies.

Although the topics seem different, they all analyze the damage done by the particular way we have organized ourselves economically. Questioning the concept of "ownership" translates into the progressive movement's suspicion of "concentration of wealth." We agree.

My friend Jesse Gordon (a CPPAX board member whose political advice is extraordinary) has pointed out a problem with the slowly accumulating critiques of our way of life, of our government and money system: They don't say how to help. What we can do to make it better? While others will lure you into voting for a savior, or worshiping one in a temple, or work out the chains of causality regarding some public policy issue using factor analyses — well, those might define a process, but what can we actually *DO* to make it better?

II / What is limiting our progress: the three poisons

The three poisons in the center of the wheel of life, the bird, snake and pig, representing the three Buddhist poisons of greed, hatred and delusion.

We have a chance to make the world we live in into the paradise our ancestors taught us we would inherit for a life well-lived, to reach for the planets around distant stars, to end diseases, poverty, hunger, fear, and war. But to do all this I believe we have to overcome the brainwashing that taught us exploitation of the weak and the earth is in our interests and that we have no power to change the authoritarian private and public empires.

The sources of all our sufferings are the three poisons of greed, hatred, and delusion. They are driven by fear. We are embarked on a great struggle to replace them with generosity, love and science. The three poisons are connected: greed led to amassing wealth and power which uses delusion and war to control what we think, sowing the seeds of hatred. What weighs in the balance in our struggle to free ourselves from these is our survival as a species.

III / The Architecture of Power

Our world has a shape, an architecture, that defines what is supported and what is not, what can be done and what is prohibited. It is fashionable to equate what is allowed as "legal," and what is legal to be "just," but this is simply not so.

The social architecture of our world is the way power is distributed, maintained, used and accumulated. A Boston University sociology professor one night stared at me in disbelief at my naiveté, because as a student I thought justice would always win. "It's about power, not justice," he said.

For thousands of years the world, plagued by the three poisons, has been run and owned by a handful of rich men who have most of the world's wealth and whose interests fundamentally differ from those of over 99 percent of the people on our planet. In other words, by oligarchs. The roles of public policy and religion, socialization and law, armies and media, child rearing and education are designed to maintain the relationships of power between factions and subgroups of the world population. To protect the pyramids of power.

For centuries, education cultivated the acquisition of skills without critical thinking, for empires need technicians to function, but cannot afford thinkers who question the socioeconomic order. Even today the road to freedom is defined as going to college and working hard — which deflects the energies of the poor toward climbing the pyramid of power, rather than getting rid of the pyramid. And that effort to climb mostly fails, while increasing the wealth and power of those at the top.

It is no surprise to me that when I went to Harvard there was a saying that politics is a fight between graduates of Harvard and graduates of Yale. The educated elite, the Pharisees for the corporations, know who they are, know what the limits of their discourse are, and know the reduction into obscurity that befalls any who stray from the accepted, safe interpretations of reality they are in charge of disseminating.

Look, for example, at the banker bailout of 2008, which was widely opposed but passed anyway. This disconnect between the people who live in a country and the decisions made by supposedly democratic governments is the result of the efforts to maintain the financial and social inequalities that are the defining characteristic of our societies.

The system itself *inevitably* leads to those who own capital accumulating more and more wealth resulting in larger and larger inequalities of opportunity, power, and resources. Previous upheavals without reforms did not change the inevitable growth of the same inequalities over time with the same results. Killing the king without getting rid of the kingdom just meant a new king.

In the United States, we find the top 1% owns over half the wealth and a third of the income — fifty times the wealth were it to be spread evenly and thirty times the income if were to be spread evenly. And this type of unequal distribution of wealth and income have been pretty much the same for the past three hundred years. It is a result of how our economies actually work, and without interventions like progressive taxation, and taxation on wealth, can continue indefinitely.

This unequal distribution of wealth might not mean much if opportunities to get rich were equally available to everyone and if the decisions made to keep the pyramid of power intact were sustainable. Neither is true.

Everyone having an equal opportunity to get rich is a myth that stabilizes our society. It misidentifies people who work hard to earn a lot of money with the rich. Most people define upward mobility in terms of getting a higher paying job— a bit like defining freedom as choosing which corporate jail you will be in. This myth has its equivalent in our so called 'democracy' in which political freedom is defined as picking between rich candidates for public office already chosen to run by the political elite.

How did this happen? What keeps it like this? Can things change? And what can we do to help make the world a better place?

Let's begin with the costs of keeping it going the way it is now.

IV / Costs of keeping things the way they are

For those who rule the world, the interlocking megacorporations of the rich who own most capital and income, the goal is straightforward: to maximize short term profits and keep ownership of productive capital, using the state to support this goal.

The first thing to check out are the costs – the unintended consequences of our decisions and systems. The costs go by other names like unemployment, humanitarian crises, global warming, the end of codfish on Georges Bank, crumbling infrastructure, and so forth.

This does not mean that they don't do good things from time to time, but for the most part this is incidental to their main function: to maintain the pyramid of power as it presently exists. It also does not mean that as the pyramid grows that there are no benefits to those at lower levels because it is in the nature of that growth that the bigger the pie the more possibilities of getting a bite. However the scale of inequalities also grows and the diseconomies of scale, i.e. the social costs, trend upward as well. One way to think of this is that a rising tide drowns anyone who doesn't have a boat.

There would not be room to list all the hidden costs of our socioeconomic systems here, but a few might be useful as a starting point for discussion: Let's take as one example we can use as a model — the heavily subsidized practice of identifying, getting, refining, selling and burning fossil fuels. This industry, which could not exist without support from government, profits a handful of megacorporations themselves controlled by a handful of powerful men. The "green movement" identified a cost of using fossil fuels to create energy – increased levels of CO_2 which in turn causes global warming, leading to a host of ecological catastrophes. But indirect consequences include support for Saudi kings who are amenable to giving rich oil companies the crude beneath the desert while funding militant fundamental Islamic jihadists, for example.

I would like my readers to understand my motivation: my goal is constructive, even though much of my analysis sounds destructive. I envision a society where these underlying issues are fixed: but first we have to recognize the underlying issues.

I critique a lot about America today — but I envision Americas as the *SOLUTION* to these problems more than their *CAUSE*. America today is the only society in the history of the earth that has enough people, enough brains, enough power, and enough resources to actually *SOLVE* the crises that the world is facing.

America can, basically, save this planet and its people from a horrible future. And I'm quite optimistic that it will. The reason I'm so critical is precisely because America is the last best hope. Thermonuclear war is not a recoverable event; nor is global warming, nor any of the other extinction-level events we face now or will soon face – and which humanity faces for the first time. America can save us from that. And only America can save us from that.

An intangible cost: the increase in fragility: Pretend that in 1800 you put a circle around Boston and asked: how long could people survive without any transport of goods or services across that circle? Suppose that circle was say, ten miles in diameter. The answer is: many years. If that circle were drawn around Boston now, death and chaos would happen rapidly. Electric power would fail given the lack of local generation, food supplies would disappear once storage facilities are used up, cars and trucks would stop without gasoline, medicines would grow scarce and so forth. It is not profitable, given the so-called market system, to maximize the flexibility of the economy which would require redundant systems dependent upon multiple sources of power, production, and raw materials. In monetary systems where profit is god, redundancy is sin.

The bankrupt judicial system: The judicial system, including judges, police, prosecutors and jails is supposed to deliver justice and enforce a framework of rules that ostensibly maintains order and civility. This not its actual purpose.

Our judicial system, like all of our institutions, has as its primary job the support of existing hierarchies. This is deeper than the often-observed bias of the system toward those with money and power. Its institutional structure is consistent with our cultural scaffolding reflecting an adversarial model of the universe (e.g. God and Satan, good and evil, right and wrong etc.) There is a lot written about criminal justice. I agree that it's criminal.

Poverty: In the absence of intervention, poverty is the result of the pyramid game which relies on it to maintain low wages and provide society with workers who do work no one else wants to do. If you teach that working hard gets you "ahead" (meaning above others), and define personal status as elevated when not doing certain types of work which are taught to be demeaning, then you need people desperate enough to work for peanuts at anything you need done in order to get these jobs done and make the most profit you can.

Atomization: Atomization is useful to our system for several reasons. First, it's a lot harder to deal with individuals who unite into a group and make a common demand than one individual who can be characterized as mentally aberrant. Second, you sell a lot more if everyone has to own one of whatever you are selling than if there is sharing, which is an annoying habit among people who live in families and groups with solidarity and social connections.

Waiting for a savior: If you successfully indoctrinate people into believing that everyone is self-made, the Ayn Rand school of philosophy, this will lead to an endless search for a savior. If you get taught that you get ahead through your own actions, not as part of a team, you begin to direct hope toward individuals, the search for superman. If we are taught that history is the consequence of great actions by powerful men who strut across the stage we should not be surprised people will hope, desire, and pray for a savior. This is destined to fail of course, as no one man or god has ever saved the world nor could they, but the endless series of stories from Superman to Christ.

The emergence of the security state: Constant fear, and the end of "freedom" is a cost of the system. I remember George McGovern saying in a rally in Atlanta at Morehouse College that "those who practice imperialism abroad bring fascism home." Fear breeds fear and there is nothing so fearful as fear. It destroys everything it touches. The fear and the resultant security state are costs of the system based on lies that feed the greedy security complex. The "security" systems increase our insecurity, endanger us and take away our freedom — the costs keep getting bigger.

V / What keeps us from fighting
for our own interests

There are a set of interlocking institutionalized mechanisms that keep us climbing over each other in a hope to reach the top of the pyramid of power.

Religion: Religion performs its function of stabilizing anger toward the rich in several ways. It promotes obedience to higher authority indirectly reinforcing the orientation of the masses toward obeying government and leaders; it teaches that the failure to have money or power is the result of the sin of disobedience. Religion also teaches children that there is pie in the sky when they die, or virgins, or a better reincarnation that fits in well with the idea that not getting to be rich is your own fault.

The illusion of choice: Choice is an illusion. The propaganda from which we have been indoctrinated from childhood into believing all sorts of nonsense that has only one function — to keep us in our place — has many heads. Is choosing which jail and what color of cell and which set of institutional rules among institutions that differ in unimportant details mean you are free?

Wage slavery: By creating a society in which we should "work for a living," not only must we compete to get a job and look, sound, dress and talk like what the boss wants, but workers will hesitate to ever criticize the company they work for or organize against it or tell the truth if they think it might endanger their jobs. Do you really believe the 2008 meltdown of the US economy was not a predicted, understood outcome of the behavior of the financial institutions that created it by the people who worked at those institutions? We have never really liked whistleblowers because they rock the boat; they make what must be invisible visible and this is unacceptable on principle to power. If you don't believe me ask Edward Snowden or Julian Assange. \

Assimilation: One of the most powerful and poignant, sad and effective ways to disarm change is assimilation. It is built on the very foundation of our species for we are creatures that needs affinity and reinforcement of belonging to a group. Once I walked through the Fenway, meeting a girl whose long dress marked her as one of the people of "the movement," and I was invited to go naked on stage at the Wilbur theater in downtown Boston in a production of the musical "Hair." It was performed by an unpaid group of ragamuffins to raise consciousness about the war in Vietnam. Years later in New York in Manhattan Robert and I went to the high cost production of "Hair" — now entertainment, not support for any political movement. "Hair" got assimilated. The first "Hair" was a part of the change we wanted to seek. The second was the selling of retro — once real and now sold as memories.

The gay movement whose incarnations were about sexual freedom transformed slowly from wanting to be part of the legitimate world led to gay soldiers, owning each other in monogamy, and working for companies. Hardly a radical agenda. The movement for freedom was assimilated and by absorbing and legitimating a version of its demands took away the energy and the focus to actually transform the world. There was once a private club where sexual misfits protected and understood each other. Now, like "Hair," the movement was adopted and in adopting it, it was legitimated and turned into a eunuch.

With gay marriage, we now have the right to do exactly what everyone else has the right to do. Perhaps we are a little better off, but that is not what the fight was about. We are still in a world which controls our bodies, equates sex with sin, demonizes those who play differently, and the underground was decimated.

Propaganda: If your power is from people voting for you, such as in a democracy, then you need to control the mind and the elections. All ruling elites doctor their history, but the United States goes further: It cultivates the image that it is superman — powerful but not to be feared for it protects the weak and uses its power to fix what's wrong. This idea is rammed into people's head with an unending campaign that uses movies, radio, television, elite intellectuals and whatever else money can buy, by retrofitting history to misrepresent America and its behaviors to avoid questioning from its own people.

Propaganda goes a lot further than screwing up history. It teaches lies about the society we are in making it difficult for us to know what to support or how. Among other lies sold to the Americans are:

- *Lie: Unions are bad things that take away your money and are clumsy, corrupt things.* Never mentioned are their central roles in ending child labor, establishing the 40-hour work week, forcing companies to have pension plans and paid leave, forcing companies into higher pay for overtime work, and hundreds of other worthwhile things.

- *Lie: In Vietnam America was protecting the people of the South from the invasion of the communist North.* In reality the USA bombed the hell out of the South long before the North had one soldier on the ground in the South. The USA fought a war killing millions to keep democracy from coming to Vietnam for fear the lesson that poor countries can become free from what the companies that run the USA want might spread to other countries.

- *Lie: The "drug war" is a war against addictive drugs that destroy lives.* In actuality the "drug war" is the most astonishing money making scheme in recent memory and has nothing to do with any genuine concern about the harm caused by addictive drugs. To underline the lack of real concern, virtually no state in the USA has treatment-on-demand for people trying to get rid of an addiction.

- *Lie: The U.S.A. supports democratically-elected governments around the world.* Fact is the USA is the world's most dependable supporter of dictatorships, having interfered in the internal affairs of over 60 countries since World War II, supporting dictators over elected governments in the vast majority of cases.

Three sifts: There are three habits of mind that work in concert — three ways that ideas were vetted, three sifts through which ideas are sorted out which when used together will always end up allowing only those ideas that do not endanger the systems under which we live. The three sifts ensure that when an intellectual upheaval occurs it will be contained, to avoid it endangering the power of the existing system.

Discounting emotion: In the intellectual community, emotion is itself viewed as irrational. In real life the emotion tells you exactly what is wrong. If a landlord arsoned his apartment building while children were sleeping in it, the reaction to those hysterical about their children's deaths would be to calm them down because the explanation must be homosexuals or prostitutes — and crying and yelling does not help identify the problem. But in fact it does. This story is not a made up metaphor — it is what actually happened in Fenway in the arson years during which a conspiracy of powerful people burned down buildings to make money on the fire insurance. And the reactions of the police were that the street prostitutes and homosexuals were burning down their own homes.

Two sides to every story: The two-sided sift is that there must be two sides to every story. This equal time for the two sides tends to reduce the urgency to change anything. During the struggle for gay liberation, the handful of gay Republicans were given equal time in the media with the hundreds of thousands of Massachusetts Democrats, creating the impression that the efforts were bipartisan, notwithstanding the surveys taken by ten gay newspapers over years showing that 85% of all gays surveyed voted the same way: Democratic.

Pilot study it to death: If by chance some idea or info got past both sifts there was a final one: Let's study it to death. Let's do a pilot program which will never actually change anything — but we can all feel good about doing an experiment which we are assured if it succeeds will transform the way the system works — but in reality the window-dressing pilot program remains a pilot until the issues die down.

VI / What we can do about it

The examples can go on forever. What brings them together — the point of noticing these things — is to realize that the source of all these distortions is the same, from the themes of films to the news stories we read or watch on television, from the once-every-four-years choosing a President to the choices of bathroom fixtures, to the drudgery of work to the lack of work because all of these things belong to a religion — state capitalism.

The point is to notice that all of these things work together to support the pyramid of power that has dominated, distorted, and destroyed us for thousands of years in one form or another. To understand, to see this, is to look behind the curtain and stop being afraid of the Wizard. To leave the land of Oz. To free ourselves from slavery.

Today there is a second superpower — the only adversary of the oligarchy — the people whose labor produces all the things we call the economy and politics and policy and religion and thought. It is us. There will be no savior. Just us.

Measuring Tools: We have some tools available to measure whether an action might be helpful in freeing us: if an action is directed at getting rid of a rule or institution that decreases freedom it is a good action. If an action is directed at supporting a rule or institution that increases freedom it is a good action. Anything that increases the accountability to people on the part of elected or non-elected officials is a good thing.

Taking Action: People often wonder where the second superpower's fundamental power comes from. That's easy: the oligarchy requires two things from us: our money and our work. Stopping either one puts real pressure on the system and will lead to negotiations that may improve our lives.

Start in your backyard: have a barbecue. Learn about the people who live near you. Talk about what is going on locally and how it connects to the larger world. For example, there are local radio and television stations on cable owned by the neighborhood. It's time to meet, say, over dinner, and create together a local show where local people and even local officials can talk about local issues. Or a local webpage. To the extent that local people use these tools three things happen:

- People get used to the idea that people get to communicate their own experiences with each other directly, and that there are local issues that we need to deal with.

- Local politicians will in fact respond to some extent to whatever this peoples' media talks about because it might affect votes —I know I spent a lot of time reacting to the media.

- And finally it gives a vehicle to loosening up the mind. The enemy creates most of the cacophony that we are subjected to so we need to create a media that responds to us.

The good news about state capitalism is precisely how inefficient it really is. It is locally that we have the biggest clout. I remember that teaching a fifth grade class about saving whales is what led to Boston boycotting fish from Iceland until it signed the whale treaty which Ronald Reagan could not get it to do. It will not be easy to organize in such a way that we all win our freedom, but it can be done step by step.

In general, anything that replaces any aspect of the system with one we control increases our freedom. This reduces the power of the system over our lives. Gay marriage and gay rights; women's right to vote and go to college and own property; the 8-hour work day and minimum wages; health care for all; the end of child labor; building and sanitary codes; the end of putting poor people in jails for being unable to pay bills; the existence of a public school system and fire department; elected local officials; garbage collection; recycling and clean water; drugs that actually work; an end to the dominance of cisgenderism; neighborhood newspapers; and zoning restrictions — these were all the creation of organized people on the local level taking action to make life better for all of us.

We can do more. And we can because we have each other. And together we are very powerful.

Index

A

ACT UP: the AIDS Coalition to Unleash Power; ii:185-6, ii:230, ii:280-2, iv:15, iv:95-6
    photo: ii:282
Ainspan, Ron: Scondras college friend; boyfriend of Copper Coggins; i:5
Albritton, Rogers: Philosophy Professor at Harvard University; i:47-8, i:67, i:73, ii:192
Allyson, Sasha: owner of *Bay Windows*, a Boston gay community publication; iii:185-6
Altamari, Mike: Neighborhood activist and artist; i:74, i:129-31, i:136, i:141, i:145,
    i:153, iv:214-5
    photos: i:129, i:153, iv:215
ANC: African National Congress, South African Liberation Movement; ii:77-80, iii:193
Ansara, Mike: head of *Fair Share*; head of Harvard SDS; i:168
Apuzzo, Virginia "Ginny": Democratic Party organizer; Deputy Director of the New York
    State Consumer Protection Board; ii:113, ii:193-7
    photos: ii:196-7
Aquino, Corazon: resident of Massachusetts, then President of the Philippines; ii:17
Arroyo, Felix: Boston City Councilor citywide; i:158
Arson investigations: *see* Fenway arson investigations
Assimilationism: idea that gays can be "straight-lite" instead of inherently different
    (contrast to Liberationism): i:14, i:169, ii:6, ii:14, ii:28, ii:168, ii:180,
    iii:105, iii:135, iii:185, iii:195, iv:5-8, iv:23, iv:55-6
Atkins, Chet: chair of the Democratic State Committee; ii:82

B

Babets, Don: First openly gay assistant to State Senator Bill Owens;
    Scondras campaign manager; i:56, ii:71, ii:97-8, iii:23-4
Bacon, Smoki: Boston socialite and activist; iii:181-2
    photos: iii:182
Baird, Allan: Teamster official and Harvey Milk supporter; ii:106-7
    photo: ii:106
Barrios, Jarrett: Scondras staffer; openly gay State Senator; iii:135, iii:142
    photos: ii:32, iii:184
BCOA, Boston Center for Older Americans; i:21, i:96, i:103, i:107, i:114, i:127, i:131
Beal, Bob: real estate supporter and Scondras supporter; ii:115
Beal, Eugenie: opponent candidate for City Council district 8; i:171, i:201
Belafonte, Harry: singer, songwriter, and social activist; ii:80, iii:193, iv:170
    photo: ii:80
Bellotti, Frank: Massachusetts attorney general; i:139-40, i:144, i:154, i:190, ii:31, iii:163
Berk, Lee: founder of Berklee Performance Center; i:142, ii:184, iv:47
Berlandi, Joseph: Fenway Project Director, representative of the BRA; i:109-10
BLGPA, Boston Lesbian and Gay Political Alliance: i:188, ii:211
Bloomingdale, Gwen: lesbian activist; scion of the retail store family; iii:9, iii:16, iv:26
Bolling, Bruce: Boston City Council colleague; first black President of Boston City Council;
    ii:29, ii:70, ii:120, ii:123, ii:220, ii:273, ii:293, iii:6, iii:62, iii:101-3, iii:143
Bolling, Royal Jr.: State Rep. and brother of Bruce Bolling; ii:120

Bolling, Royal Sr.: State Senator and father of Bruce Bolling; i:142
Borge, Tomás: Interior Minister of Nicaragua; ii:85
Bozzotto, Domenic "Dom": leader of Hotel Workers Union Local 26; ii:105,iii:132, iii:174
BRA: Boston Redevelopment Authority (now the Boston Planning & Development
        Agency); i:82, i:102-6, i:109-11, i:116, i:122-3, iii:26, iii:38, iii:188, iii:195
Braude, Jim: Cambridge City Councilor; New England Cable Network News reporter; iv:145
Britt , Harry: Succeeded Harvey Milk as San Francisco County Supervisor; i:177-8
Bryant, Anita: anti-gay activist; ii:151, ii:225, ii:261
Bucke, Rev. Gerald: West End community activist; i:105, i:111-2, i:164
Bulger, Billy: president of the Massachusetts Senate, 1978-1996; i:14
Bunker, Archie: bigot from 1970s TV show, "All in the Family"; ii:297
Burbank, Liz: Fenway community activist; i:153
Byrne, Garrett: District Attorney of Boston; i:188
Byrne, Jim: Boston City Council colleague; i:6, ii:29, ii:121, ii:292, iii:91-2, iii:100

C

Caffrey, Andrew: Federal District Court Judge; i:124-5, i:192-3
Campbell, Bob: *Boston Globe* architectural critic; i:257-8
Carr, Howie: *Boston Herald* columnist; i:6, ii:23, ii:223-5, ii:300, iii:30, iii:172, iii:181,
        iii:191, iv:53-5, iv:191
Casazza, Joe: head of Boston's public works department; ii:199
Case, Father Robert: priest; Fenway community activist; i:75, i:99, i:109-12, ii:184, ii:236
Cathcart, Kevin: GLAAD activist; i:151, ii:45
CCLSF, Committee for Civil Liberties and Sexual Freedom; ii:218-22
Chávez, César: labor activist & founder of the United Farm Workers; i:15,
        ii:92-6, ii:241, iii:192
        photos: ii:96
Chomsky, Noam: MIT professor and political writer; i:67, iv:219
Clapprood, Marjorie: State Rep.; radio host; ii:201, ii:280
Coggins, Copper: Scondras BFF from college; i:5, iii:41
Commerford, Betty; Social worker in Mission Hill; iii:195
Condlin, Robert: Boston College Law School faculty; i:111
Contras: U. S.-backed militia opposing the Sandinista government; ii:81-4, ii:109, ii:190,
        ii:206, ii:238, iii:72, iii:193, iv:170
Coors, Peter: beer magnate, target of the Coors boycott; ii:101-4, ii:188-91, ii:249-52, iv:6
Cox, Helen: Fenway community activist; ii:46
CPPAX, Citizens for Participation in Political Action; i:90, iv:220
Crisp, Quentin: British writer and raconteur; i:13
Cristiani, Alfredo: President of El Salvador; iii:62-70
Cronin, Mike: Boston City Council candidate against incumbent Jim Kelly; iii:126, iii:143
Crumb, Fritz, director of the BCOA; i:96

D

Daher, George "Eddie": Chief Judge of the Boston Housing Court; ii:111
Dapper; *see:* O'Neil: Albert
Day, Debbie, Christian Scientist activist: i:97, i:117
D'Elia, Christopher: manager of Deak-Perera currency company; ii:78

DeMaria, Alfred "Al": Assistant Commissioner of the State Department of Public
       Health; iv:9, iv:16-8, iv:112, iv:213
D'Escoto, Miguel: priest; official of the Sandinista government; ii:83
DiCara, Larry: Former Boston City Councilor; ii:51, ii:231
DiFronzo, Anne: the "first lady of East Boston"; i:163
Don't-ask-don't-tell policy; i:164, iv:46
Dobson Affair (and Donald Dobson); ii:220-4
Dotterman, Gary: Scondras staffer; AIDS activist; i:200, ii:31-2, ii:34-7, ii:101,
       ii:145, ii:182, ii:199, ii:213, ii:217, iii:192, iv:198
       photo: ii:32
Duberman, Martin: historian in New York, author of "*Stonewall*"; i:179-80, iii:169-70
Dukakis, Kitty: First Lady of Massachusetts; ii:back cover, ii:15,
Dukakis, Mike: Governor of Massachusetts, i:2, i:142, i:147, i:162-3, i:194, ii:15, ii:55,
       ii:98, ii:108, ii:116, ii:182-3, ii:207, ii:214, ii:261, ii:267, ii:270-5, ii:280,
       ii:285, ii:297-9, ii:310, iii:21, iii:33, iii:52, iii:105, iii:182

E

Eagan, Margery: *Boston Herald* reporter; iii:82, iii:134
Epperly, Jeff: editor of *Bay Windows*, a Boston gay community publication; iii:186-7

F

Fadem, Randy: Fenway community activist with dog, Zapata; i:75, i:99, i:102
Fallaw, Tom: Scondras friend at Harvard; i:46, iii:155
Family Protection Act: Scondras legislation for domestic partner benefits;
       i:21, ii:191, iii:44-7, iii:130-5, iii:143
Fauci, Tony: immunologist; Reagan appointed to AIDS at NIH; ii:127, iv:20, iv:28
Feder, Don: *Boston Herald* columnist; ii:234-5, iii:47
Feinstein, Dianne: Member of San Francisco Board of Supervisors with Harvey Milk (q.v.);
       later Mayor of San Francisco and U.S. Senator; i:177
Fenway Health Center; i:89-91, i:96, i:189, ii:50, ii:60, ii:171, iii:32, iii:38-9, iii:188
Fenway arson investigations; i:129-47, i:157, i:160, i:188, ii:30, ii:233, iii:23-4,
       iii:172, iii:194, iv:230
Fierstein, Harvey: gay playwright and actor; best known for his drag role in
       the play "Hairspray"; ii:241, ii:281-3
Fiscus, Glen: Scondras' opponent in City Council race; ii:231-2, iii:142-3
Fitzgerald, Kevin: State Rep. from Mission Hill; ii:110, ii:202, iii:28, iii:147
Flynn, Ray: Mayor of Boston; i:6, i:13, i:166, i:192, i:198, i:200, i:202, ii:13, ii:21, ii:26,
       ii:55-8, ii:67, ii:74, ii:94-5, ii:110-1, ii:117-9, ii:128, ii:131, ii:156, ii:198, ii:210,
       ii:234, ii:253, ii:266-73, ii:286, ii:292-3, ii:302, ii:309-10, iii:11, iii:22, iii:31-4,
       iii:36-40, iii:45, iii:52-61, iii:86, iii:91-5, iii:100, iii:109, iii:120, iii:127, iii:135,
       iii:141, iii:193
       photos: ii:27, iii:110
Flynn, Shelagh: wife of Mayor Flynn; ii:31
FMLN (Farabundo Martí National Liberation Front, the freedom fighters of El Salvador):
       iii:62-4, iii:67, iii:70-3, iii:79-81
FPA: *see* Family Protection Act

Combined index for i:The Beginning; ii:The Kiss; iii:The Coup; and iv:The Long Way Home

Frank, Barney: first openly gay member of Congress from Massachusetts; i:157, i:190, ii:37,
ii:51, ii:55, ii:201-2, ii:212, ii:227-8, ii:234-5, ii:276, ii:297, iii:2, iii:7, iii:161, iii:176,
iii:181-2, iv:103, iv:112
photo: iii:182
French: *see* Wall, French (Scondras staffer)

G

Gallagher, Tom: State Rep. from Allston-Brighton; ii:122
Gandhi, Mohandas "Mahatma": political leader of India; i:155, ii:213, iii:195, iv:91
Garland, Judy: actress and singer; i:22, i:177, i:179
Garneau, Ernie: Fenway tenant activist; i:134
Gates, Bill; philanthropist and founder of Microsoft; iv:21
Gaydar: ii:57, ii:61, iii:164, iii:183
GCN: *Gay Community News*, a Boston-based weekly newspaper; i:162, i:165-6, i:172-3,
i:197, ii:11-2, ii:62, ii:175, iii:185-6
Gilbert, Galen: Fenway community activist; Scondras campaign treasurer; now
director of the Water Table Trust; i:171, ii:118, ii:203, ii:222
GLAAD: Gay & Lesbian Alliance Against Defamation, legal organization to defend LGBT
people; i:151, ii:45
Goldsmith, Larry: reporter at *Gay Community News*; i:173, ii:12
Gordon, Jesse: political activist and editor of this book; i:2,ii:1, iii:3, iv:2, iv:198-9, iv:220
Gore, Al: Vice President and environmental activist; iv:219
Guide, The, gay news magazine; i:200, ii:218, iii:126

H

Hall, Jackson (Jack): Scondras staffer; ii:10, ii:31-2, ii:53, ii:92
photo: ii:32
Hattam, Nick: poet and friend of Scondras; ii:16, iv:159-60
Hay, Harry; founder of Mattachine Society; i:181, ii:68
Heilman, John: Mayor of West Hollywood California; i:177
Hennigan, Maura: Boston City Council colleague, ii:29, ii:59, ii:104, ii:121, ii:142,
ii:158, ii:204, ii:210,
Heritage Foundation: conservative think tank; ii:191
Hernandez, Peggy: *Boston Globe* reporter; ii:221, ii:270, ii:304
Higgens, Carol: Scondras high school crush; homecoming queen; i:32
Hirschfeld, Magnus: founded the Scientific Humanitarian Committee in Germany
and organized the first Congress for Sexual Reform; i:181
Hoffman, Abbie: 1960s radical; i:127
Hoffman, Julius: right-wing Judge; i:125, iii:179, iii:256, iv:322-3
Holland (the Netherlands): ii:289, ii:309, iv:29, iv:152
Holmes, Dan: chef and founder of the Downtown Café; ii:94, ii:145
Hougen, Ed: minister and founder of gay news magazine *The Guide;* i:200
Hughes, Langston: poet and social activist; ii:58, ii:63-5, iii:161
photo: ii:65
; i:173, i:179, i:214, i:219
Hurley , John J. "Wacko": anti-gay activist; iii:157
Huynh, Marylyn: political activist Robert called Marylyn Spacecheck; i:30-1, iii:29

I

Iannella, Chris: Boston City Council colleague; i:111, ii:29, ii:122, ii:280-1, ii:293, ii:301,
 iii:12, iii:62-3, iii:122, iii:280, iii:293, iii:301
Isaacson, Arlene: Co-Chair of Massachusetts Gay and Lesbian Political Caucus; i:157

J

Jack: *see* Hall, Jackson (Scondras staffer)
Jackson, Bob: Boston firefighter; ii:172-3
Jackson, Rev. Earl: anti-gay activist; iii:105-6
Jackson, Jesse: political activist; candidate for president, 1984 and 1988; i:15, i:73,
 ii:8, ii:259-63, ii:267, ii:283-4, ii:296-9, ii:310, iii:182, iii:194
 photos: ii:260, ii:284
Jackson, Michael: singer; ii:17-8, ii:20, ii:26
John Birch Society: anti-Communist advocacy group; ii:190
Johnson, Helene: Boston community activist and state rep candidate; i:188
Johnson, Lyndon: President from 1963 to 1968; i:72, i:78, i:96, i:111, ii:161
Jordan, Robert: *Boston Globe* reporter; ii:13
Joshi, Shashank: M.D. in India; iv:76-8, iv:85
 photo: iv:76
Jurkowitz, Mark: reporter for *the Boston Ledger*; i:202

K

Kallmann, Gerhard: Boston architect; ii:258
Kameny, Frank: Early gay rights activist; i:181
Kaven, Bob: openly gay Chris Iannella aide; ii:122, ii:301
Keane, Tom: City Council opponent who unseated Scondras; Rep. Moakley's staffer;
 iii:165-7, iii:171, iii:177-81, iii:186, iii:190, iii:195-6, iv:8
 photo: iii:171
Kelly, Frank: Boston vice squad police officer; ii:88
Kelly, Jim: Boston City Council colleague, i:6, i:193, ii:26, ii:29, ii:84, ii:98, ii:110,
 ii:122, ii:133, ii:225, ii:281, ii:288, ii:302, iii:10, iii:53, iii:99-103, iii:120-1,
 iii:128, iii:143, iii:158, iii:173, iv:91
Kennedy, Edward "Ted": Senator from Massachusetts; i:14, i:124, ii:138, ii:140,
 ii:274, iii:92
Kennedy, Joe Jr.: U.S. Rep.; father of U. S. Rep. Joe Kennedy III; ii:139-40, iii:62-4,
 iii:67, iii:83, iii:189, iii:195
Kennedy, John F.: President and Senator from Massachusetts; i:23, i:32, i:52-5, i:67,
 i:168, i:196, iii:160, iv:54
Kennedy, Robert F.: Senator from New York; i:79, ii:36
Kennedy School of Government and Library: Harvard University, i:104, ii:108
Kerry, John: Senator from Massachusetts; i:126, i:183, i:198, ii:202, iii:62-4, iv:103, iv:112
Ketover, Dede: staffer in mayor's office; AIDS activist; ii:148
Keverian, George: speaker of the Massachusetts Statehouse; iii:7-8
Kimmel, Daniel, campaign volunteer and copy-editor of this book; ii:256-7

King, Mel: Director of the New Urban League of Greater Boston; candidate for Mayor;
        i:7, i:137-8, i:155-6, i:161, i:178, i:198-200, ii:8-9, ii:13, ii:21, ii:78-80,
        ii:130, ii:235, ii:243, ii:259, iii:17, iii:57, iii:189, iv:218
        photo: ii:80
Klavens, Dr. George: Scondras psychiatrist; i:60-1
Kozachenko, Kathy: first openly gay person elected to public office; i:177
Kramer, Larry: gay playwright; founder of ACT UP; ii:185-6, ii:209, ii:230
Krebs, Robert: architect; Scondras' life partner (major citations); i:2, i:18, i:153, ii:14,
        ii:31-2, ii:37-45, ii:48-50, ii:72, ii:283, iii:65, iv:184-5
        photos: ii:cover, ii:32, ii:48,

L

LaFontaine, David: activist with Boston Gay and Lesbian Political Alliance; ii:211
Langone, Freddy: Boston City Councilor from the North End; ii:58, ii:233
LaRouche, Lyndon: perennial candidate & founder of LaRouche movement: ii:131, ii:151
Lennon, John: founder of *The Beatles*; i:69, i:71
Levenson, Norman: real estate developer; Fenway landlord; i:134, ii:109-10
Levine, Marsha: co-founder of the Boston Lesbian and Gay Political Alliance; i:178, i:187
Liakos, Dennis: Fenway landlord convicted of arson; i:132-3
Liberationism: idea that gays are inherently different from straights and those differences
        should be respected; ii:168, ii:168-70, iii:23, iii:45, iii:170, iv:230
Log Cabin Republicans: gay conservative political group; iii:99, iii:195
Lucas, Peter: columnist in the *Boston Herald*; i:173
Lyons, Pat & John: Fenway real estate and nightclub owners; ii:102

M

Maguire, Ann: City of Boston gay liaison; i:187-8, ii:67, ii:288
Malewezi, Justin: Vice President of the African Republic of Malawi; iv:100,
        iv:111-2,iv:141-6, iv:150
        photo: iv:111, iv:142
Mandel, Fred: Boston Human Rights Commission Director; ii:92, ii:200, ii:228,
        iii:156, iii:193, iv:5
Mandela, Nelson: leader of the African National Congress; first black President of
        South Africa; ii:80, ii:227, iii:193, iv:100, iv:121, iv:137-8
        photo: iv:121
Mapplethorpe, Robert: photographer and gay activist; iii:95-103
        photo: iii:96
Martin, Gaye: Fenway activist; i:129-31, i:136, i:146, i:153
Martorelli, Tom: Fenway Health Center board member; i:89
Matewan: Scondras familial home in West Virginia; i:40-4, iii:37
Mattachine Society: early pro-gay rights groups, founded in 1950s; i:181, ii:68
Mbeki, Thabo: President of South Africa who denied that HIV caused AIDS; i:6, iv:94,
        iv:100, iv:116-21, iv:124-5, iv:131-3, iv:135, iv:144
        photos: iv:200, iv:121
MBTA: Metropolitan Boston Transit Authority, Boston's train system, known
        as "the T"; i:183, ii:7, ii:98, ii:136-41

McCormack, Mike: Boston City Council colleague; i:6, ii:29, ii:51, ii:86, ii:121, ii:215,
       iii:6, iii:31, iii:88,
        photo: ii:215
McCormick, Dale: Lesbian and Gay Political Alliance, Maine State Senator; ii:163, iii:107
        photo: iii:107
McDonough, Will: *Boston Globe* reporter; ii:190-1
McFeeley, Tim: founder of the Bay State Stonewall Democrats; i:187
Mead, Margaret: anthropologist, i:76-7, i:84
Medoff, Peter: public health / AIDS activist; ii:208, ii:228, iii:148, iii:156, iii:189, iv:8-9
Menino, Thomas: City Council colleague and Mayor of Boston, 1993-2014; i:101,
       ii:29, ii:104, ii:120, ii:123, ii:216, ii:270, iii:25, iii:173, iii:177, iii:188, iv:12, iv:146
Milaiko, Vinni: social worker; i:82
Milk, Harvey: San Francisco elected official; one of the first openly gay politicians;
       i:158, i:177-8, i:187, i:198, ii:75, ii:101, ii:106-7, iii:2, iii:12, iii:161, iii:170, iii:190
Mills, Jack: Fenway activist and Scondras staffer; i:134, i:153, ii:31-2, ii:51, iii:64
        photo: ii:32
Mitzel, John: founded the Calamus Bookstore; i:301
Moakley, Joe: U.S. Representative for Boston; i:6, ii:121, iii:62-4, iii:70,
       iii:165, iv:18, iv:103, iv:112
Molesworth, Jack, Scondras' opponent in City Council race; ii:231-2
Molson, John: Social activist and beer mogul; iv:140
Monroe, Laura: Holocaust survivor and YWCA activist; ii:158
Montgomery, Harold: Fenway elder activist; i:102
Moon, Parry: MIT math professor, husband of Domina Spencer, father of Euclid; iii:49-50
Moore, Mike: community activist and arson investigator; i:160, i:167
Mosely, LeBaron: Scondras gay black Harvard classmate; i:63
Mulligan, Joe: city's Corporation Counsel, the chief lawyer for city of Boston; ii:72, iii:92
Munshine, Dave, Scondras City Council staffer and SFAC staffer; iv:8, iv:26

N

Nazi Germany: anti-gay aspects, and neo-Nazis; i:68, i:73, ii:188, ii:239, ii:261,
       ii:269, iii:146, iii:160, iv:198
Near, Holly: LGBT activist and singer; ii:284
Neville, Jean: President of the Mental Patients Liberation Front; iii:147
Nhu, Madame: Wife of South Vietnamese dictator Diem; i:54
Nicoletta, Daniel: photographer and partner of Harvey Milk; ii:107
Nimoy, Leonard: *Star Trek* actor and Boston native; i:107
Nixon, cat owned by Scondras and Robert Krebs; ii:23, ii:300, iii:148-9
Nixon, Richard: President 1969-74; i:54, i:71, i:79, i:107, i:111, i:117, ii:90, iii:127, iv:32
NLRB: National Labor Relations Board; iii:90, iii:93
Noble, Elaine: first openly lesbian elected official in U.S.; member of MA state House of
       Representatives; i:157, i:177-8, i:188, ii:106, ii:249, iii:2, iii:172, iv:24
Norris, Chris: lawyer and Scondras staffer; ii:31-2, ii:145, iii:60
        photo: ii:32
North, Oliver "Ollie": Reagan National Security Council staffer; implicated
       in Iran-Contra scandal; ii:81-2, iv:170
Nucci, John: President of Boston's School Committee; Boston City
       Council colleague; iii:47, iii:143

O

O'Bryant, John: Dean of Northeastern U.; Boston School ..Committee President; i:7, i:198
O'Connor, Peter J.: staffer at federal Office of Economic Opportunity; i:111
O'Neil, Albert "Dapper": Boston City Councilor, 1971 to 1999; i:6, i:13, i:164, i:192,
        ii:29-30, ii:58-9, ii:70-1, ii:73, ii:81-2, ii:91, ii:120, ii:131-3, ii:155, ii:175,
        ii:200-1, ii:204-7, ii:210, ii:214, ii:217, ii:222-5, ii:234, ii:268, ii:280, ii:288,
        ii:304-5, iii:12, iii:19, iii:22, iii:57, iii:63, iii:82, iii:88, iii:92-102, iii:128, iii:131-2,
        iii:139, iii:173, iii:193, iv:5, iv:91
O'Neill, Thomas Phillip "Tip": Representative for Boston in the U.S. House, 1953 to 1987;
        i:14, i:146, i:154, ii:84, ii:234, iii:83
Ortega, Daniel: leader of the Sandinistas; President of Nicaragua; ii:81-6,iv:170
Osborne, Arthur: New England chair, AFL-CIO; ii:103-5, ii:130
Owens, Bill: State Senator from Roxbury; iii:24, iii:28

P

Parks, Bob and Theresa: Mission Hill activists; i:202, ii:217-8
Parks, Rosa: civil rights activist; i:15, ii:237, iii:119, iii:170
Passafaro, David: staff director for the Boston City Council; ii:81
Pennington, John: Harvard anti-Vietnam activist; i:70, iv:169
Perkovic, Paul: publisher of HUG newsletter (Harvard University Gays); i:169
Perrelli, Vince: staffer at Fenway Health Center; i:91, i:96, ii:50
Phillips, Lou Diamond, Latino movie actor and labor activist; i:15, ii:94, iii:339
Phinney, Frederic: Publisher of the *Boston Ledger*; ii:188-9
Piketty, Thomas: author of *Capital in the 21st Century*; iv:219
Powers, Jack: Boston arts adviser, owned "Stone Soup" poetry club; iv:158-60, iv:164-6
        photo: iv:158

Q

Quilty, Dennis: Back Bay lawyer who ran for state rep; i:171, i:187-90, i:201-2
Quiroga, Jorge: reporter for Channel Five news; i:191

R

Radical Faeries: gay organization founded by Harry Hay (q.v.); i:49
Rappaport, Jerome "Jerry": real estate developer nicknamed the "14th councilor";
        i:104-6, ii:119, ii:121, ii:215, ii:293, iii:91
Reade, Charles E.: friend of Robert; volunteer for Scondras campaign; died of AIDS; iv:13-5
        photo: iv:14
Reagan, Nancy: First Lady of the United States; ii:162
Reagan, Ronald: president of the United States, i:14, ii:26, ii:81-6, ii:95, ii:127, ii:136,
        ii:151, ii:155, ii:207-9, ii:214, ii:230, ii:238, ii:267-8, ii:292, ii:298-9, iii:9, iii:48,
        iii:72, iii:90-3, iii:118, iii:149, iii:172, iii:193, iv:8, iv:20, iv:170, iv:232
Rechner, Carl: Planning Director of the Christian Science Church; i:115-7
Reeves, Ken: openly gay Mayor of Cambridge; iii:35, iii:182, iv:145, iv:197-8
        photo: iii:182
Reinstein, John: legal director of the Civil Liberties Union of Massachusetts; ii:286
Rezendes, Mike: Writer for *East Boston Community News*; i:168

Roache, Francis "Mickey": Boston Police Commissioner, 1985 to 1993; Boston City
        Councilor, 1996 to 2002; ii:109, ii:147, ii:176, iii:10, iii:100, iii:168
Robert: *see* Krebs (when unattributed with a surname, "Robert" refers to
        Scondras' partner Robert Krebs)
Robinson, Randall: Boston-based anti-apartheid lawyer and founder of Trans Africa; ii:79
Robinson, William: Massachusetts House minority leader; ii:108
Rofes, Eric: writer and co-founder of BLGPA, i:187
Romero, Oscar: martyred Archbishop of El Salvador; iii:64-5, iii:72
Roosevelt, Franklin and Eleanor: President and First Lady of the United States;
        i:23, ii:6-10, ii:36, ii:55, ii:108, ii:202, ii:263, iii:161
Roosevelt, Mark: Boston City Council candidate defeated by Scondras, later Democratic
        nominee for Governor; i:171, i:198, i:200-1, ii:6, iii:25, iii:28, iii:141
        photo: iii:43
Roosevelt, Teddy: President of the United States; ii:6
Rosaria: *see* Salerno

S

Salerno, Rosaria: nun: Boston city council colleague; Fenway community activist; i:75, i:99,
        I:100, ii:11, ii:184, ii:198, ii:202, ii:232-6, ii:270, ii:277-80, ii:287, ii:292-3, ii:304,
        ii:310-2, iii:6, iii:38, iii:57, iii:62, iii:167, iii:176-7, iii:182, iv:26-7
        photo: iii:182
Salk, Jonas: Inventor of polio vaccine in 1955 & AIDS vaccine in 1987; i:6, iv:24-5, iv:214
Salk, Peter: son of Jonas Salk; M.D. at Salk Institute; iv:25, iv:139-41, iv:153, iv:214
        photo: iv:139
Sandinistas: members of the Sandinista National Liberation Front, a political
        party in Nicaragua; i:14, ii:81-6, ii:206, ii:238, iii:193, iv:170
Sarantos, Father John: Greek Orthodox priest in Lowell; i:49, ii:87
Schorow, Stephanie: author of *Boston on Fire*, a 2003 book; i:129
Scondras, Dorothea (mom) nee Coravos; i:2, i:11-3, i:20, i:25-6, i:46, i:49, i:62, i:75,
        i:127, i:152, i:163, i:173, ii:18, ii:23, ii:87, ii:138, ii:211, iii:59-61, iii:155,
        iii:172, iv:178, iv:191-2, iv:198
        photo: i:25
Schulte, Steve: gay model and Mayor of West Hollywood California; i:177
Scondrasistas: nickname for supporters of David Scondras, named after
        the Sandinistas (q.v.); i:6, ii:86, ii:89, ii:187, iii:6
Search For A Cure: anti-AIDS organization led by Scondras; i:6, ii:106, iii:2, iv:cover,
        iv:3, iv:6, iv:15-8, iv:23-4, iv:70-1, iv:80-2, iv:87, iv:112, iv:135, iv:139-40,
        iv:144-6, iv:149
Secoy, Edward: National Consumer Law Center, defended the FPA; iii:131
Selover, John: Public Relations Director of the Christian Science Church; i:98, ii:289
SFAC: Scondras organization, *Search For A Cure* (q.v.)
Shamsi, Ed: Boston landlord and anti-rent control activist; ii:126, ii:141-2, ii:158, iii:48
Shannon, Jim: Massachusetts member of U.S. Congress; ii:50, ii:202, iii:62, iii:95
Silber, John: B.U. President, candidate for Governor; ii:100, ii:272
Slowey, Dominic: activist with Mass. Charter Public School Association; i:171
South Africa: Republic of, site of 1994 overthrow of apartheid white minority government,
        Ii:77-80, ii:84, ii:151, iii:193, iv:31, iv:94-5, iv:100, iv:102-3, iv:116-28,
        iv:131-40, iv:144, iv:151, iv:170

Spear, Alan: State Senator in Minnesota, first elected official to come out as gay,
          ex post facto; i:158, i:178, ii:249, iii:2, iii:161
Spencer, Domina: neighborhood activist and mathematician, wife of Parry Moon; iii:48-9
Spencer, Jim: Joe Kennedy staffer; now runs The Campaign Network; ii:139
St. Clair, James Vincent: chair of the St. Clair Commission, formerly lawyer for
          Richard Nixon during impeachment; ii:90
St. Clair Commission: conducted investigation of Boston Police; iii:127-30, iv:9, iv:174
Steinberg, David: Scondras staffer; ii:32, ii:200
          photos: ii:32, ii:200
Stonewall: gay club in NYC where 1969 riots marked the beginning of the gay
          rights movement; i:58, i:178-80, ii:238, ii:284, iii:169-70
Stowe, Joannie: elderly constituent; ii:91
Stravinsky, Igor: Russian-born composer and pianist; i:68
Stuart, Charles: murdered his wife but accused a Mission Hill resident; iii:51-5
Studds, Gerry: Representative for Boston MA in the U.S. House, 1983 to 1997; first openly
          gay member of Congress: i:196-7, ii:227, iii:161, iii:186, iv:54
Sullivan, Dan: lawyer for Fenway community lawsuits, i:111, i:122-4
Sullivan, Neil: Mayor Flynn's chief public policy aide; ii:266, ii:275, iv:11

T

T, the: *see* MBTA, Metropolitan Boston Transit Authority
Taylor, James: singer; i:107
Terrigno, Valerie: City Councilor of West Hollywood CA, and later Mayor; i:177
Thurston, Ernie: Scondras college friend; boyfriend of Copper Coggins; i:5
Tierney, Joe: president of Boston City Council; Scondras City Council colleague:
          i:105-6, i:111, ii:29-30, ii:53-4, ii:73-4, ii:121-3, ii:136, ii:210, ii:235
Tierney, Steven: co-coordinator of the Massachusetts Gay Political Caucus; i:157, i:188
Tietcher, Edward: Fenway resident; i:205
Timilty, Joe: State Senator & Boston mayoral candidate; i:143, ii:29, ii:120, iv:12
Tramont, Ed: head of special projects at NIH; iv:19-20
Trask, Anna: Scondras campaign volunteer; NARAL activist; wife of Jack Hall; i:175
Travaglini, Robert "Trav"; City Council colleague, 1984-92; State Senator, 1992-2007;
          ii:29, ii:59, ii:120, ii:270, ii:293
          photo: iii:cover
Trumka, Richard: president of the United Mine Workers; iii:33, iii:37
Tye, Michael: Ray's son and AIDS activist; ii:102
Tye, Ray: owner of United Liquors (beer distributor); ii:102, ii:106, ii:190, ii:250-1

U-V

Vara, Henry: owner of RamRod and other gay clubs; i:14
Vargas, Maria Luisa: Legal Counsel for the Sandinistas (Nicaragua); ii:86
Volvovitz, Frank: creator of first AIDS vaccine; iv:9, iv:15, iv:26

W-X

Wald, George: Nobel laureate in Biology and anti-apartheid activist; i:79
Wall, French: Scondras staff aide; i:13, ii:10, ii:193, ii:217-23, ii:232-6, ii:248, ii:282

Waterflow, Annie: a.k.a. Susan Bruckner, Fenway community activist; i:153
Waterhouse, Robert: Greyhound bus employee killed while on strike,
        namesake of Waterhouse Bill preventing strike-breaking; iii:89-94, iii:109
Webb, Marc: staffer at Boston Redevelopment Authority; i:82
Weld, William: Republican Governor; ii:100, ii:138, ii:211, iii:140, iii:174-5, iv:18
White, Dan: assassin who killed Harvey Milk; i:177
White, Kevin: Mayor of Boston, 1968-1984; i:105, i:143, i:160-2, i:184, ii:6, ii:37, ii:259
Whiting, Rosemary: Scondras staffer and volunteer coordinator; ii:31-3
        photo: ii:32
Williams, Jerry: Boston radio personality; i:172-4, ii:280

Y

Yacino, Michael: Director of the Gun Owners Action League; local NRA activist;
        iii:14, iii:61
Yancey, Charles: Boston City Councilor colleague representing Roxbury and Mattapan;
        ii:29, ii;77, ii:100, ii:120, ii:222, ii:271, ii:293, iii:6, iii:62, iii:82,
        iii:103, iii:128, iii:135

Z

Zanger, Marc; writer for the *Boston Real Paper*; i:136, i:139
Zeibekiko: Greek dance; i:13
Zinn, Howard: social activist and politics professor at Boston University; iv:164
Zobel, Hiller: Judge on Superior Court of Massachusetts; iii:157-8